SUPER SKIN

Moisture!
pg. 55

SUPER SKIN

A LEADING DERMATOLOGIST'S GUIDE TO THE LATEST BREAKTHROUGHS IN SKIN CARE

NELSON LEE NOVICK, M.D.

Clarkson N. Potter, Inc. / Publishers

With special thanks to my office manager, Barbara Jerabek, for a yeoman's job of managing the business of the office by day and critiquing and proofing this book by night.

Publisher's Note: This book contains recommendations to be followed within the context of an overall health-care program. However, not all recommendations are designed for all individuals. While the book discusses certain issues and choices regarding skin care, it is not intended as a substitute for professional medical advice. Before following these or any other health-care recommendations, a physician should be consulted.

Many products mentioned in this book are trademarks of their respective companies. Every effort has been made to identify these trademarks by initial capitalization. Should there be any errors or omissions in this respect, we shall be pleased to make the necessary corrections in future printings.

Published by Clarkson N. Potter, Inc., 201 East 50th Street, New York, New York 10022, and distributed by Crown Publishers, Inc., New York

CLARKSON N. POTTER, POTTER, and colophon are trademarks of Clarkson N. Potter, Inc.

Manufactured in the United States of America

Library of Congress Cataloging-in-Publication Data

Novick, Nelson Lee.
Super skin : a leading dermatologist's guide to the latest breakthroughs in skin care / by Nelson Lee Novick.
p.   cm.
1. Skin—Care and hygiene. I. Title.
RL87.N695   1988
646.7'26—dc19   88-12678 CIP
ISBN 0-517-57035-1

Design by Jan Melchior

10   9   8   7   6   5   4   3

*T*o my wife
and closest friend, Meryl,
for continuous support and
continual encouragement in all my
pursuits; and to my five sons,
Yonatan, Yoel, Ariel, Daniel, and
Avraham, who grace my life with
true meaning, purpose, and joy.

CONTENTS

PREFACE ix

P A R T   O N E / THE BASICS OF GOOD SKIN CARE

O N E

THE MAKEUP AND BREAKUP OF SKIN 3

T W O

SUN SENSE 14

T H R E E

CLEAN, NOT SQUEAKY CLEAN 31

F O U R

MOISTURIZERS: "HOPE IN A BOTTLE" 42

F I V E

CHOOSING COSMETICS: READ THE LABEL 57

S I X

GOOD HEALTH = A MORE BEAUTIFUL SKIN 75

P A R T   T W O / COMMON SKIN PROBLEMS

S E V E N

WHO SAYS ACNE IS JUST KID STUFF? 93

E I G H T

COMMON SKIN RASHES 110

N I N E

COMMON SKIN INFECTIONS 127

CONTENTS

TEN

SKIN GROWTHS: THE HARMLESS AND THE BAD 142

PART THREE/
MAKING A GOOD THING BETTER

ELEVEN

HELPING NATURE: COSMETIC SURGERY 167

TWELVE

HAIR—TOO MUCH OR NOT ENOUGH 187

THIRTEEN

GOING TO EXTREMITIES: HEALTHY NAILS AND FEET 206

FOURTEEN

SPECIAL CARE FOR SPECIAL PLACES 229

FIFTEEN

SEX AND YOUR SKIN 237

SIXTEEN

PREGNANCY AND YOUR SKIN 255

SEVENTEEN

GOOD SKIN IS POSSIBLE AT *ANY* AGE 272

EIGHTEEN

WHAT'S ON THE HORIZON 285

INDEX 295

PREFACE

*I*t was toward the end of my postgraduate specialty training in internal medicine that I decided to pursue a career in dermatology. At first, a number of my medical colleagues didn't take me seriously. Some of them maintained that a career in skin care was not really an appropriate calling for a "true" physician. The prevailing sentiment was that a dermatologist is merely a "pimple doctor" who never faces emergencies or deals with matters of greater concern than treating a "teenage girl with a big zit on her face the night before the prom."

The reality, of course, is that skin is a vitally important, complex organ that is affected by many genetic and environmental factors and is subject to a wide variety of conditions and diseases, some 1,000 of them, in fact. These problems can run the gamut from simple dry skin, eczema, and hives to grave skin cancers, such as malignant melanoma.

Just as you cannot live without your heart or lungs, you cannot live without your skin. Many skin problems can be quite serious, physically or psychologically debilitating, and even life-threatening. To appreciate more fully the importance of healthy skin to overall health, you need only visit the bedside of a severe burn victim. Today, along with continued investigations into the causes, prevention, and treatments of common skin conditions such as acne, itching, and eczema, dermatologists are in the vanguard of AIDS and cancer research.

While the impact on life and health of serious, widespread skin conditions can be easily appreciated, the impact of less serious skin problems on the quality of a person's life is often not so readily understood either by friends or families of the sufferers. For example, pimples are often the butt of callous humor, yet the potential impact of a supposedly harmless skin condition such as acne, which does not ordinarily affect a person's general health and is largely of cosmetic importance, should not be taken lightly; the psychological consequences of severe acne or post-acne scarring upon a person's self-confidence and self-image can last a lifetime. In the same way, as we age, the contribution of skin wrinkling and sagging to low self-esteem and lower quality of life is beginning to be recognized more fully. One recent study suggested that younger-looking people may actually live longer. Clearly, appearance counts.

Dermatologic science is on its way to making it possible for all of us to have healthier and younger-looking skin. While much remains to be learned about the skin, much is already known. Many conditions can be prevented or improved by simple home skin-care measures and routines. Others require the professional care of a dermatologist. Finally, a number of new, and in most cases simple and relatively inexpensive, in-office, cosmetic surgical procedures are now available to make us more attractive and younger looking.

While so many new and exciting things are going on in the field of skin care, much of this information is *not* filtering down to the general public. Magazine, television, and radio ads for skin products, whose aims are to sell you on this or that "magical" cream or lotion, can be confusing or misleading. Unfortunately, many consumers rely on these sources for their information. In addition, so-called skin-care specialists abound. Skin has become big business and advice is readily dispensed by a host of nonexperts. Beauticians, cosmetologists, facial and sauna entrepreneurs, and massage therapists, to name a few, freely extend their advice and testimonials on this or that potion or technique that they swear will make you younger overnight.

The proliferation of nonscientifically-based beauty books attests to just how big a business the skin-care advice game has become.

This book answers the public's need for a medically and scientifically based guide on skin care. It is not a beauty book, although its aim is to help you keep your skin healthier and younger looking. It is a no-nonsense guide for adults, aimed at saving its readers time and money. The material has been organized and written with two themes in mind: *educating* and *protecting* you, the consumer of skin-care products, treatments, and cosmetic surgery.

Throughout the book great effort is made to help you separate facts from fears and fantasies. The subject matter of each chapter is based upon current medical information and my clinical experience in treating thousands of patients in private practice and addressing the questions and concerns they express most often. During the past several years, I have had the opportunity to work with a number of consumer affairs reporters on a variety of public health concerns, most notably in the areas of misinformation and misrepresentation in the cosmetic and skin-care product industry. I have also written a number of articles on these subjects in newspapers and popular magazines. The consumer advocacy approach throughout the book reflects my experiences and concerns in these areas.

To help you in the marketplace, I suggest a variety of cosmetics and drugs by generic or brand name for a number of different skin problems and conditions. These are brands with which I have had considerable personal experience and ones that I have found to be most consistently useful. However, this should not be misconstrued as an endorsement of these items. The products mentioned are certainly not the only ones available for managing the conditions described, nor should exclusion of any product from this book be taken to imply lack of efficacy or safety.

Since this book is intended for a wide audience, the descriptions and explanations of all medical and surgical therapies are purposely of a more general nature. Naturally, if you have any specific questions about drugs or cosmetics, you should discuss them with your dermatologist.

Time and again it becomes apparent that there are few real shortcuts in life. You have to invest a little time and effort to get what you want. It's the same with caring for your skin. You simply cannot make the most of your time, your looks, and your money if you don't know some basics about skin and the problems that can afflict it. It is my hope that this book will provide you with all the informaton you need to be an informed consumer and dermatological patient, and to take those first initial steps toward achieving truly super skin.

PART ONE

THE
BASICS OF
GOOD
SKIN CARE

THE MAKEUP
AND BREAKUP
OF SKIN

Skin is more than just what meets the eye. Its structure and function, its anatomy and physiology, are quite complex. What happens within and to your skin can have an impact on your physical and psychological health. It follows, then, that the more you know about your skin, the better able you will be to evaluate skin-care products and to appreciate the rationale for the medical and cosmetic skin-care treatments discussed in this book or prescribed by your dermatologist. And by taking the time to learn a few facts about your skin, you will be more likely to preserve your health—and appearance.

For most people, the effects of aging on the skin are first noticed sometime between the ages of twenty and thirty. Medical and technological advances have resulted in increasing numbers of our population surviving into old age. It is estimated that by the year 2000 there will be about 31.8 million Americans aged sixty-five years and over. As a result of our longer life spans, most of us will be confronted with the effects of skin aging for decades longer than past generations. Given our youth-oriented society, it is not surprising to find that, as people stay healthy longer, they wish to remain younger-looking longer. This chapter give the facts about what *really* happens within your skin as you age.

NORMAL SKIN

You may be surprised to learn that your skin is the largest organ of your body, measuring approximately 20 square feet and weighing, on average, between 7 and 9 pounds. Normal, healthy skin is a complex organ composed of many layers. At its thickest (back, soles of feet, and palms), your skin measures approximately ⅛ inch. At its thinnest (eyelids), it measures only ¹⁄₂₅ inch. Among its many important functions, skin not only protects the inside of your body from the assaults of the outside environment, but it also serves as the primary regulator of body temperature.

Skin is divided into three layers: the *epidermis, dermis,* and

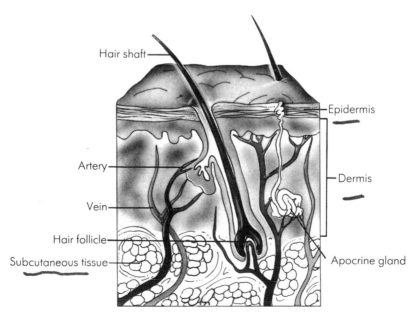

Figure 1.1   Cross-section of normal skin

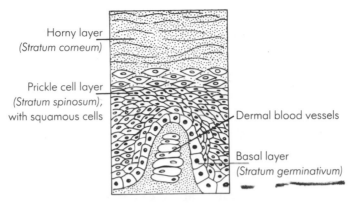

Horny layer
(Stratum corneum)

Prickle cell layer
(Stratum spinosum),
with squamous cells

Dermal blood vessels

Basal layer
(Stratum germinativum)

Figure 1.2   Close-up of epidermis

subcutis. Each of these layers has its own unique functions. Figures 1.1 and 1.2 display cross-sectional representations of normal skin.

The epidermis (Figure 1.1) is the highly cellular uppermost layer of your skin. It is no thicker than a page in this book and is composed of fifteen to twenty layers that overlap near the skin surface. As you can see, the epidermis is itself subdivided into three layers. The bottommost layer is appropriately called the *basal layer,* because the cells composing it form the *base* of the epidermis. The basal layer may also be called the *Stratum germinativum* because the cells in this layer continually germinate ("give birth to") new cells.

The layers of the epidermis undergo a continual process of birth, life, and death. As older cells are shed at the skin surface, new cells are formed in the basal layer. These newly formed cells grow, mature, and divide to produce more cells. Finally, they make a two-week migration upward through the epidermis to the surface of your skin, replacing older cells being shed there.

The basal layer is not composed exclusively of basal cells. It hosts another important class of cells called *melanocytes,* the pigment-producing cells of your skin. They produce the *melanin,* which is responsible for imparting a color to your skin. Usually, every sixth cell in the basal layer is a melanocyte.

Racial differences in skin color are attributable to genetically determined differences in the amount and distribution of melanin. As a rule, people with darker skin possess more melanin in their epidermal cells than people with fair skin. In addition, the melanin within the skin cells of dark-complected people is more densely arranged; by contrast, melanin is more sparsely arranged in people with fair skin.

Sunlight stimulates melanin production and a suntan is nothing more than sun-induced melanin production. More than simply imparting color to your skin, melanin protects you by absorbing the sun's damaging ultraviolet rays. Unfortunately, this protection is far from complete; long-term sun exposure can result in premature aging of the skin and the development of skin cancers (chapters 2 and 10).

The top layer of the epidermis consists of a sheet of nonliving cells called the *Stratum corneum,* or the *horny layer* (which gets its name from the fact that when tightly compacted, its cells become tough, like the horn of an animal. In fact, the horns of mammals are made of the same protein material, *keratin,* which makes up the horny layer of human skin). The surface of the horny layer is somewhat acidic and is referred to as the *acid mantle.*

Horny layer cells are constantly shed at the skin surface, remaining there about two weeks and replaced from below. Any abnormal accumulation of horny cells on the surface of your skin, for any reason, can result in skin ashiness or flakiness. Skin ash is particularly troublesome to people with dark skin because of the sharp contrast in color between the gray ash and the surrounding skin.

The horny layer of your skin serves several extremely important functions. It is not only the major physical barrier to the environment, but, to some extent, is also a shield against the sun's harmful ultraviolet rays. More important, it effectively prevents the penetration of most environmental substances that come in contact with your skin or are applied to it. In general, only those substances possessing a molecular size smaller than the size of water molecules can readily penetrate this epidermal barrier. This is the main reason why, contrary to what cosmetic manufacturers would have you believe, your skin cannot "eat up" or "drink up" such substances as collagen, elastin, vitamins, or nutrients—ingredients that are often contained in many of the fanciest, most expensive moisturizers and cosmetics. The molecular structure of these ingredients is simply too large to pass through your skin. (More about this in chapter 5.)

The middle, and thickest, layer of the epidermis is called the *Stratum spinosum* or *prickle cell layer,* owing to the spiny, hairlike, prickly-looking processes, or projections, that link the cells in this layer. The cells within the prickle cell layer are known as *squamous* cells. Essentially, squamous cells are basal cells that have matured and migrated upward within the epidermis.

Beneath the epidermis lies the dermis, the cellular and largely fibrous and elastic supporting layer of your skin. It contains the important fibers *collagen* and *elastin,* which are the subject of much advertising hype by moisturizer manufacturers. Collagen and elastin are the complex proteins responsible for the support and elasticity of the skin. They enable your skin to regain its shape after being stretched or pulled. Both proteins are composed of large, complex molecules, far too large to be "eaten up" or "drunk in" by your skin (thereupon to "replace lost natural protein"), as some ads suggest.

The dermis is home to other important skin structures as well. The tiny, twiglike sensory nerve endings that allow you to sense, for example, something as soft as a wisp of cotton on your skin or subtle changes of temperature are located high in the dermis, as are the nerve endings that allow you to feel pressure, vibration, and pain.

Skin nutrition and oxygenation are supplied by the numerous tiny arteries, veins, and capillaries coursing upward through the dermis. These vessels branch from larger vessels situated more deeply in the body. Incredibly, each square inch of the dermis houses 15 feet of small, nutrient-providing blood vessels. Their constriction and dilation, in response to extremes of heat and cold, are responsible for keeping your body temperature constant. These small blood vessels also keep your skin healthy and viable and remove metabolic waste materials (Figure 1.1). As a rule, nutrients cannot be supplied to your skin by topical application. In other words, applying vitamins, minerals, fruits, or vegetables, or any cream or lotion concoction, to your skin in hopes of getting these additives *into* your skin is a waste of your time and money.

The subcutis, or fatty layer, lies below the dermis and is the bottommost layer of your skin. The fatty layer functions both as a cushion for your vital internal organs and a reserve energy storage site for the body. The amount and distribution of fat throughout the body is believed, in most cases, to be an inherited family trait.

SPECIAL SKIN STRUCTURES

The skin houses several other important structures. These include hairs, hair follicles, and three kinds of sweat glands. *Hairs,* which are nonliving, fibrous strands, are, like the horny layer of the skin, composed primarily of the protein keratin. *Hair follicles,* located at the base of the hair shaft, generally in the deep dermis or subcutis, are the living reproduction parts of the hair.

The skin contains three types of sweat glands—the *sebaceous, apocrine,* and *eccrine glands.* The sebaceous glands, or oil glands, lie to the side of the hair follicles. Sebaceous glands produce *sebum,* or natural skin oil, which is actually a complex mixture of a number of different fats and waxes. The oil you feel on your face on a hot, humid day is sebum. Approximately three thousand oil glands are contained in each square inch of forehead and facial skin.

Sebaceous glands are located primarily on the scalp, face, chest, and back, although they may be found elsewhere on the body. Present from birth, these glands mature and begin to secrete sebum actively following puberty. Sebum is secreted through a small duct leading directly from the oil gland into the hair shaft, and travels upward to the skin surface through the hair follicle. Dead cells and other debris within the hair follicles are also "washed" to the skin surface by this process. Sebum coats your skin, locking in its natural moisture and preventing it from drying out.

Apocrine glands are located primarily in the armpit, genital and anal areas, and around the belly button. These glands are heavily coiled and are usually situated deep within the subcutis. They produce a milky sweat that when broken down by bacteria on the skin causes body odor. Apocrine glands secrete their contents into the upper portion of the hair follicle, and from there the secretions exit to the skin surface.

In other mammals it is believed that apocrine glands produce body odors that serve as a sexual function to attract mates. In humans, however, the function of these glands remains unknown. They are present in the skin from birth, but do not mature and secrete until the onset of puberty. Periods of heightened emotional stress appear to stimulate their secretions.

Like apocrine glands, eccrine glands are generally situated in the subcutis, and are heavily coiled. Unlike sebaceous and apocrine gland secretions, however, eccrine sweat exits the skin through its own pores rather than through the hair follicles. Exercise, hot weather, fever, and emotional stress are known to stimulate eccrine sweating. Your skin contains between 2 and 3 million eccrine sweat glands; they are located over the entire body, but are highly concentrated on the palms, soles of the feet, and armpits. In these areas, and on the forehead, sweat production appears to be more strongly linked to emotional and stress factors than to heat stimulation. Since eccrine sweat is largely water, these glands are normally not responsible for body odor.

The watery, colorless sweat produced by eccrine glands functions to regulate body temperature. Sweat evaporation at the skin surface lowers body temperature. In addition, sweat can help to eliminate small amounts of waste salts and other substances from the body. However, some people suffer from a profuse sweating condition known as *hyperhidrosis*. This condition, which often requires medical treatment, can pose a severely compromising and embarrassing social problem for sufferers (chapter 14).

Finally, a word about the all-important subject of *pores*. A pore is the lay term for the opening of your oil or sweat glands at the skin surface. (The medical term is *follicular orifice.*) The size of your pores is largely determined by heredity. Unfortunately, although there are a number of toners, astringents, and foundations that claim to be able to shrink dilated pores, no product is yet available that can actually accomplish this for more than a few hours. If you have acne or oily skin, which can make your pores appear wider, consult your dermatologist.

THE COSMETICS CON

Dermatologists frequently reserve the term *skin type* for a person's relative sensitivity to sun exposure (chapter 2), a classification that you will see is of tremendous lifelong importance. The phrase *skin type,* however, has become very much a part of common parlance and is often used in a much different way at sales counters and in cosmetics ads. For most people, skin type has come to indicate whether they have normal, oily, or dry skin, or skin that combines these qualities.

Most dermatologists, however, prefer to deal with the specific condition of each area of your skin. The characteristics of your skin, your skin type, can vary considerably depending upon a number of factors. In fact, your skin type often varies from one part of your body to another. Your chronological age, the season and climate, the level of nervous tension you may be experiencing, and the stresses of illness or pregnancy may influence your skin type. Because of these variations, it is of little practical value to classify skin types.

Interestingly, nondermatologists often get into trouble when they try to pigeonhole their clients into these categories. For example, there is an extremely common form of facial eczema called *seborrheic dermatitis* (chapter 8), which typically causes scaling around the nose and in the eyebrow areas. Cosmetologists and facial specialists frequently misdiagnose this condition as dry skin and "prescribe" oily creams and lotions to treat it. Since the flaking from seborrheic dermatitis does *not* stem from dryness, oily creams frequently make the condition worse. In my own practice, I have had quite a number of patients show up in my office for the first time with active seborrheic dermatitis after having had the wrong cream recommended for "their skin type."

You should be especially wary of what I like to call the skin-type trap. After a facial, you will often find that the salon sales people pitch the products they used on you during the treatment. They may even try to persuade you that their particular "special regimen" or "complete line" of cosmetics is the only "right one for your skin type." What's more, while the facial may have cost you only $35, the "complete" cosmetic line or skin-care program often runs somewhere between $80 and $200. You may also be told that substitutions of any other cosmetics from elsewhere would diminish the benefits. This simply is not so. You *can* substitute. Second, even if the cosmetics are right for you today, your skin may change tomorrow or the next day and you could end up stuck with a lot of expensive potions. Finally, and even more important, if a skin condition you have has mistakenly been attributed to your skin type, applying the wrong cosmetics can worsen the condition.

Those one-product-does-all cosmetics intended for use on "combination skin" should be viewed with similar skepticism. It is very difficult, as you might imagine, to make one product that can both moisturize dry skin and dry oily skin. The ingredients would run counter to each other. Instead, choose products that deal with each problem separately, and if you have any problems or questions about how best to care for your skin, consult with your dermatologist.

SKIN AGING

During the past few years, we have discovered that skin is actually subject to two distinct aging processes: *chronological aging* and *photoaging*. Chronological skin aging is simply the inherited tendency to age. Clearly, some people seem to be more fortunate than others when it comes to how fast their skin ages. Photoaging, also known as *solar-induced aging,* results from sun damage. You may be surprised to learn that the changes associated with sun damage are now believed to be more prevalent and more profound than those attributed to the natural aging process. (More about sun damage in chapter 2.)

CHRONOLOGICAL (NATURAL) SKIN AGING

Most people could easily describe the outward appearance of an aging face: changes in facial shape; increased prominence of certain features, such as the nose; decrease in the vertical height of the mouth; recession of the gums and teeth; and loss of hair and skin color. In addition, you frequently find accentuation or wrinkling of the natural action lines of the face, sagging, jowl and pouch formation, generalized dryness (often severe), and laxity and inelasticity of the skin.

Dermatologic researchers and others interested in the aging process are actively investigating the precise nature of the structural and functional alterations in the skin that account for aging. Although we have learned much in the past decade, we do not, unfortunately, have all the answers yet. We do know that as skin ages, it tends to produce fewer new cells, and that damaged cells are repaired less quickly and less effectively. At the same time, cells in the horny layer lose some of their ability to adhere to one another. The epidermis and dermis become thinner, and the horny layer becomes less protective, dryer, and rougher. Furthermore, melanocytes become fewer in number, accounting for the development of patchy areas of skin-color loss.

Aging also results in changes in the fat distribution of the skin. Thinning of the subcutis occurs in certain areas, particularly the face, hands, feet, and shins, which means that the skin no longer feels as thick as it did before. Fat is typically redistributed to the waist in men and the thighs in women. At the same time, basal metabolism slows and life-styles become increasingly more sedentary. These changes result in the appearance and persistence of unsightly bulges.

Age affects both hair color and hair growth. Hair graying and whitening, like skin color loss, is linked to age-related decreases in melanocyte numbers and functioning. Most people (women as well as men) also experience thinning of their hair, perhaps a slowing growth rate of their hair, and even the thinning of the caliber of their hairs in certain locations. Conversely, in some areas, such as the ears, nose, and eyebrows of men, and upper lip and chin of women, previously fine, barely perceptible hairs often become thicker, more visible, and cosmetically compromising.

Equally dramatic changes in the dermis occur with natural aging. Cell numbers generally decrease and the dermis becomes thinner; as a consequence, the dermis is less capable of retaining its moisture content. In addition, the number of dermal blood vessels decreases and nerve endings become abnormal, leading to altered or reduced sensation. Wound healing is likewise generally compromised and there is usually a reduced ability to clear foreign materials and fluids. Finally, increasing rigidity and inelasticity of dermal collagen and elastin fibers contribute to wrinkling and sagging of the skin. Although some people mistakenly maintain that the loss of tone in the muscles responsible for chewing, laughing, eating, and so on contributes to the development of wrinkles and sags, this is untrue. Performing muscle toning or isometric exercises has absolutely no beneficial effect in eliminating or reducing wrinkles and sags.

Finally, the amounts of eccrine and apocrine sweat secretion become diminished with age as the number of eccrine glands and the size of apocrine glands decrease. As a consequence, the need for antiperspirants and deodorants is lessened. Sebaceous gland output diminishes, contributing in part to the generalized dryness and roughness so characteristic of aging skin.

The more you know about your skin and what happens to it as the years go by, the less likely you will be to fall for exaggerated or phony claims for skin-care products or services. You will also find this information useful for better understanding the chapters that follow. Simply knowing something about skin basics enables you to be a more discriminating consumer, which in the long run can save you a lot of time, money, and dashed hopes.

SUN SENSE

*M*ost people continue to mistake the effects of photoaging for those of chronological aging. However, there is no longer any doubt that sun damage not only adds to, accelerates, and exaggerates the effects of chronological aging, but also causes distinct and irreversible changes of its own.

THE HABIT THAT'S SO HARD TO BREAK

During the past couple of years, there has been an intensive public education program in the media stressing the potentially damaging effects of cumulative sun exposure. Such efforts receive the full endorsement of the National Cancer Institute, American Cancer Society, and Skin Cancer Foundation.

Despite these efforts at public education, however, most Americans lust still for that "healthy," golden tan. A recent study demonstrated that more than 80 percent of Americans are aware that sun exposure is unhealthy but that only half of them were taking steps to protect themselves. An it's-not-going-to-happen-to-me attitude was expressed by more than 60 percent of those polled.

It used to be that having a tan was considered a sign of poverty. Only peasants and field hands who were forced to work long, hard hours outdoors had tans. Lily-white skin signified wealth and the good life. Women of the leisure class took great pains to cover their skin and protect themselves from the sun with parasols.

In the 1920s, attitudes were reversed and suntans became fashionable, due in part to the influence of designers such as Coco Chanel. A golden tan meant that the person bearing it had the money and leisure for vacations in the sun and such sports as tennis, golf, skiing, and sailing. Unfortunately, tans have yet to go out of fashion. Most people, regardless of how much money they have, feel that they must return from a vacation with a deep tan in order to have something to show for it or to prove that they had a wonderful time. "Oh no! I simply cannot come home without at least some tan" remains a common refrain.

Sunshine, like the great outdoors and country air, is supposed to be healthy for you. But does the sun really do you any good? Certainly, sun bathing is not without its benefits; it gives many people a psychological uplift. Equally without debate, a tan is not only attractive, it can mask acne blemishes, scars, discolorations, and other skin irregularities.

No doubt most of you have been taught that sunlight is responsible for stimulating in your skin the production of vitamin D, which is essential for regulating calcium metabolism and the growth and maintenance of strong bones. In fact, all the vitamin D benefits that can be obtained from the sun can be derived from a daily *fifteen-minute* exposure to it. However, even that is not necessary; with the exception of those living in underdeveloped countries, most of us get enough vitamin D through what we eat, even those who exist on fast-food diets.

When I was a child in the mid 1950s, it was common for mothers to send their children out into the sun to "dry up" colds. Actually the sun has no curative powers. In fact, it is well-known that sun exposure can trigger herpes virus infections of the lips ("cold sores"), chicken pox, and even warts. And people with the condition known as *lupus erythematosus* should definitely avoid sun exposure, since overexposure can precipitate a serious flare-up of the disease, resulting occasionally in death.

The sun is also responsible for causing certain allergies. Some people are allergic to sunlight itself and may develop red blotches or bumps, hives, and small blisters. For others the combination of sunlight and a particular perfume, cosmetic, soap, detergent, or topical medication can cause an allergic reaction. Similarly, a number of commonly prescribed internal medicines make certain people more sensitive to the sun and lead to skin irritation or allergy. Dermatologists refer to such rashes as *photosensitivity reactions*. Some of the more common drugs responsible for photosensitivity reactions are listed in Table 2.1. Notice that these include birth-control pills, a number of antibiotics and antifungals, tranquilizers, diuretics, antidiabetic medication, and anticoagulants.

There are many other medications that may cause photosensitivity problems. If you have an unusual reaction to sun exposure, check with your doctor.

Sunlight cannot cure acne, as some people believe. In fact, many people who claim to have improved their acne by suntanning may find that they break out in numerous whiteheads four and six weeks after sun exposure. The whitehead formation is believed to result directly from ultraviolet light–induced damage and consequent clogging of pores. So far as a suntan's ability to mask blemishes, there are certainly far safer and more satisfactory ways to accomplish this cosmetically, as outlined in chapters 5 and 11.

As though skin cancer formation were not enough, the sun has been linked to still other unhealthy effects. These include ultraviolet light damage to the skin cells' genetic material, suppressing your skin's immune system, perhaps by damaging certain important cells that migrate there or by suppressing the skin's production of *growth factors,* substances known to stimulate immunity. Such effects may contribute to skin cancer formation. Furthermore, cataracts, or opacifications of the lenses of the eyes, have been associated with lifelong exposure to ultraviolet rays.

TABLE 2.1

COMMON PHOTOSENSITIZING DRUGS

ANTIBIOTICS

- Chlortetracycline (aureomycin)
- Doxycycline (vibramycin)
- Fulvicin U/F (griseofulvin)
- Minocin (minocycline)
- Tetracycline (tetracycline)

ANTIDIABETIC
MEDICATION

- Orinase (tolbutamide)

ANTIDEPRESSANTS

- Elavil (amitriptyline)
- Norpramin (desipramine)

BIRTH CONTROL PILLS

- Estrogen (estrogen)
- Estrogen and Progestin (oral contraceptives)

DIURETICS

- Diuril (chlorothiazide)
- Hygroton (chlorthalidone)
- Lasix (furosemide)
- Esidrix (hydrochlorothiazide)
- Dyrenium (triamterene)

TRANQUILIZERS

- Librium (chlordiazepoxide)
- Thorazine (chlorpromazine)
- Haldol (haloperidol)
- Navane (thiothixene)

If the above-mentioned effects of sun tanning do not deter you, the cosmetic problems it causes may. The deleterious effects of sun exposure accumulate through the years and are largely irreversible. Put another way, at the end of the summer your tan will fade, but the damage never will. The leathery, hidelike appearance of skin on the face, V of the chest, backs of hands, and nape of neck is a direct result of ultraviolet light damage to the skin's collagen and elastin proteins. Sunlight also promotes a fishnetlike display of "broken" blood vessels of the face, neck, and chest. "Liver" spots or "age" spots have nothing to do with liver disease or age but are the aftermath of accumulated sun damage, as are freckles and areas of mottled discoloration. Other areas may lose their color altogether. In addition to brownish blotches, gray, yellowish, and reddish discolorations may also occur. Sun-damaged skin tends to be drier, more pebbly and nodular. In the final analysis, it seems that nature intended vegetation to bask in the sun, not people.

An easy means for comparing the effects of natural aging with those of sun-induced aging is to examine your buttocks. This much maligned, often ignored, area of your anatomy is a site that has probably never been exposed to the light of day. Precisely because it has not been exposed to the sun through the years, the skin there is generally less mottled, less dry, less wrinkled, smoother, and more supple. The fact that you often find striking differences between exposed and unexposed areas is a persuasive argument for sun protection as one of the best methods of preventing skin aging.

Paradoxically, consumers spend millions of hard-earned dollars each year for products claiming to be anti-age, anti-wrinkle, to rejuvenate, and to firm up their skin. They spend millions more for cosmetic surgery to eliminate wrinkles and tighten sagging skin. Yet many of these same people fail to take heed when warned not to fry themselves in the sun and neglect to follow a few simple measures to protect themselves when outdoors (see below). Appropriate sun protection is by far the single best anti-wrinkle remedy available.

Many sun worshippers frequently ask me whether it is all right for them to get "just a little tan." In a recent survey, in which 51 percent of those polled reported using a sunscreen last year to minimize the dangers of sun exposure, less than 40 percent reported "prevention of tanning" as a reason for doing so. To emphasize the dangers of tanning, I usually distribute three brochures to my patients, the titles of which, I believe, say it all: *Tan Now, Pay Later; Suntan Minus Sunburn Still Equals Sun Damage;* and *Today's Handsome Tan Is Tomorrow's Wrinkle and Skin Cancer.*

I try to impress upon my patients that sun tanning is to the skin what cigarette smoking is to the lungs and heart. I would like the FTC and FDA to require all advertisements for fun-in-the-sun Caribbean and south-of-the-border holidays and all sun products that encourage people to go out and tan to carry the following warning:

THE SURGEON GENERAL HAS DETERMINED THAT SUN TANNING IS DANGEROUS TO YOUR HEALTH. SUN TANNING MAY

LEAD TO THE DEVELOPMENT OF PREMATURE AGING, SAG-
GING, WRINKLING, AND DISCOLORATION OF YOUR SKIN
AND THE DEVELOPMENT OF SKIN CANCERS.

THE GOOD NEWS

At this point, you're probably thinking about swapping your
upcoming vacation cruise to the Bahamas for a trip to the Arctic
during the six-month winter darkness. But wait—there is some
good news. Complete abstinence from the sun is neither practical
nor desirable for most of us. Knowing your skin type, wearing
proper clothing, using the appropriate sunscreens, and following a few sensible rules can help you make your sun exposure
safe.

SKIN TYPES

Most of us have a general idea of how sensitive we are to the
sun's rays. There are those of us who always burn and never tan,
and there are those who always tan and never burn. Between
these two extremes lie a number of gradations. There are currently six skin types used by dermatologists to measure individual susceptibility to sun exposure:

TABLE 2.2

SKIN TYPES	
TYPE I	TYPE IV
• Always burns; never tans (i.e., extremely sensitive)	• Always tans; sometimes burns (i.e., minimally sensitive)
TYPE II	TYPE V
• Always burns; sometimes tans (i.e., very sensitive)	• Always tans, never burns (i.e., not sensitive)
TYPE III	TYPE VI
• Sometimes tans; sometimes burns (i.e., sensitive)	• Black skin (i.e., not sensitive)

In general, people with blue eyes and blond hair exhibit type I or type II skin. Blacks, on the other hand, are usually type VI.

Skin types can generally be grouped along ethnic lines. People of Celtic (Scotch-Irish), Scandinavian, or North European extraction usually fall into skin types I or II. Those of Mediterranean backgrounds, such as Italians, Spaniards, and Greeks, are often type III, IV, or V. East Asians and Hispanics frequently have type V skin, and sub-Saharan Africans, type VI.

Naturally, people within any ethnic or racial grouping may vary in their susceptibility to the sun. For example, you might find light-complected blacks having type II or type III skin or Northern Italians with type I or II. Ethnic dilution through intermarriage is believed to play a great role in the evolution of such variations. Because of these variations, no matter what your ethnic background, *it is important to know your specific skin type.*

CLOTHING: THE FIRST LINE OF DEFENSE

Even if you long ago joined the ranks of the enlightened and have given up sun bathing and oily sun-tanning lotions (which offer no protection), you may not be aware of the many other ways you expose yourself to risk. A ten-minute walk between buildings at noon, a twenty-minute picnic lunch or coffee break on the steps of your office building, a half hour of gardening, or even your daily brisk constitutional can put your skin at risk of permanent sun damage. These "innocent" minutes add up to irreversible changes. For that reason you must protect yourself at all times. And by protection, I don't mean just protecting your face. The sun's rays are as damaging to the skin of your body as they are to your face.

Choosing the right clothes for outdoor work or play is important. Broad-brim hats, large sunglasses, long-sleeved shirts, and long pants offer optimal sun protection. Light-colored, light-weight, tightly woven cotton clothing is best for comfort and sun protection. While dark clothing is generally more efficient at absorbing the harmful rays, it also absorbs more heat and is less comfortable for warm weather wear. Loose woven fabrics let too much light through, and wet, clinging clothing can transmit ultraviolet light. Thus, if you tend to perspire heavily or don dry clothing directly over a wet body at the beach or poolside, beware.

Your choice of sunglasses is also important. Take care to choose them with more than just fashion in mind. Recent evidence confirms that dark glasses do indeed reduce glare, but by cutting down on light and allowing your pupils to dilate, more potentially damaging ultraviolet rays may reach the delicate retinas of your eyes. Eye specialists believe that the effects of such ultraviolet radiation can accumulate and may cause permanent visual damage and loss. To choose the safest and most effective sunglasses, consult your eye-care specialist. In general, yellow or rose-colored sunglasses are less effective and less safe than dark green, dark brown or gray-tinted polarized lenses.

SUN BLOCKS AND SUNSCREENS

Besides the visible light you see, the sun emits several different types of radiation. *Ultraviolet light A (UVA)* and *ultraviolet light B (UVB)* are two important types of invisible light rays that pierce our atmosphere and reach the surface of the earth. Both are dangerous to your skin and are responsible for tanning and burning. A third, and potentially even more damaging ultraviolet light, *UVC,* is fortunately screened out by our atmosphere. It has only recently been suspected that still another kind of invisible light, *infrared radiation (heat radiation),* may also contribute to sun damage.

After the use of protective clothing, sunblocks and sunscreens are your next line of defense against the sun's rays. *Sun blocks* are products intended to block out ultraviolet light completely by scattering or reflecting it away from your skin. They are available in ointments, creams, or lotions and usually contain either *titanium dioxide, zinc oxide, kaolin,* or *talc.*

Although sun blocks are as a rule very effective products, their thickness, greasiness, and tendency to discolor clothing limit their usefulness. Most people reserve sun blocks for particularly sun-sensitive regions such as the nose, lips, or below the breasts. Zinc oxide ointment, the familiar thick, white nose coat, has for years been the hallmark of the lifeguard. Sun blocks can occasionally cause a prickly heat rash or a pimplelike reaction on the skin (*folliculitis*) by clogging pores. To make sun blocks more esthetically pleasing, several manufacturers now make flesh-colored or multicolored formulations. RV-Paque and A-Fil creams are examples of effective flesh-colored sun blocks. Le-Zink, a relatively new line of sun-block preparations, comes in many bright colors.

A *sunscreen* is a barrier product that works by absorbing harmful ultraviolet radiation, rather than scattering it away from your skin. While there is as yet no conclusive evidence that sunscreens can prevent any of the long-term damaging effects of sun exposure, many investigators now believe they can. We do know for sure that when used appropriately they can prevent sunburn and reduce or prevent tanning.

Sunscreens are not considered cosmetics and are classed as drugs by the Food and Drug Administration. Until recently, PABA and its derivatives were the most commonly used sunscreen ingredients. A wide variety of effective ingredients have now been added to the list. To date, the FDA has approved twenty-one different sunscreen ingredients, including *para-aminobenzoic acid (PABA)* or PABA derivatives (*padimate-O* and *padimate-A*), *benzophenones, cinnamate* derivatives, *salicylates,* and *sulfonic acid* derivatives.

The FDA has made it easier to choose sunscreen products by requiring that manufacturers label their products with SPF, or Sun Protection Factor, numbers. The higher the number, the more protection the product affords you. For example, if you would normally burn after twenty minutes in the first blush of the spring sun, it would take ten times twenty minutes (or more than three hours) to get to that same degree of sunburn under the same conditions if you used a sunscreen with an SPF of 10. As a rule, sunscreens with an SPF of 8 or less provide minimal protection. Those with SPFs between 8 and 15 provide moderate protection. Maximum protection sunscreens are considered those with SPF numbers of 15 or higher. Table 2.3 includes some of the SPF-15 or higher products, which contain the most widely used sunscreen ingredients.

In general, the fairer and more sensitive your skin, the higher the SPF sunscreen you should choose, i.e., those with type I or II skin should use maximum protection sunscreens, those with type III or IV may use sunscreens with SPFs of 8 or higher, and dark-skinned blacks generally need no sunscreens at all.

Although active research in this area continues, the perfect sunscreen has not yet been created. Since the currently available sunscreens are much more effective for blocking out UVB than UVA, you will unfortunately find that you can still tan while

TABLE 2.3

COMMON SUNSCREENS AND THEIR INGREDIENTS SPF 15 or Higher (Maximum Protection)	PABA	PADIMATE-A (PABA-ESTER)	PADIMATE-O (PABA-ESTER)	BENZO-PHENONES	CINNAMATE	SALICYLATE	SULFONIC ACID
Total Eclipse		+	+	+			
Bain de Soleil-15			+	+			
Coppertone-Supershade-15			+	+			
PreSun 15	+		+	+			
Block Out 15			+				
Hill Shade Lotion	+						
Sol-bar Plus 15			+	+			
Sundown Sunblock-15			+	+		+	
Ti Screen				+	+		
PreSun 29				+	+		
Solbar PF				+	+		
Pabanol	+						
Clinique-19							+

using them. It's a common story in my private practice for patients to return from vacation with a deep tan even though they routinely, liberally, and properly applied their sunscreens every day. UVA exposure is the reason for this and the amount of UVA in summer sunlight may be as much as one thousand times that of UVB. Finally, the fact that none of the currently available sunscreens is capable of reflecting infrared rays creates an additional problem: the more potent the sunscreen you use, the more likely you will be to remain outdoors longer, and the more potentially harmful infrared radiation you will receive.

Most experts believe that severe sun damage is largely irreversible, but one prominent researcher demonstrated recently with laboratory animals that the regular application of potent sunscreens not only prevented further ultraviolet light—induced damage, but allowed sun-damaged skin to repair itself, despite continued sun exposure. Results such as these are certainly encouraging but await confirmation in humans.

Sunscreens, particularly those containing PABA or its derivatives, can sometimes cause problems themselves. They occasionally sting when applied to the skin, especially the face, while sunbathing. They can stain clothing yellow or yellow-orange. Alone or in combination with sunlight they can also cause skin allergies. Even more important, they can make some people allergic to such common topical anesthetics as benzocaine and procaine, or to hair dyes containing para-phenylenediamene, or to oral sulfonamide antibiotics. For these reasons, I usually advise my patients to use a maximum-protection, PABA-free, fragrance-free sunscreen, such as PreSun 29. For those of you with an acne tendency, make certain that the sunscreen you choose is *noncomedogenic*—that is, it has been tested and shown not to trigger acne.

Since it has been estimated that 70 percent of the damage inflicted by the sun during your lifetime is from simply being outdoors or merely sitting by a window, from mid-April to mid-October, when the sun is high in the sky and its rays more direct, you should routinely apply a sunscreen during those months. Be sure to use sunscreens when skiing; high altitudes and thin air permit more ultraviolet light damage, and snow and ice can reflect as much as 90 percent of the sun's rays.

For best results, apply your sunscreen between fifteen and thirty minutes *prior* to sun exposure, preferably while in a dry, air-conditioned room, to allow the sunscreen enough time to adequately bind to your skin. You should reapply it after every two hours of vigorous exercise, since perspiration can dilute its benefits. Reapplication does not increase the length of time you can stay out in the sun, however; it only reinstates the original SPF potency. Use sufficient amounts of sunscreen to form a protective film on your skin; do not rub it in. For added precaution, sunscreens should also be reapplied *immediately* after swimming, even though many of them claim to be insoluble.

Don't neglect to apply sunscreen to all the exposed areas of your skin and especially to the tops of your ears, hairless portions of your scalp, and other sensitive areas. You would be surprised to find out how many people protect only their faces, forgetting that the rest of their skin is just as vulnerable to the ravages of the sun. And today's low-cut summer clothing requires that you apply your sunscreens all the way down the cleavage line. Lips are especially sensitive to sun damage, so remember to protect them with lip balms containing high SPF ingredients (such as PreSun, Total Eclipse, and Chapstick-15). Finally, keep babies six months and younger out of direct sunlight altogether; after six months, you can start applying sunscreens with SPFs of 15 or higher to them regularly. It's never too early to begin.

Don't confuse sunscreens with suntan products containing mineral oil, mineral oil and iodine, baby oil, cocoa butter, and coconut oil. Unless these lotions also contain active sunscreen ingredients, they do nothing more than lubricate your skin. They may in fact make matters worse by focusing and concentrating the sun's rays on your skin.

TIPS FOR SAFE SUNNING

• Avoid outdoor exposure during the hours from 10:00 A.M. to 3:00 P.M., when the sun is directly overhead. This does not mean that you need not use a sunscreen before or after those hours. Sun-induced damage can occur all day long.

• Take extra care during particularly hot, humid, or windy days. These conditions are known to enhance the harmful effects of ultraviolet radiation.

• Also beware of cloudy bright days. They tend to be cooler and darker, tempting you to stay outdoors longer and use less protection. Ultraviolet rays can pierce clouds and cause a serious sunburn.

• Use sunscreens *before* swimming, as well as after—ultraviolet light can penetrate up to 3 feet of water. In addition, water droplets on your skin can act like small magnifying glasses to intensify the sun's rays.

• Don't let your guard down in shady places. Use sunscreens even if you intend to sit under the boardwalk, a beach umbrella, or a shade tree. Sand, water, and concrete reflect between 40 and 60 percent of the sun's rays.

• *Never* use sun reflectors. They concentrate the sun's harmful rays and also focus them on areas ordinarily protected from the sun's rays, such as your eyelids, earlobes, and underside of the chin.

If, after all is said and done, you still insist on getting a tan, do it prudently. Start with a higher SPF sunscreen for about two days, then cut back to a lower SPF sunscreen until you achieve the color you wish. At that point, return to using the higher SPF product; once you have a tan, you will get enough of the UVA through the sunscreen to maintain it.

For those of you who wish to be more scientific about sun exposure, there is now a new kind of ultraviolet light–sensing device or sun-exposure meter. These devices are pocket-size and can be programmed with your skin type and with the SPF of the sunscreen you use. The sensor is supposed to alert you to possible overexposure. A beep tone sounds when you need to seek out the shade.

Finally, since sun ordinarily dries out your skin and causes peeling, be sure to use a moisturizer regularly (chapter 4), especially after your bath or shower.

ARTIFICIAL TANNING AGENTS

BRONZERS AND SKIN STAINS

What should you do when you want that golden tan, but you're already convinced that tanning is out? Artificial tanning agents are one possible answer. These types of products are generally safe, since they do not require outdoor exposure to create the appearance of a tan. Two major classes of safe tanning agents are *bronzers* and *skin stains*.

Bronzers contain water-soluble pigment that is simply deposited on the skin. No chemical reaction occurs between the skin and the colorant. Being water-soluble, bronzers may be washed off with soap and water if you don't like the effect. This is the main advantage of bronzers over skin dyes, but it is also their major drawback. If you happen to like the color of your "tan," continually having to reapply the bronzer can become a nuisance. While "tanning" your skin, bronzers by themselves offer no actual protection from the sun's rays. If you go outdoors, you must follow the sun precautions already discussed.

Skin stains, sometimes referred to as quick-tanning agents, provide a longer-lasting effect. Most of these contain the chemical *dihydroxyacetone (DHA)*, a harmless skin dye that chemically binds to your skin and stains the upper part of the horny layer a brown or reddish-brown color. The major advantage of DHA tanning agents is that the color lasts longer and you need only reapply the tanning agent every three or four days. Your "tan" is lost as the stained cells of the horny layer are naturally shed or washed away.

The longer-lasting aspect becomes a disadvantage if you happen to dislike the color of your "tan" because you are stuck with it for several days. For that reason, I strongly recommend that you first apply a small amount of these products to a small, hidden area of your skin as a test. If you like the resulting color, you can then apply it to any area you wish to appear tanned. Several coats are usually needed to achieve the desired color. **Warning:** As with bronzers, no matter how deeply "tanned" these agents make you appear, they provide no real protection from the sun. You must use appropriate sunscreen protection to prevent a serious burn. Some products combine artificial tanning agents with sunscreens. Examine the labels carefully.

TANNING PILLS

Beta-carotene and *canthaxanthin,* chemical relatives of vitamin A, protect people from photosensitivity reactions to *visible* light *(photoprotection).* They are the only ingested chemicals known to do so. Their protective effect usually requires a minimum of six weeks of therapy. Although how these chemicals actually work remains a mystery, it is believed they may act as an antioxidant.

Beta-carotene and canthaxanthin, either alone or in combination, are the main constituents of many of the so-called tanning tablets available in Canada and Europe. Oral use of beta-carotene and canthaxanthin is being actively promoted by body builders and others in the health game as a safe means of tanning. Beta-carotene is a natural constituent of many plants, including such common fruits and vegetables as oranges, carrots, tomatoes, and mushrooms. It is also used as a food additive in butter, cheese, and in chicken feed to provide yellower egg yolks. Neither chemical has been approved for use in the United States as a tanning pill.

Unfortunately, when applied to your skin or taken orally, beta-carotene and canthaxanthin do not protect against ultraviolet radiation; they have only been demonstrated to be effective in absorbing visible light radiation. Furthermore, if ingested in high doses, these substances accumulate within the skin and fatty tissue and turn it a deep yellow or orange-brown. In fact, ingesting large quantities of tanning capsules can result in *hypercarotenemia,* a condition in which the skin, including the palms of the hands, turns quite yellow. Hypercarotenemia by itself is harmless. However, the yellowing of the skin can be so intense that people with hypercarotenemia occasionally have been confused with patients suffering from a more serious illness, *hepatitis (jaundice)*. The safety of consuming large amounts of these substances remains unknown.

Another kind of tanning pill contains the photosensitizing chemical *8-methoxypsoralen*. Psoralens, originally used solely in topical preparations for their fragrance, were found to be photosensitizing and have been more recently employed as therapeutic agents for such conditions as psoriasis (chapter 8).

In blond or freckled people who suffer from painful, blistering reactions to sunlight, oral 8-methoxypsoralen has been used to help enhance resistance to sun damage. The protective effect is believed to result from the chemical's capacity to increase both the thickness of the skin and melanin production. People who are extremely sensitive to the sun and who are allergic to sunscreens are advised to take two or three capsules of the chemical for a two-week period before prolonged sun exposure. Naturally, this regimen should only be carried out under the supervision of a dermatologist.

Psoralens are found in a number of European sunscreens advertised as tan-promoting lotions. While they do promote tanning, they may, according to some researchers, also promote the development of skin cancers. For that reason, the FDA has not approved their use in sunscreens in this country. Avoid them.

TAN-ACCELERATOR LOTIONS

Another class of tan-promoting potions to avoid are those billed as presunbathing *tan accelerators*. These are a new class of suntan product that is intended to be applied to your skin each day for several days *before* sunbathing. They are supposed to promote a faster, deeper tan. Such products usually contain an impressive list of chemical names including the amino acid *tyrosine*, a natural substance involved in the normal production of melanin and the tanning process. Manufacturers' claims for the efficacy of tan accelerators remain unproven; a recent independent study of these products failed to demonstrate any augmentation of tanning. Indeed, it is doubtful that sufficient amounts of tyrosine can penetrate to the level of the skin where it could enhance melanin production. Even more important, however, is the issue of whether tan accelerators should be used at all. The answer is, of course, that any product encouraging sun exposure, sunbathing, and sun tanning, either explicitly or implicitly, should be avoided.

TANNING PARLORS

The increasing numbers of tanning salons and "sun" centers are another manifestation of the ongoing tanning craze. Insofar as tanning salons permit year-round exposure, they are potentially more dangerous than the sun. In 1986, there were nearly 10,000 tanning salons in the United States, representing nearly a 33 percent increase over 1985. Approximately 2 million Americans frequented them. A typical tanning booth is 3 feet square and has walls composed of fluorescent lights. Interestingly, tanning machines have even been ferried in house trailers to the beaches of California and Florida so that vacationers could acquire "quick tans" without spending much time on the beach.

Prior to 1985, tanning salons, having switched in most cases from UVB to UVA, claimed to be "safer than the sun." It has since become illegal for tanning salons to make that claim. While it is true that sunburn is less likely with UVA sources, it is still possible. In addition, the other dangers of ultraviolet radiation remain very real. As of September 1986, the FDA requires manufacturers of tanning devices to affix a warning label on all their machines. I echo the FDA concern and strongly caution you against using them. For similar reasons, you should also avoid sunlamps.

CLEAN, NOT SQUEAKY CLEAN

Your skin is a daily battleground in an ongoing war with dirt, airborne pollution, cosmetics, oils, dead skin cells, and perspiration. Cleansing your skin is the defense. Strong soaps, hot water, and superscrubbing were once the prescriptions of the day, but scientific thinking on proper skin cleansing has changed over the last decade or so. In general, vigorous scrubbing with soap and water are no longer routinely recommended. Gentleness in skin cleansing is now advised.

Because heavy and greasy substances such as cosmetics and dirt can be difficult to remove, adequate skin cleansing usually requires more than just plain water. You need to use some kind of cleansing agent. All soaps and cleansers work by dissolving grease and allowing it to be rinsed off with water. If you've ever tried to remove petroleum jelly from your hands with plain water, you probably have noticed that it seems to repel the water. Soaps and detergents contain chemicals called *emulsifiers* or *surfactants,* whose molecules have the special ability to lock onto both grease and water. These chemicals allow greasy substances such as skin oils and dirt to be soaped up and then rinsed away with water.

The range of cleansers for face and body includes a variety of soaps, soapless soaps (synthetic detergent soaps), cleansing creams and lotions, and washable creams and lotions. Manufacturers of these products spend many millions of dollars on advertising to persuade you that their particular product can do miraculous things for your skin, i.e., rejuvenate your skin and make you younger looking in X number of days or fight wrinkles or give your complexion that special blush or glow. Bear in mind, however, that no matter which soap or cleanser you ultimately decide to use, you will be wasting your time and money if you purchase it in the belief that it will do more than merely help keep your skin clean and feeling fresh. In fact, all soaps and cleansers are actually irritating to the skin!

While their performance and effectiveness vary little, the retail prices of the various brands of soaps and cleansers may differ dramatically. Bar soaps, for example, may range from less than 20 cents per bar to nearly 9 dollars per bar. Packaging and fragrance together account for about 30 percent of a soap's price. Besides price, durability—how slowly or quickly a particular brand of soap melts away in your soap dish—is about the only other important difference between bar soaps. Incidentally, a soap need not lather well to be an effective cleanser, although most people seem to prefer those that lather richly.

The well-stocked shelves of our supermarkets and drugstores attest to how wide the selection of skin cleansers really is. Choosing the right one depends upon your individual needs. However, owing to the wide range of choices, your final selection will most likely also be influenced by your personal preferences for product color, fragrance, feel, and your taste for luxury.

The aim of this chapter is to help you make an informed choice. To this end, I have divided cleansers into several categories, including toilet soaps, superfatted soaps, soapless soaps, washable creams and lotions and liquid soaps, deodorant soaps, soaps with additives, and bubble baths. Alcohol-based products, such as astringents and toners, are also discussed. The remainder of the chapter is devoted to proper washing and bathing.

SOAPS, CLEANSING LOTIONS, AND BUBBLE BATHS

TOILET SOAPS

Toilet soap, which is available in opaque bars, is plain old soap and is composed of the salts of animal or vegetable fats and olive oils (tallow). Palm kernel or coconut oils are often added to enhance lathering. About half of all currently available toilet soaps are *milled* soaps. Milling is the process by which soap chips are thoroughly blended and then compressed by machinery into bars to ensure that moisture is removed and the basic ingredients and additives are evenly distributed. Ivory is probably the best-known brand of toilet soap.

In general, toilet soaps do what they are supposed to do—that is, they help to clean off grease, grime, and cosmetics. They also tend to be quite inexpensive. However, these soaps as a rule are rather alkaline and have the potential to be irritating; overusing them can lead to irritation by affecting the skin's acid mantle. Fortunately for most people with normal skin, natural skin acidity returns to normal very shortly after the soap is rinsed off. If you have especially sensitive skin, or if you are using drying acne medications, however, you may find basic toilet soap too irritating.

Finally, there is an additional problem with toilet soaps for those who live in a hard-water area—that is, one where the water contains naturally high amounts of calcium or magnesium minerals. Sticky and potentially irritating residues resulting from the chemical interaction between toilet soap and hard water may be deposited on your skin and in sink basins. If you choose to use toilet soaps under these circumstances, I advise you to rinse your skin with copious amounts of water. Using synthetic detergent soaps (pages 34–35) or conditioning your water are alternatives.

SUPERFATTED SOAPS

Superfatted soaps are essentially toilet soaps to which moisturizers such as cold cream, lanolin, mineral oil, olive oil, cocoa butter, and other neutral fats have been added. The amount of fatty material added varies widely among different brands. While most soaps ordinarily contain less than 2 percent fat, superfatted soaps contain somewhere between 5 percent and approximately 15 percent fat. The fatty moisturizers in superfatted soaps are intended to counter the degreasing effects of the soap —a difficult task to accomplish. Some people complain that superfatted soaps deposit a greasy residue on their skin and leave them feeling unclean, but there are many who do prefer these soaps, finding them gentler to the skin. For those of you who like superfatted soaps, I have found Purpose, Dove, and Basis satisfactory.

Transparent soap is a special form of superfatted soap. In addition to a higher fat content, often in the form of castor oil or resin, these soaps contain ingredients such as glycerin (at least 10 percent more than other soaps), alcohol, and sugar. The higher glycerin content is responsible for the soap's soft consistency and transparency.

Transparent soaps do not seem to be any better for sensitive skin than other superfatted soaps. In fact, because glycerin (in high concentrations) and, even more so, alcohol may draw water from the skin, these soaps can paradoxically be too drying for some people. For this reason, transparent soaps are best reserved for individuals with sensitive but oily skin.

In general, transparent soaps lather poorly. Moreover, they frequently melt into unmanageable globs if you leave them in the soap dish. However, you can extend their life by drying them after each use. Neutrogena soap is a well-known brand of transparent soap.

SOAPLESS SOAPS

Also called *synthetic detergent soaps, cakes,* or *bars,* soapless soaps are derived from petroleum materials, fatty acids, and other substances. Cosmetic and pharmaceutical chemists have attempted to formulate detergent soaps to make them less irritating, less alkaline, and richer lathering than plain toilet soaps. Most soapless soaps perform satisfactorily and have the additional benefit, as I mentioned earlier, of not interacting with hard water to leave scummy residue on your skin or in the sink. In contrast with transparent soaps, they lather reasonably well and usually don't melt as readily in the soap dish. They also don't leave the greasy film that many people complain of after washing with superfatted soaps. For these reasons, and especially because they tend to be gentler than toilet soaps, I generally recommend soapless soaps for most of my patients who have normal, dry, or sensitive skin. Lowila cake is one product that I found quite satisfactory as an all-purpose skin cleanser.

WASHABLE CREAMS AND LOTIONS AND LIQUID SOAPS

Washable creams and lotions share many of the same ingredients as bar soaps, but in general tend to be more expensive. They are basically moisturizers to which soaps or detergents have been added. Moisturizing ingredients are the major components of washable creams; washable lotions are simply washable creams to which more water has been added to make them thinner and easily spreadable. Both are intended to be rinsed off with water.

These days, some of the major cosmetic manufacturers seem to be focusing their attention on liquid soaps, which are also made to be rinsed off with water. Liquid soaps have a higher soap or detergent content than washable lotions and usually contain glycerin. They tend to be more expensive than their bar counterparts but possess no particular advantage over them, although they come in pump dispensers and are convenient to use.

Washable lotions can be helpful for some people. If you have dry or sensitive skin, you might try alternating the use of regular soap and a washable lotion, cleansing with soap in the morning and the washable lotion at night. Or, you might use soap one day and a washable lotion the next, depending upon your individual needs. Because they contain moisturizers, I do not advise washable creams or lotions for persons with excessively oily skin as they may aggravate the condition. Cetaphil lotion is a very useful washable lotion.

Washable lotions and liquid soaps should *not* be confused with cleansing creams or lotions. These are primarily moisturizers used mainly for cleaning purposes. Basically they are variations on the old cold-cream formula and are meant to be applied and then *wiped off* with a facial tissue or soft towel, rather than washed off with water. Liquefying creams are simply cleansing creams that contain oils and waxes that melt upon contact with skin heat. Otherwise, they differ little from cleansing creams and have no special properties. The word *liquefying* makes great ad copy, but that's all.

Like many moisturizers, cleansing lotions (and liquefying creams) tend to be greasy, and can leave a film on your skin; in addition, because they contain little or no detergent, they generally clean poorly. Cleansing creams and lotions can be useful, however, for removing makeup, particularly oil-based or heavy theater makeups and powders. If you use them for makeup removal, I suggest you follow with a gentle soap and water cleansing. They may also be useful if you have extremely dry or sensitive skin and absolutely cannot tolerate any form of soap or detergent cleanser. Overall, I seldom recommend cleansing lotions.

DEODORANT SOAPS

Deodorant soaps, which are intended to suppress or mask body odor, contain two major types of ingredients: antiseptics for controlling bacteria and perfumes. Body odor results from the action of skin bacteria on the secretions of the apocrine sweat glands (as discussed in chapter 1). The apocrine sweat itself is odorless; the bacterial breakdown products of apocrine sweat are the culprits of body odor. To slow bacterial growth, the major brands of deodorant soaps contain the antiseptics *triclosan* or *triclocarban*. Deodorant soaps tend to be drying, and since apocrine glands are not found in facial skin, you do not ordinarily need to use deodorant soaps on your face. However, they make excellent body soaps, especially if you tend to perspire heavily. Occasionally, your dermatologist may recommend using them as part of the treatment regimen for certain skin infections such as folliculitis.

Deodorant soaps can be problematic. They may cause allergic eruptions or rashes in people with sensitive skin. In addition, the antibacterials in them can be absorbed into your bloodstream through the skin. While the amounts absorbed are minimal, the long-term effects of this absorption remain unknown. Finally, the perfumes in some of these soaps can be irritating. I recommend deodorant soaps only if you have a very difficult odor problem or if you are advised to use one by your dermatologist. For most people, washing with basic toilet soap usually proves satisfactory for cleansing and odor control. Dial and Safeguard are two well-known brands of deodorant soaps.

SOAPS WITH ADDITIVES

An array of so-called organic, herbal, and other natural additives, medications, and abrasive particles have been added to soaps and cleansers supposedly to provide additional benefits. In general, despite the ad copy, these soaps do little else for you than part you from your money.

Fruit, vegetable, and herbal soaps amount to nothing more than, in the words of the Immortal Bard, "sound and fury, signifying nothing." The "natural" or organic ingredients, fruit juices, vitamins and minerals, and so on, are supposed to conjure up images of healthy living; the advertisements for them usually show people enjoying life outdoors and looking incredibly fresh on a sunny spring day in the country. In actual fact, herbal, fruit, and vegetable soaps clean no better than conventional soaps and provide no additional benefits.

During the soap manufacturing process, the herbs, fruits, or vegetables added to these cleansers are strained, sterilized, alcohol-purified, and mixed with preservatives. By the time the process is complete, the end product is so far removed from the original natural ingredient that artificial colorings and fragrances must be included to simulate the real thing. The bottom line: Unless you are crazy about the artificial smell and color of herbs, fruits, and vegetables in your soaps, don't waste your money on them.

Medicated soaps are cleansers that contain topical drugs in addition to the cleansing agent. They are advertised as being helpful for treating a variety of common skin conditions. These soaps may contain sulfur, resorcinol, salicylic acid, benzoyl peroxide, or antiseptics—the medications successfully used to treat a number of medical conditions such as acne, bacterial and fungal infections, and certain forms of eczema. In order to be of value, however, a medication must remain in contact with your skin for an extended period of time. Since soaps are intended to be lathered up quickly and rinsed off almost immediately, the ingredients in them do not remain on your skin long enough to do much of anything. In addition, medicated soaps tend to be drying and irritating. If you have a specific skin condition, see your dermatologist. Don't play around with soaps.

Abrasive cleansers, or *exfoliating cleansers* as they are also known, contain tiny particles or grains that are supposed to abrade your skin mildly and slough off the surface layer of dead cells. Some abrasive soaps may contain as much as 25 percent pumice (ground volcanic rock); this is intended to leave you with a smooth, glowing complexion. For many people, abrasive soaps can be too harsh and drying, but if you have extremely oily skin, you may find them helpful when used occasionally. However, if you have acne or other types of inflammation, the use of these abrasives can aggravate your condition. Abrasive cleansers should be used with great care. If used too often or too vigorously, or if used in conjunction with certain potent antiacne medications, your skin may become very dry, flaky, or cracked; in extreme cases, "broken" blood vessels may even result. Once again, I suggest that you consult with your physician before using these kinds of cleansers.

BUBBLE BATHS

Bubble bath products are simply detergent cleansers that contain ingredients capable of making your bathwater foam. Appealing as a bubble bath might seem, however, sitting for prolonged periods of time in the degreasing detergent environment of a bubble bath can be quite irritating, especially for people with sensitive or dry skin or eczema. You should use no more of the detergent than is recommended by the manufacturer—do not dump in half the bottle. An overconcentrated solution of bubble bath can irritate skin and mucous membranes. Be sure to distribute the bath product thoroughly before going into the tub. A moisturizer should be applied after the bath. If any skin irritation develops, stop using the product and consult your dermatologist.

BEYOND SOAP:
ALCOHOL-BASED PRODUCTS

Fresheners, toners, bracers, astringents, and clarifying lotions are intended to cleanse and freshen your skin and shrink pores. However, they actually do little more than make your skin feel *temporarily* cool, tight, and tingly.

Fresheners, toners, and *bracers* are essentially clear, liquid alcohol solutions. The alcohol in them helps dissolve dirt, oils, and cosmetics. In addition, the evaporation of the alcohol causes the cooling and tightening sensations of the skin that people experience moments after applying these products. Glycerin is frequently added for its cooling and moisturing effects.

Astringents, also called *pore refiners* or *refining lotions,* contain more alcohol than fresheners and toners. They may also contain other ingredients to enhance their cooling, tingling, and tightening functions, such as *zinc* and *aluminum salts, witch hazel, acetone, boric acid, menthol,* and *camphor.* The addition of these chemicals causes a slight irritation and swelling of the openings of your pores, tightening them temporarily. Virtually the same effect can be obtained by pinching or patting your cheeks. Mint, eucalyptus, and lemon fragrances are often added to astringents to increase product appeal.

Since astringents can be irritating to dry or sensitive skin, I generally do not recommend them. However, they may be of some value for persons with oily skin who want to remove excess oil between regular skin cleansings.

Clarifying lotions are water, alcohol, and glycerin solutions to which certain keratin-dissolving chemicals have been added for smoothing your skin. These may include *salicylic acid, resorcinol,* and *benzoyl peroxide,* all of which are helpful antiacne ingredients. They may also contain *papain,* a keratin-dissolving enzyme, which is extracted from papaya plants. Clarifying lotions can be highly irritating, especially to dry or sensitive skin, so I suggest avoiding them. If you need any of these ingredients, your dermatologist can prescribe or recommend a host of other more effective medications that contain them.

PROPER WASHING AND BATHING

Americans are the most overbathed, overwashed people in the world. If cleanliness is next to godliness, we should be pretty near the seventh level of heaven by now. Most people shower or bath *at least* once a day and, for relaxation, love to soak in very hot water. But is so much washing, showering, and bathing really necessary or good for you? The answer is *no.*

Madison Avenue would have us believe that if we skip even one washing, we're not only going to look and feel dirty, but even worse, we're going to offend others. The "don't you wish everyone did?" idea adds to our body odor paranoia. Yet the truth may surprise you. The armpits, groin, anal, genital, and foot regions of the body are the *only* significant odor-producing areas. If you were to sponge bathe these areas each day with just a water-dampened cloth to wipe away sweat and odor-producing bacteria, you would not smell. And so long as you continued to sponge bathe in this manner you wouldn't smell, even if you never bathed or showered at all. But of course, washing isn't simply about smell, it's also about dirt and sweat (the kind that soaks you during exercise, say) and the need to *feel* clean. And face it—there aren't too many of us who wouldn't opt for a shower on a hot, sticky day! Many people "need" to shower or bathe daily just to relax; others can't conceive of *not* doing it every morning upon arising.

Fortunately, those of you with normal or oily skin are probably resilient enough to rebound from your daily cleansing frenzy. On the other hand, if you have dry or sensitive skin, daily, or even worse, twice daily showering or bathing has the potential for causing significant irritation. Bathing tends to be even more drying than showering because people tend to sit and relax for long periods in a tub.

To prevent skin abuse in the name of cleanliness, you should wash gently, and not more than twice each day. Wash with your fingertips only and use the gentlest soap that does the job. Whenever possible, shower instead of bathe, use lukewarm rather than hot water, and stay in only as long as it takes you to clean yourself. Concentrate on the odor-producing areas of your body; let plain water rinse off the rest of you. Your skin is not a greasy steak plate and does not need harsh soaps, superscrubbing, detergents, and hot water to get it clean. Always pat your skin dry; don't buff it with a towel. If you find that your skin remains dry and sensitive, limit showering to every other day or even every third day and just sponge bathe the odor-producing areas. Avoid wash cloths or abrasive polyester sponge pads or cloths. These merely abrade and irritate your skin. Finally, follow with a moisturizer regularly.

MOISTURIZERS: "HOPE IN A BOTTLE"

*M*any years ago, Charles Revson, the founder of Revlon Cosmetics, commented that the cosmetics industry "sells hope in a bottle." In no area of the huge cosmetics industry is this more evident than in the moisturizer market. Consumers spend more than 2 billion dollars each year for moisturizers, which range in price from less than $1 per ounce to between $30 and $90 per ounce. Some of the industry's wildest claims and biggest advertising hypes involve moisturizers.

Ads for moisturizers frequently use alluring terms such as "deep energizing," "nourishing," "toning," "pore-shrinking," "skin-firming," "anti-aging," "anti-wrinkling," and "cellular-energizing" to describe their products. Some fabulously expensive moisturizers, which contain some of the most exotic-sounding ingredients and which are sold exclusively at selected, "fine" stores, are being touted as almost magical skin restorers and revitalizers. It is no wonder, then, that William Safire was given to observe in the *New York Times* that the word cellular has become the moisturizer manufacturers' new hard "sell-ular."

A definition is in order here. A *cosmetic* is any product whose purpose is to enhance or beautify the skin. A *topical medication,* on the other hand, is a product that affects the structure and function of the skin. Moisturizers, which can also be called *lubricants* or *emollients,* are cosmetics; they serve to sooth, smooth, and soften your skin—nothing more. No matter what you hear or read about them, *moisturizers can neither retard nor reverse the skin aging process.*

However, for many people, regular use of moisturizers for the prevention of dryness and irritation and for the maintenance of smooth, supple skin constitutes an extremely important part of proper skin care that should not be neglected.

In this chapter, I explain what smooth, supple, and moist skin is, then I address the problem of dry skin—who needs a moisturizer—and common ingredients in moisturizers, a discussion that is intended to demystify the bewildering array of products available today. There's a brief discussion of bath oils and bath oil pearls, and then finally I give tips on how to choose the right moisturizer.

THE GOAL:
SMOOTH, SUPPLE, AND MOIST SKIN

Smooth, supple, and moist skin results from a complex interaction between three major skin elements: its natural water content, oil gland production, and the presence, in varying amounts, of special substances called *natural moisturizing factors* (NMF). Your skin's water content is the most important determinant of skin texture. Ordinarily, the horny layer of the skin is the crucial layer for moisture and contains between 10 and 30 percent water. The maintenance of optimal water content of the skin depends heavily upon the presence of the skin's protective oil layers or *lipid film.* This vital layer is derived primarily from two sources: from secretions of your skin's oil (sebaceous) glands and from substances present in the walls of the dead skin cells of the horny layer.

Natural moisturizing factors are substances produced by the body (or synthetically in the laboratory) that act to attract and hold on to water at the skin surface. They are thought to work by binding water in place or by helping the skin's cellular proteins arrange themselves so that they better absorb and hold on to the water. NMFs include *urea, phospholipids,* and *lactic, malic, pyruvic, glycolic,* and *pyrollidone carboxylic acids.*

DRY SKIN

Dry skin is by far the most common human skin affliction. It has been estimated that in the course of our lifetimes, every single one of us will be affected by it to varying degrees. Under the electron microscope, normal skin appears to have a dramatically jagged outline, but to the naked eye, normally hydrated skin appears perfectly smooth and scale-free. When the horny layer of your skin for any reason becomes too dry, fine flakes begin to appear. If the problem persists or worsens, coarser and more adherent flakes appear, which are then shed in clumps at the surface. If dryness becomes more severe, you can generate a little shower of flakes by simply rubbing or scratching your skin. Dermatologists often use the terms *xerosis* or *asteatosis* to refer to any severe dry-skin condition. Aging skin is particularly prone to dryness and will be discussed in chapter 17.

The reasons that some people suffer from dry skin more than others are not completely understood yet, but the common link among all forms of dry-skin problems seems to be an abnormal shedding of cells from the horny layer of the skin. Under normal circumstances, single cells are shed from this layer; in dry skin conditions, clumps of tightly bound cells are shed. Contrary to conventional wisdom, there is little evidence that dry, roughened skin contains substantially less water than normal skin, although there is believed to be a progressive decline in skin water content as we age. However, individuals predisposed to rough, spiky, scaly-looking skin will find their condition worsened by any measures that dry the skin, such as overwashing or using harsh soaps. Yet, adding water to the surface of scaling skin by applying a moisturizer immediately after your bath or shower can dramatically alleviate the condition.

Dry skin, particularly when severe, can predispose you to a variety of complications. In general, dryness leads to the thickening and stiffening of the horny layer of your skin. This in turn leads to an increase in evaporative water loss through the horny layer, which then leads to the formation of skin splits and cracks (fissures). Fissures tend to be itchy and sore and make you prone to further irritation, eczema, and even infections.

Manufacturers of the concoctions that are supposed to be anti-aging and anti-wrinkling take advantage of the average consumer's basic lack of knowledge about skin, not to mention wishful thinking. But no matter what the ads try to make you believe, dryness is *not* responsible for the development of wrinkles or premature skin aging. To be sure, dryness can accentuate wrinkles, so if you have this problem, by all means use a moisturizer regularly, although it won't make your wrinkles disappear permanently.

A new moisturizing drug, Lac-Hydrin Lotion, was introduced recently. It contains the equivalent of 12 percent lactic acid, a potent moisturizing ingredient and NMF, and is available by doctor's prescription only. As a topical drug, Lac-Hydrin Lotion required FDA approval, which means it had to demonstrate not only safety but also efficacy. It has been found to be effective in dealing with many stubborn dry-skin conditions and appears also to work at the skin's deeper levels. Moreover, Lac-Hydrin's effects on the skin have been observed to continue from three to fourteen days after its last application. As a rule, the effects of conventional, nonprescription moisturizers last only as long as the moisturizer remains on your skin.

With the introduction of moisturizing drugs such as Lac-Hydrin, I believe that we are now on the threshold of developing a whole new class of "cosmeceutical" products that will be capable of affecting the structure and function of the skin. Research is actively continuing in this area, and we may soon be able to realize some or all of those wonderful results that hyped cosmetics have long been claiming possible.

WHO NEEDS A MOISTURIZER?

Not everyone needs to use moisturizers. If you have oily skin, you can usually do without them. On the other hand, if you have dry or sensitive skin, you would do well to use them. I routinely recommend moisturizers for older people whose skin tends to be drier, but people of any age who are exposed to prolonged periods of cold, chapping, harsh weather conditions, indoor heating, or air-conditioned rooms may also benefit from their use. A relative humidity above 40 percent is usually sufficient to maintain skin moisture; anything below that can dry out your skin. Overzealous and too frequent sun exposure and skin cleansing, or the use of harsh or alkaline soaps, scrub brushes, or irritating cosmetics, may likewise necessitate the use of moisturizers.

In addition, there are a number of medical conditions and treatments that can dry or irritate the skin, for which moisturizers are often recommended. Acne medications, those for so-called "teenage" acne and adult acne, even when used properly, often leave your skin a shade on the dry side. Moisturizers can help and dermatologists often advise using them as part of the treatment regimen. *Diuretics* ("water pills"), commonly used for treating high blood pressure and other forms of heart disease, premenstrual fluid accumulation, and inappropriately for crash dieting, may deplete the skin of moisture. Here, too, moisturizers can help.

Finally, several common skin conditions, though not caused by dryness, are frequently accompanied or triggered by it. These include certain forms of eczema, psoriasis (see chapter 8), and a less common dry-skin problem, *ichthyosis*. The daily use of moisturizers can play an important part in their management. However, if what appears to be a simple dry-skin problem doesn't improve with the regular use of moisturizers, you should consult with your dermatologist. Many potent prescription topicals are available for ameliorating tougher dry-skin and eczema problems.

COMMON INGREDIENTS IN MOISTURIZERS

Moisturizers today are composed primarily of two things: *occlusive ingredients* and *humectants*. Occlusive ingredients are those that lock in the moisture already in your skin. Humectants are ingredients that attract water as it passes through the horny layer of the skin, as well as from the surrounding air.

OCCLUSIVE MOISTURIZING INGREDIENTS

Animal fats, vegetable oils, and mineral oils are all occlusive ingredients. Animal fats include lanolin, and mink, turtle, and codfish oils. Lanolin, which is a derivative of sheep oil glands, is a very common ingredient in moisturizers. Hydrous wool fat was and is a frequently used form of lanolin, although many other lanolin derivatives are now used also. Closely resembling the makeup of your own oil gland secretions, lanolin usually does not interfere with your skin's normal functioning. Unfortunately, people with sensitive skin are frequently allergic to lanolin and its derivatives. Further, lanolin may clog pores and trigger acne breakouts. Mink and turtle oils are no better than simple lanolin, but some moisturizer manufacturers make subtle use of the association between the richness of mink coats and mink oil moisturizers. Similarly, they attempt to play upon the notion that since turtles live so long, their oils may have age-retarding or age-reversing properties. These claims amount to nothing more than advertising gimmicks.

Olive, safflower, corn, wheat germ, palm kernel, apricot, and sesame seed oils are all examples of common vegetable oils found in many moisturizers. These polyunsaturated oils can make satisfactory occlusive ingredients, but they are generally not as effective as either animal fats or mineral oils. In the case of vegetable oils, sales of some products benefit from the subtle association with the health benefits of consuming polyunsaturated oils for your heart. Unfortunately, when applied to the skin, these oils provide no special benefits.

Cocoa butter is another vegetable oil commonly found in moisturizers. A solid fat derivative of the roasted seeds of the cacao tree (the source of chocolate and cocoa), cocoa butter melts at room temperature. Although an effective moisturizing ingredient, I seldom recommend it because it can irritate sensitive skin.

Petroleum derivatives and plain mineral oil are examples of mineral oils. For more than a hundred years, petroleum jelly or petrolatum, as dermatologists often refer to it, has been an excellent occlusive moisturizer. In fact, even today it remains the paradigm of effectiveness among occlusive moisturizers against which all other newly developed moisturizers are compared. Petroleum jelly has the additional advantage of being very inexpensive, and allergies to it are rare. If you have extremely sensitive skin and are easily irritated by commercial moisturizers, you might try petroleum jelly. However, most people find it too greasy and messy to use regularly. It can also clog pores and trigger acne flare-ups. Some products include petrolatum in their formulations in order to capitalize on its benefits while minimizing its drawbacks.

Minerals oils are also quite effective moisturizers, though they can be irritating to people with very sensitive skin. In addition, like petroleum jelly, they are messy to use and can aggravate acne. As a rule, I seldom recommend them.

HUMECTANT MOISTURIZERS

Glycerine, propylene glycol, butylene glycol, urea, lactic acid, lecithin (a phospholipid), and *sodium pyrollidone carboxylic acid* are examples of common humectants. Today, humectants are increasingly being used in moisturizers, either alone or in combination with other humectants or occlusive ingredients. These substances help to loosen scales, are very effective even for stubborn dry-skin problems, and are non—acne aggravating. In fact, they are also particularly useful for countering the drying effects of many topical antiacne medications. Some humectant-containing moisturizers come in varying concentrations. In general, the more severe your dry-skin problem, the higher the concentration of humectant you require. I have already mentioned the prescription moisturizing drug Lac-Hydrin Lotion. Other useful, nonprescription moisturizers that contain humectants include Aquacare-HP, Carmol-10, and Ultramide lotions.

INGREDIENTS TO WATCH OUT FOR

Certain ingredients, when included in moisturizers, add much to the ad copy and a lot to the price, but little to the benefit of the product. These include *amino acids, collagen, procollagen, elastin, hyaluronic acid, proteins, DNA, vitamin E (tocopherol)*, and *vitamin A*. Other frequently hyped ingredients include *hormones* and *placental extracts;* herbal and other unusual ingredients, such as *algae, aloe vera, allantoin,* and *liposomes,* and *eggs, milk, honey,* and *royal bee jelly.*

AMINO ACIDS, COLLAGEN, ELASTIN
HYALURONIC ACID, PROTEINS, AND DNA

Amino acids are the building blocks of proteins, and proteins are in turn the structural building blocks of your body. Collagen and elastin are the major supporting and elastic fibers in your skin. As these fibers age or are damaged by ultraviolet light and normal wear and tear, they are replaced by newly synthesized collagen and elastin. To do this, your cells utilize the amino acids from the foods you eat. However, ad copy notwithstanding, collagen, elastin, or other proteins and amino acids cannot get into the skin through topical application. The molecules of these substances are simply too large to penetrate your skin. Thus, any moisturizers containing these substances are no more effective than the oils or humectants they contain. Although some people contend that moisturizers containing collagen spread more smoothly and have a satiny feel, they don't moisturize any better. In my opinion, these moisturizers are not worth their often extremely high prices.

Collagen in moisturizers must not be confused with the injectable collagen preparations, Zyderm and Zyplast, used by dermatologists for treating wrinkles and depressed scars (chapter 11). The collagen material in these preparations is injected with a needle precisely where it is needed in the deeper level of the skin.

Hyaluronic acid, a natural component of the nonfibrous portion of the dermis, has been getting a lot of play in the past year or two. As an ingredient in moisturizers, however, it remains unproven. Like collagen, it enhances the feel of the products that contain it by acting as a humectant. Unfortunately, there's no magic there.

DNA, which stands for *deoxyribonucleic acid,* is the building block of our genetic material and is essential for cellular repair and regeneration. Recently, some manufacturers have been pitching the rejuvenating benefits of DNA-containing cellular extracts in their products. There is no evidence to support these claims.

VITAMINS E AND A

Vitamin E, or as it is sometimes also listed on cosmetic ingredient labels, *tocopherol* or *tocopheryl acetate,* is another highly promoted additive. For several years now, people have been consuming large amounts of vitamin E for everything from curing cancer and revitalizing a waning sex drive to speeding wound healing and rejuvenating skin. Despite the fact that its benefits remain largely unproven, many people continue to break open vitamin E capsules and apply the material directly to their skin. Others use commercially available moisturizers containing vitamin E. Like collagen and elastin, the vitamin E molecules are too large to pass through your skin. Moreover, vitamin E use is not without its potential side effects. I have treated a number of patients who had developed severe allergic reactions to the vitamin E they were applying to their skin.

Vitamin A has also been incorporated into moisturizers as an anti-aging, anti-wrinkle medication. Research has recently suggested that retinoic acid, a vitamin A derivative, is capable of retarding or reversing some of the effects of photoaging (ultraviolet-light, sun-induced aging). *Retinol,* a vitamin A derivative found in a number of moisturizers, is believed to be oxidized on the skin to *retinoic acid.* Even if they did work, these moisturizers would require months of continuous daily use before any significant benefits could be realized; in addition, their use would be required indefinitely thereafter to maintain the benefits. The jury is not yet in on these moisturizers, and we have only the manufacturers' in-house studies to support the claims for them.

The question arises whether these types of moisturizers, because they purport to alter the structure of your skin, should be reclassified as drugs. If they were reclassified, the manufacturers would have to submit their data on these moisturizers to FDA scrutiny. The FDA is currently in the process of filing such action against a number of major cosmetic houses, the outcome of which most probably will follow a long legal battle.

HORMONES AND PLACENTAL EXTRACTS

Some expensive moisturizers also contain hormones, typically estrogens in amounts so small that the moisturizers remain under the category of cosmetic, rather than drug. However, such small amounts of added hormones effect little or no recognizable benefit. The hormones contained in moisturizers may act to attract water, but their benefits are of such a limited nature that, in my opinion, their use is not justified.

Placental extracts are another big hype. In moisturizers these ingredients allegedly supplement the vitamin and hormone content. The manufacturers of these products take advantage of the belief that since the placenta nourishes the developing embryo, an extract of it can nourish and rejuvenate aging skin. Placental extracts can do no such thing.

HERBAL AND OTHER UNUSUAL INGREDIENTS

Although the use of algae herbs and vegetable extracts may sound appealing, none of these ingredients has been demonstrated to impart any real benefits to moisturizers. Algae is a simple form of plant life, such as pond scum or seaweed. Aloe vera is an extract from the succulent aloe plant leaf and is virtually 100 percent water. Other popular preparations include extracts of almond, avocado, cucumber, camomile, jojoba, ginseng, lime, lemon, peach, and wheat germ. Allantoin, a colorless crystal derived from uric acid and found in many creams, is believed to disrupt the skin's surface structure, leading to greater water penetration. Here again, the benefits remain unproven.

LIPOSOMES

Liposomes are one of the newest entries in the fountain of youth arena. According to one recent theory, cellular aging involves the rigidification of skin cell membranes. Liposomes, which are tiny bags of fat and thymus gland extract suspended in a gel, are supposed to merge with your aging skin cells, revive them, and add moisture to them. Current scientific understanding does not support the rigidification theory. The cell membranes of young and old persons are alike. As a result, it is likely that liposome-containing moisturizers represent nothing more than another expensive allure.

EGGS, MILK, HONEY, AND ROYAL BEE JELLY

These ingredients are other favorites of some moisturizer manufacturers. Without question, eggs are nourishing for the embryo, milk nourishing and life-sustaining for infants, and honey and bee jelly nectar for bees. When applied to the skin, however, they do little for you, although they may give a moisturizer a smoother consistency or a lush look.

BATH OILS AND BATH OIL PEARLS

In general, I have no serious objections to the use of bath oils. They can supplement other measures for moisturizing your skin. Bath oils are simply moisturizers intended to be placed in your bathwater or on your skin during a shower. Fragrances are frequently added to enhance your bathing experience. However, most of the moisturizer deposited on your skin in this way gets rubbed off when you towel-dry yourself, and most of the potential benefits of moisturizing in this way are lost. Moreover, the perfumed ingredients may contribute to dry skin. In addition, bath oils can make the bathtub and floor quite slippery and pose a serious hazard if you do not take proper precautions when using them. Older people should take special care in this regard. As a rule, the use of conventional moisturizers applied to your skin directly following your bath or shower, while your skin is still damp (not dry), is more effective.

Bath oil beads or pearls consist basically of small amounts of bath oils that have been incorporated into gelatin capsules. These capsules dissolve and release their contents in hot water. In addition to bath oil, the capsules frequently contain at least 10 percent fragrance and coloring. Often the pearly color that gives these capsules their name is due to the presence of titanium dioxide—coated mica particles. In general, the effects of bath oil beads—or more appropriately, the relative lack of them—are roughly the same as for bath oils. However, if you enjoy pampering yourself every now and then, go ahead. As with bath oils, you should use a moisturizer after your bath.

HOW TO CHOOSE THE RIGHT MOISTURIZER

At last count, the marketplace and cosmetic counters were flooded with more than 350 brands of general moisturizers and several hundred other special moisturizers for the face. Given the claims and testimonials for the success of each of these, and the often wide disparity in retail prices among many of them, the simple act of purchasing a moisturizer can make your head spin. To add still more confusion to this already confusing situation, manufacturers produce specific moisturizers for almost every area of your body. There are moisturizers intended only for your face, moisturizers for the eye area, the neck and décolletage, and moisturizers for the rest of your body. There are also heavier night creams and lighter day creams.

Happily, you need only follow a few simple rules to find a

moisturizer that's right for you. In general, choose a moisturizer that does not feel greasy. The bottom line for any moisturizer is if you don't like the feel of it, you won't use it.

Moisturizers differ not only in the kinds of oils they contain, but also in the proportions of oil and water used to make them. Water-based moisturizers contain more water than oil, whereas oil-based moisturizers contain more oil than water, and oil-free moisturizers may contain synthetic moisturizers in place of oil. People with dry skin and no acne problems can use oily moisturizers. A quick way to get a sense of whether a moisturizer is water- or oil-based is merely to rub a small amount on the back of your hand. Those that are water-based will cool your skin as the water in them evaporates; by contrast, those that are oil-based will warm your skin by absorbing the heat.

MOISTURIZING INGREDIENTS AND ACNE-PRONE OR OILY SKIN

AVOID	OKAY TO USE
Acetylated lanolin alcohols	Beeswax
Cocoa butter	Corn oil
Heavy mineral oil	Cottonseed oil
Isopropyl esters	Isostearyl neopentate
Isopropyl myristate	Light mineral oil
Lanolin	Octyl palmitate
Lanolin fatty acid	Propylene glycol
Linseed oil	Safflower oil
Oleic acid	Sodium lauryl sulfate
Olive oil	Spermacetti
Petrolatum	
Stearic acid	

If you have acne-prone or oily skin, you should choose water-based or oil-free products. In addition, you should avoid moisturizers containing potentially acne-aggravating ingredients and choose instead those with ingredients that can actually benefit your skin.

Any moisturizers that contain potentially irritating substances should be avoided. Because a number of people develop allergies to lanolin, I usually advise my patients to steer clear of products containing it and its derivatives. *Parabens* are other potential problem causers. Among the most frequently used preservatives, parabens are found in many different products and for a goodly number of people are irritants. For that reason, I advise my patients to look for paraben-free moisturizers.

Fragrances should also be avoided. There is no good reason for a moisturizer to contain fragrances—they add nothing to its lubricating benefits and may be potentially allergenic or irritating to a fair number of people. If you desire a particular scent, using a separate perfume or cologne, which you can apply to a few spots where you want it, is preferable.

The moisturizer you choose should also be convenient to purchase and use. You should be able to buy it at your local supermarket or corner drugstore, not just in department stores or at an expensive skin salon. Moreover, you don't need separate moisturizers for each area of your skin, or one moisturizer for the day and another for the night. The moisturizer you choose should cost no more than a few dollars for several fluid ounces, so that you can use it liberally over your whole body, if necessary.

The choice of cream or lotion form is largely up to you. A lotion is simply a cream to which more water has been added to make the product go on smoothly and easily. If you have exceptionally dry or flaky skin, you may do better to choose a cream, which is heavier. However, many people find creams too thick and greasy. I generally recommend an all-purpose moisturizing lotion such as Moisturel. In sum, if you enjoy using more expensive moisturizers with exotic additives, it's perfectly all right— so long as you know that you are spending your money for advertising, fancy packaging, and fragrances. The extra dollars will not confer upon you magical overnight cures for aging skin and wrinkles.

TEN TIPS FOR HEALTHIER AND YOUNGER-LOOKING SKIN

The tips that follow summarize the ground covered in the last chapters. Naturally, if you have questions, you should discuss them with your dermatologist.

If you follow these guidelines closely and regularly, you will be on your way toward achieving healthier and younger-looking skin. Until these tips become second nature, you might tack a copy of them near your bathroom mirror.

1. For adequate sun protection, use protective clothing; broad-brimmed hats; wide, dark gray or green polarized sunglasses; and sunscreens with high SPFs.
2. Between mid-April and mid-November apply sunscreens routinely; avoid sun exposure between 10:00 A.M. and 3:00 P.M.
3. For greatest effectiveness, apply sunscreens liberally fifteen to thirty minutes *before* sun exposure, and then reapply after heavy exertion or swimming.
4. Avoid overscrubbing your skin—and do not wash more than twice a day.
5. Use only your fingertips to wash; avoid polyester scrub brushes or washcloths.
6. Use gentle soaps—soapless soaps or superfatted soaps.
7. Gently pat your skin dry after washing; do not vigorously towel dry.
8. Use moisturizers regularly to treat dry, sensitive skin, especially during cold weather or after sun exposure.
9. For best results, moisturizers should be applied immediately following a gentle skin cleansing, while your skin is still moist to wet rather than completely dry.
10. For oily or acne-prone skin, use oil-free or water-based moisturizers.

CHOOSING COSMETICS: READ THE LABEL

*C*osmetics are big business. Each year, more than $1.5 billion is spent on cosmetics, mostly by women, and this figure is expected to continue rising. Makeup's popularity has been attributed to both our society's emphasis on physical beauty and the psychological needs of the consumer. At their best, cosmetics serve to highlight a person's features while deemphasizing others. This chapter is not intended to teach you how to be a makeup artist or even how to apply makeup. To that end scores of beauty books have been written by beauticians and cosmetologists. Instead, I am interested in giving you the basic information needed to choose the safest, most effective products for the least money and to see beyond advertising hype.

U.S. law stipulates that cosmetics are products applied to the human body for cleansing and promoting attractiveness. They are not topical medications and should not be confused with them, although I believe many cosmetic manufacturers today, particularly those promoting so-called anti-aging moisturizers (chapter 4), try to capitalize on this confusion. In contrast with a cosmetic, a topical medication is a drug whose purpose is to affect the structure and function of your skin.

The difference in definitions has profound implications for you, the consumer. We all know that the federal government regulates the sale of both cosmetics and drugs. But did you know that a cosmetic manufacturer need only prove to the government that its product is safe for use on humans? It need *not* prove that it does what it claims to do. For example, if a cosmetic claims that it can "nourish" your hair and give it "life," the manufacturer has only to demonstrate that most people won't be hurt by using its product; however, if a drug company claims that its product can grow hair on bald heads, the product must go through years of testing to prove that it is not only safe for humans to use, but that it can also grow hair in at least some cases. Because existing legislation does not require the cosmetic manufacturer to prove that you will be helped by the product, the burden for choosing the right cosmetics falls squarely on your shoulders. Once again, it's a case of caveat emptor or "Let the buyer beware."

This brings us to another problem. The vast number of cosmetics that are available today and the enormous variations among the prices of these products make choosing the right products difficult. We are constantly confronted with different brands of cosmetics that seem to share many of the same ingredients, but that differ markedly in price. The price differential can be as little as a few cents or as much as $70 or $80, depending upon the item. To further complicate the matter, there are different brands that share the same basic ingredients but differ in their additives or preservatives. Some are packaged in modest wrappers or containers and make only simple claims for their benefits. Others sport the fanciest of trimmings, touted by their advertisers as God's gift to the human race and sold for exorbitant prices.

THE KEY TO CHOOSING COSMETICS

Fortunately, there is a better way to choose cosmetics than relying on trial and error, testimonials from friends and relatives, pure luck, or ad copy. The key lies in being able to read and understand cosmetics' ingredient labels. The Food and Drug Administration requires that all American-made cosmetics display a product ingredient label and specifies that the ingredients must be listed in order of their relative amounts in the product. This means that the first ingredients listed on the label make up most of the product and those listed last are present in the smallest quantities. For example, the first ingredient in many moisturizers is *water*. That's right. No matter how expensive a particular moisturizer is, or what the ads claim it will do for you, most of what you would be getting from that product is water.

Just knowing this simple fact about the order of ingredients on the label can be quite helpful when comparing brands. For example, if ingredient X, let's say vitamin E, is being hyped for healing wounds and soothing rashes, you know you won't be getting a lot of it if you find it near the end of the list. In fact, often you will find that the ingredient(s) that gets all the media hype is the one that is contained in the smallest amounts in the cosmetic. Knowing this, you have to weigh whether a small amount of extra ingredient is worth the often tremendous difference in price between the fancy product and its nonfancy counterpart with fewer exotic-sounding additives.

Unfortunately, cosmetic labels can be confusing. For one thing, while the FDA does require that the major ingredients be listed in their relative amounts, it does not require that the *exact* amounts be listed. This can make for problems when choosing between competing costmetics. Let's say that one cosmetic contains 20 grams of ingredient X, 5 grams of ingredient Y, and 1 gram of ingredient Z, and that its competitor actually contains twice as much of each ingredient. In both cases, the ingredient label would read X, Y, Z, yet you would have no way of knowing that one product contained so much more than the other of each ingredient.

A second problem with ingredient labels is that the law does *not* require that all minor ingredients be listed. To protect manufacturers from having to divulge trade secrets, the law does not require that specific flavorings or fragrances be listed. The manufacturer may simply use the words *flavorings* or *fragrances* to indicate their presence. This can be troublesome if you happen to have an allergy to a particular fragrance or flavoring and wish to avoid purchasing products that contain it.

The names of ingredients present another problem. Many cosmetic ingredients may have three names: a common name, a chemical name, and a trade name. Under present regulations, the particular name of an ingredient chosen for use on the ingredient label is left up to the manufacturer. As a result, comparing the ingredients of one product with those of another can be difficult. For example, *eugenol* not only sounds fancier than *carnation oil*, but you might think that a product containing it would do something extra for you.

At this point, you may be thinking that an ingredient label will be helpful only for ingredients such as water or mineral oil, which everyone can recognize. What are you supposed to do with those other tongue-twisting chemical names such as methyl-propyl paraben, for example? It would seem that you would need an advanced degree in cosmetic chemistry just to pronounce the names of many cosmetic ingredients, let alone understand how they affect the particular item you want to buy.

To make your job easier, I have included a list (Table 5.1) of many of the most commonly used cosmetic ingredients, as well as what they are supposed to do for you. These ingredients are used in the preparation of a wide variety of makeups. If you bring a copy of this list to the store, you will find reading ingredient labels much simpler. In time, you will grow familiar with the more common ingredient names and won't need to rely on the list.

Of course, the list is only helpful to a point. In the remainder of this chapter, you will learn more ways to turn the ingredient label into your best friend when shopping. The merits and draw-backs of many ingredients are discussed, and you will find out how to bypass confusing chemical names and target what is most important—i.e., those ingredients that are supposed to work for you.

COSMETIC INGREDIENTS

To be a savvy shopper, there are only three kinds of ingredients in any cosmetic with which you need to concern yourself. "Stop right there! How could that possibly be?" you're probably saying to yourself. "Everyone knows that some cosmetic labels list ten or twenty different ingredients." Nevertheless, all those fancy-sounding ingredients in most cosmetics can be lumped into three basic categories: (1) *Ingredients that do something for you*, (2) *ingredients that aren't intended to do anything for you*, and (3) *ingredients that you are told (or mistakenly believe) may do something special for you, but really don't*. I refer to those ingredients that really do something for you as *active ingredients*. Those that are necessary only to the cosmetic I prefer to call *inactive ingredients*, and those that are all fluff and no substance I label *exotic ingredients*.

ACTIVE INGREDIENTS

No matter which types of cosmetics you buy, the most important point you want to know is what the product is actually going to do for you. For example, if you are looking for a good moisturizing lotion, the most important information you need is whether the product will help keep your skin moist and smooth. Thus, the active ingredients in any moisturizing lotion are those ingredients directly responsible for keeping your skin moist. In the case of a skin cleanser, the active ingredient(s) is the specific soap or detergents that is responsible for the cleaning and de-greasing action. In the case of a moisturizing sunscreen, however, where the product is intended to protect you from the sun *and* moisturize your skin, the active ingredients are the ultra-violet light absorbing or reflecting ingredient(s) *and* the moisturizing ingredient(s).

TABLE 5.1

COMMON COSMETIC INGREDIENTS BY FUNCTION

ACTIVE INGREDIENTS

EMOLLIENTS

Butyl stearate
Caprylic/capric triglyceride
Castor oil
Cetearyl alcohol
Cetyl alcohol
Diisopropyl adipate
Glycerin
Glyceryl monostearate
Isopropyl myristate
Isopropyl palmitate
Lanolin
Lanolin alcohol
Lanolin, hydrogenated
Mineral oil
Petrolatum
Polyethylene glycols
Polyoxethylene lauryl ether
Polyoxypropylene 15 stearyl ether
Propylene glycol stearate
Silicone
Squalane
Stearic acid
Steryl alcohol
Vegetable oils

HUMECTANTS

Glycerin
Lactic acid
Lecithin
Propylene glycol
Sorbitol solution
Urea

COMMON PIGMENTS
(COLORS)

Bismuth oxychloride
Carmine
Chromium oxide green
D&C and FD&C Colors
Ferric ammonium ferrocyanide
Ferric ferrocyanide
Iron oxides
Manganese violet
Mica
Titanium dioxide (white pigment)
Ultramarine blue

INACTIVE INGREDIENTS

EMULSIFYING AGENTS
(SURFACTANTS)

Amphoteric-9
Carbomer
Cetearyl alcohol (and) ceteareth-20
Cholesterol
Disodium monooleamidosulfosuc-
   cinate
Emulsifying wax, NF
Lanolin
Lanolin alcohol (laureths)
Lanolin, hydrogenated
Lecithin

Polyethylene glycol 1000 monocetyl
   ether
Polyoxyl 40 stearate
Polysorbates
Sodium laureth sulfate
Sodium lauryl sulfate
Sorbitan esters
Stearic acid
Tea stearate
Trolamine

TABLE 5.1 (CONT.)

INACTIVE INGREDIENTS (CONT.)

SOLVENTS

Alcohol
Diisopropyl adipate
Glycerin
1,2,6-hexanetriol
Isopropyl myristate
Polyoxypropylene 15 stearyl ether
Propylene carbonate
Propylene glycol

THICKENING, STIFFENING, AND SUSPENDING AGENTS

Beeswax
Candelilla, carnauba, and
   cetyl esters wax
Carbomer
Cellulose gums
Dextrin
Mannitol
Ozokerite (ceresin)
Polyethylene
Xanthan gum

PRESERVATIVES, ANTIOXIDANTS, AND CHEMICAL STABILIZERS

Alcohol and benzyl alcohol
Butylated hydroxyanisole (BHA)
Butylated hydroxytoluene (BHT)
Chlorocresol
Citric and sorbic acid
Edetate disodium (EDTA)
Imidazolidinyl urea
Parabens
Phenylmercuricacetate
Potassium sorbate
Propyl gallate
Propylene glycol
Quarternium-15
Sodium bisulfite
Tocopherol (vitamin E)

EMULSION STABILIZERS AND VISCOSITY BUILDERS

Carbomer
Cetearyl, cetyl, and stearyl alcohol
Glyceryl monostearate
Paraffin
Polyethylene glycols
Propylene glycol stearate

GELLANTS

Carbomer
Carboxymethyl cellulose
Hydroxymethyl cellulose
Methyl cellulose

POWDER FORMERS

Bentonite (hydrated aluminum
   silicate clay)
Magnesium aluminum silicate
Magnesium silicate
Magnesium stearate
Talc

EXOTIC INGREDIENTS (ADDITIVES OF UNPROVEN VALUE)

Algae
Allantoin
Aloe vera
Collagen
Eggs
Elastin
Flavorings
Fragrances (except in perfumes,
   colognes, and toilet water)
Honey
Hyaluronic acid
Milk
Placental extract
RNA
Vitamins A and E (tocopherol)

INACTIVE INGREDIENTS

The majority of ingredients in most cosmetics are not active ingredients. If you examine Table 5.1 carefully, you will see that in many cases the ingredients in cosmetics serve multiple functins. Nevertheless, most of these functions do not directly relate to doing something to benefit you. Instead, they are needed in the manufacturing process or for prolonging the shelf life of the product. Therefore, when you see a long list of chemical names on the ingredient label, don't jump to the conclusion that you are getting something extra for your money. For your money, the active ingredients count most.

Here follows a description of some of the more common functions that inactive ingredients may serve in a cosmetic. Clearly, these types of ingredients are important, but they don't actually do anything for you. *Solvents,* such as water or alcohol, are carrier liquids and are needed to dissolve other chemicals. *Emulsifying agents* keep oil and water mixed in order to create creams and lotions. *Emulsion stabilizers* prevent oil and water from separating. *Preservatives, antioxidants,* and *chemical stabilizers* prolong shelf life by suppressing germs, preventing product degradation by oxygen, and preventing unwanted chemical interactions between individual ingredients. *Viscosity builders* and *thickening, stiffening,* and *suspending agents* give body to certain cosmetics. *Gellants* are special kinds of thickeners; when combined with alcohol, acetone, or water, they produce gels that liquefy upon contact with your skin. Finally, *powder formers* are any ingredients specifically used to make powdery products, such as powder blushes and powder eyeshadows.

It now should be plain that when you are looking for a good cosmetic, the most important thing to do is compare the active ingredients in the products. For example, it should make no dramatic difference to you which preservative the manufacturer uses to prolong the shelf life of a moisturizing lotion (assuming, of course, that you are not allergic to the preservative in question). Instead, what counts is which moisturizing ingredient(s) they include (e.g., lanolin, petrolatum, mineral oil, or lactic acid, etc.).

Furthermore, if you didn't know better, you might conclude that a moisturizing lotion containing the chemical *butylated hydroxyanisole (BHA)* is better than a competitor containing benzyl alcohol. (It may be tempting to think that a substance with a long chemical name possesses some special properties that its shorter or more familiar sounding counterpart doesn't.) However, by checking the list, you find that BHA, like benzyl alcohol, is simply a preservative and, as such, serves no moisturizing function at all.

EXOTIC INGREDIENTS

Exotic ingredients are additives that are unnecessary or of doubtful or unproven value. In chapter 3, I listed a number of such ingredients for which many health and beauty claims are often made. These include collagen, procollagen, elastin, vitamin E (tocopherol), vitamin D, aloe vera, allantoin, algae, royal bee jelly, eggs, milk, and honey, to name a few. In many cases, the prices of the cosmetics that include these "wonder" additives are exorbitant and the claims for their supposed benefits many and exaggerated.

If you are looking to save money and still buy satisfactory cosmetics, pass by those products containing exotic additives. Claims about the benefits of these additives usually lack independent scientific substantiation and often stem from the manufacturers' in-house testing and from the testimonials of some users. However, if money is not a major concern, I have no serious objections to their use. Other than occasionally causing allergic reactions, these ingredients pose no serious health problems.

In the following sections, I discuss common types of face cosmetics. Most of these are available either as creams or lotions, sticks, powders, or with alcohol bases. Also discussed are facial masks and hypoallergenic products. Simply knowing the *form* of a cosmetic gives you some idea of its ingredients.

CREAM-BASED MAKEUPS

FOUNDATIONS

A foundation makeup is, as the name states, the primary makeup for the face. Foundations smooth your skin, hide blemishes, scars, and other irregularities, and even out skin tones. In addition, they serve as bases for blushes and eye makeup.

Since the main purposes of foundations are to cover up and smooth, the active ingredients of any foundation are its pigments and moisturizers. In fact, foundations are simply moisturizers to which pigments (colors) have been added. Oil-free makeups contain synthetic lubricants instead of heavier natural oils such as petrolatum, mineral oil, vegetable oils, or lanolins. Water-based foundation makeups use oil-in-water moisturizer formulations, and oil-based foundations use water-in-oil formulations.

Water-based products are less likely to clog pores and are preferable for people with acne-prone skin. Unfortunately, they tend to run easily. Oil-based foundations, on the other hand, are thicker, more moisturizing, and tend to be either water-resistant or waterproof. Water-resistant makeup lasts about eight hours and won't run or streak during periods of intense perspiration or high humidity. Waterproof makeups tend to be even oilier than the water-resistant ones and usually can even withstand a half hour of swimming. People with dry or aging skin should opt for these creamier kinds of foundations.

Iron oxides, ultramarine blue, and *FD&C colors* are examples of pigments commonly used in foundations. *Pearlizers* (such as *bismuth oxychloride*), which are added to cosmetics to create a shimmering effect, may be found in some foundations. *Magnesium aluminum silicate, talc, clays,* and *kaolin* may be added to impart a matte finish to the foundation and to bring the pigments to the exact color desired. These ingredients are particularly important for muting the oily appearance of creamier foundations.

CONCEALERS

Concealers are simply creamier foundation makeups. They are generally intended for specific areas of your face, such as under the eyes (to cover dark circles, shadows, or puffiness). The active ingredients in concealers are pigments in an oil-based moisturizer. Concealers are heavier than regular foundation makeups, so you should limit their application to the areas in which they are needed if you are acne-prone.

Cream blushers are similar to concealers and consist of pigments in an oil-based moisturizer. It's best to avoid cream blushers if you have oily skin or acne problems.

CREAM EYE SHADOWS

Cream eye shadows are another variation of pigment in an oil-based moisturizer formula. In some cream eye shadows, pearlizers such as mica may cause irritation in the eye area because they possess microscopically sharp edges. Be sure to apply eye shadows with a sponge-stick or a soft, natural-bristle brush, not with your fingers.

LIQUID EYELINERS

Liquid eyeliners also follow the same formula. Inorganic pigments, such as chromium oxide greens, ferric ferrocyanide, ferric ammonium ferrocyanide, manganese violet, and carmine, are common eye cosmetic pigments. Here, though, plasticizing (film-forming) chemicals, such as *acrylates* and *acrylic copolymers,* are added to help the eyeliner adhere better to your lids and add luster and thickness to the product. Special care should be taken when putting on eyeliner. If it is applied too close to the corners or under the rims of the eyelids, severe itching, swelling, and tenderness *(chemical conjunctivitis)* may result. Permanent tattoos of the mucous membranes of the lids have also occurred occasionally from contamination by pigment.

MASCARAS

Again the active ingredients are pigments in a moisturizing base. Waterproof liquid mascaras contain heavy, oil-based moisturizing formulas to which acrylates and shellacs are often added. These serve to thicken mascaras and make them more rain- and tear-resistant. So-called *conditioning mascaras* generally have water-based moisturizing formulas and tend to be less resistant. Removal of mascara usually requires soap and water or cleansing lotions containing mineral oil. In general, you can use your favorite moisturizer for this purpose; despite the claims of advertising, special removers are not necessary.

Temporary stinging and burning of the eyes or lids during eye cosmetic application is frequently caused by evaporation of the product's volatile ingredients, such as *mineral spirits, isoparaffins,* and *alcohol.* Irritation may also result from the presence of such troublemakers as propylene glycol or soap emulsifiers. Some people who are unable to tolerate water-based mascaras may be able to use waterproof products, and vice versa.

Although it is true that loose eyelashes often fall out when mascara is applied, these hairs do grow back. Mascara does not cause permanent loss of eyelashes. In fact, with proper use, mascaras cause few problems. There are, however, two caveats: First, contact lens wearers should avoid lash-extending mascaras. These products generally contain numerous, very fine particles of rayon that can become trapped under contact lenses, causing irritation or even scratching of the eye's delicate cornea.

Second, the concentration of preservatives in mascaras purposely has been kept low so as not to irritate the eyes, but this also means that the products do not have a long shelf life, and they are not contamination resistant. Two good rules of thumb: *Never share mascara* and *discard mascara after three or four months.*

MASKING COSMETICS

Masking cosmetics are waterproof makeups made specifically to cover scars and other kinds of prominent skin discolorations, abnormalities, or irregularities that cannot be easily camouflaged by conventional foundations. They generally work best on flat irregularities and are intended for use anywhere on the body, not just the face.

These makeups are particularly useful for camouflaging "broken" blood vessels of the face; "liver spots" on the face, hands, and legs; and the small, superficial, purplish varicose blood vessels on the legs *(sunburst varicosities)*. They also are frequently recommended for disguising *port-wine stains,* depigmented skin patches *(vitiligo),* and certain kinds of disfiguring skin eruptions such as *psoriasis* and *lupus.*

Masking cosmetics are thick, oil-based preparations generally containing greater amounts of pigment than ordinary foundations. In terms of their active ingredients, they are composed of pigments suspended in oil-based moisturizers. They are durable enough to withstand the beach or a chlorinated pool, and they have the additional advantage of being excellent sunblocks, owing to their thickness. Although attempts have been made to reduce their tendency to provoke acne, I still advise people who are acne-prone to remove these cosmetics as soon as possible and certainly never to leave them on overnight.

The application of masking cosmetics is somewhat different from applying regular cosmetics. First, pat the makeup gently over the defect to be covered. Next, blend the edges with the surrounding normal skin. Finally, set the makeup with a special setting powder. When this process is complete, a regular foundation makeup, as well as any other cosmetics you wish, may be applied directly over the masking makeup. Depending upon how extensive the area to be covered, the makeup application process may require between ten and fifteen minutes. The entire routine may seem to be a hassle, but for people with disfiguring cosmetic problems, the use of these cosmetics makes all the difference in the world.

Unfortunately, masking cosmetics are usually not available at local beauty-aid stores, supermarkets, or corner drugstores, but some department stores have them. They tend to be quite expensive, especially if you need them for daily use or to cover a large area. Covermark, Dermablend, Esteem, and Dermage are four major brands.

Theater makeups (stage makeup) are similar to masking makeups in that they contain more pigment, are heavier and oilier, and are waterproof. They are made this way so as not to appear washed out under bright lights or be washed away by perspiration. Theater makeup is notorious, however, for clogging pores and aggravating acne. As a result, it should be removed as soon as possible and should not be allowed to remain on overnight.

CREAM MASKS

Masks are supposed to refresh, stimulate, "refine," firm, cleanse, and condition your skin. (When the alternate spelling, *masque,* is used the product usually retails for a higher price.) They may be applied by brush, spatula, or your fingertips. Once on your skin, they generally remain plastic (or wet) for a few minutes, after which (about twenty mintutes) they harden. They are then washed, peeled, or pried off.

Cream packs, which are similar to cleansing creams, are intended for people with dry or normal skin, but they offer no particular conditioning advantages over routine moisturizers. In general, I do not advise their use. Regular gentle facial cleansing followed by an appropriate moisturizer is generally a more effective, less expensive, and less time-consuming routine for cleansing and moisturizing your skin. However, if you wish to pamper yourself or give yourself a lift with an *occasional* cream mask facial, I have no serious objections.

STICK COSMETICS

Stick cosmetics include all lipsticks, cover sticks, pencils (e.g., eyebrow, eyeliner, and lip liner pencils), and stick blushers. The active ingredients in these items are essentially pigments dispersed throughout the heavy oil-wax base. Waxes, such as *beeswax, synthetic beeswax, candelilla wax, carnauba wax, ceresin (ozokerite),* and *cetyl* and *stearyl alcohols,* provide consistency, texture, and after-feel to these cosmetics.

LIPSTICKS

In the main, lipsticks and glosses differ little in their basic composition. So-called permanent lipsticks, which are designed to be longer lasting, contain a *staining dye* in addition to the regular pigments and pearlizers. Staining dyes not only add color but also allow other colors to adhere better to your lips. However, *eosin,* a fluorescent staining dye, also called D&C red #22, is a potent sensitizing agent, particularly in combination with sunlight, and should be avoided. A number of years ago, several lipstick pigments were found to be carcinogenic and were banned. Colors that have proven safe include D&C orange #5, and D&C red #21 and #27. Glosses usually contain lanolin or its derivatives to add shine and preserve lipstick intensity.

The fragrance and flavorings often included in lipsticks and glosses provide no additional benefits and actually may precipitate allergic reactions in sensitive people. Look for products that do not contain these unnecessary and potentially problematic ingredients.

The lips, especially the lower lip, are particularly prone to sun damage. Fortunately, the thickness and opacity of most lipsticks provide excellent sun protection. More recently, many manufacturers have added sunscreen ingredients, generally PABA derivatives, to lipsticks, and this may be of some additional benefit.

COVER STICKS

Cover sticks, which are the stick versions of concealers, are variations of the basic lipstick formula. Generally they contain a high proportion of wax to give them body and thickness. These products are recommended for camouflaging spot defects or discolorations and for lightening circles or shadows under your eyes. Some are water-resistant and all may be applied under or over your foundation or in place of it. However, cover sticks tend to aggravate acne, so avoid them altogether or use them only occasionally if you tend to break out. A vicious cycle of acne flare-ups will sometimes occur when cover sticks are applied to cover acne blemishes. If you must use them, remove them as soon as possible.

EYEBROW PENCILS, EYELINER PENCILS, AND LIP LINERS

Cosmetic pencils, like lipsticks, are simply pigments in oil-wax bases. When used properly, they seldom cause problems. Because some of these products are used near the eyes, contact lens wearers should check with their eye-care specialists to be sure that the cosmetics they have chosen will not cause problems.

POWDER COSMETICS

A wide variety of powder-based cosmetics is available. These include pressed face powders, blushers, and eye shadows. All of these products have the same principal active ingredients: pigments and powders. Certified D&C, FD&C (except in eye cosmetics), and iron oxides are the commonly used pigments. In addition, pearlizers, such as mica, guanine (from fish scales), or bismuth oxychloride may be added to create a frosted, sparkling effect. Translucent powders, intended more for blotting oil and perspiration, do not contain pigments. Loose powders are also good for blotting.

Talc, kaolin (fuller's earth), bentonite (clays), starch (polysaccharide), and *magnesium silicates, carbonates,* and *stearates* are powders typically used as fillers and compressing agents. Occasionally, *mannitol,* a complex sugar, or *dextrin,* a cornstarch derivative, are used to impart a soft feeling. In general, powder products are better for excessively oily or acne-prone complexions, for they rarely cause adverse reactions.

Face powders absorb oil, reduce sheen, and create a matte finish for cream foundations. Pressed powders generally contain some oil, such as mineral oil, and are therefore better for people with dry skin. Loose powders are preferable for people with acne-prone skin.

Powder blushes lend color and shading to your face and create contours. If you have oily or acne-prone skin, you should use powder instead of cream blushers to minimize clogging your pores.

Special care should be taken when applying powder eyeshadows. This is especially important if you choose pearlized shadows, which contain fine particles capable of irritating your eyes. Always wipe away excess powder with a clean cotton-tipped swab or cotton ball. To reduce bacterial contamination, do not use your fingers. And finally, as with all eye cosmetics, never share eyeshadows.

PACKS AND CLAY MASKS

According to the advertising, clay masks help cleanse your face, shrink your pores, and dry and peel your skin. However, long-term benefits of clay masks, like those for their cream counterparts, remain unproven. Paste or clay masks are variations of the powder formula to which water has been added. Often, abrasive ingredients such as almond meal, bran, oats, and ground pits and nuts are added. Since masks may irritate your skin, plain soap and water cleansing is preferable—and less expensive. Of course, if you have normal skin and enjoy using masks as a way of pampering yourself, I have no serious objections. Just don't overdo it.

ALCOHOL-BASED COSMETICS

COLOGNES, TOILET WATERS, AND PERFUMES

Colognes contain roughly 88 to 95 percent alcohol and between 5 and 12 percent fragrance. *Perfumes* contain about 70 to 80 percent alcohol and 15 to 30 percent fragrance. *Toilet waters* are intermediate between colognes and perfumes.

Fragrances themselves are extremely complex mixtures. Currently there are more than ten thousand different chemical essences, derived from natural animal oils or the oils of flowers, roots, and plants. And now many synthetic fragrances are commonly used. However, fragrances, along with preservative ingredients, are believed to be responsible for the majority of all adverse reactions to cosmetics. In one large study, *cinnamic alcohol, cinnamic aldehyde, hydroxycitronellal, musk ambrette, isoeugenol,* and *geraniol* were found to be the essence ingredients most frequently associated with skin reactions.

A couple of comments about fragrances are in order. The more alcohol in a product, the shorter its shelf life; hence, colognes are usually good for about six months and the strongest of perfumes for slightly more than a year. Heat and sunlight make fragrances evaporate more rapidly, so remember to store yours in cool, dark places.

HYPOALLERGENIC PRODUCTS

According to some marketing experts, in 1986 the average consumer was found to use more than twelve different cosmetics each day—a pattern of use that translates into millions of exposures of cosmetics to all kinds of skin every single day. It is truly a credit to cosmetic manufacturers that, given such wide use, misuse, and overuse of cosmetics, so few problems have been seen. Allergy to cosmetics occurred in as few as 0.3 percent of cosmetic users in one recent large survey.

The term *hypoallergenic* is frequently mistaken to mean nonallergenic, which would imply that a product has been found not to cause any allergic reactions. Unfortunately, no such cosmetic yet exists. In fact, hypoallergenic means that a manufacturer has made every effort to eliminate from its products as many of the *known* common sensitizing ingredients as possible (such as fragrances, flavorings, and certain preservatives) *and,* as much as possible, eliminate minute amounts of by-products of the manufacturing process that may contaminate the final product and render it potentially more allergenic. In addition, manufacturers of these cosmetics work closely with dermatologists to discover the source of allergies to their products by providing samples of the individual ingredients for testing. I have found the manufacturers of the following hypoallergenic cosmetic lines to be particularly responsible in these areas: Almay, Allercreme, Clinique, Dermage, and Revlon.

If you develop a problem with any cosmetic, don't despair. Once the allergic reaction has subsided, switch to another brand. Limit your selection to hypoallergenic products. If your problems persist, see your dermatologist.

GOOD HEALTH =
A MORE
BEAUTIFUL SKIN

*T*he proper use of skin-care products and choice of skin-care routines are extremely important for achieving and maintaining healthy, beautiful skin. But good skin is not merely the result of what you apply to it. Your skin is tremendously affected, both directly and indirectly, by your life-style and habits: what and how much you eat, how much or little you sleep, which types of exercises you do (or don't do), and your reactions to nervous stress or physical tension. All of these have considerable impact on your general health and your skin.

DIET

Hardly a day passes when we don't read an article or hear a news item telling us to eat this food or avoid that one for better health. We are swamped with claims for the health and beauty benefits of various foods and vitamin and mineral supplements. "Consume lots of fiber!" "Eat polyunsaturated fats!" "Take vitamin C!" Everyone seems to have a special diet and different idea of what's healthy for you, especially if they have something to sell.

What's good for your skin is usually good for your body. Without question, improper or inadequate diets can profoundly affect your skin. For example, severe vitamin C deficiency, as seen in a condition called *scurvy,* can cause bleeding gums, swelling skin, and easy bruisability. Large black-and-blue spots from hemorrhaging into the skin can appear all over the body. British sailors to this day are nicknamed "limeys," because in the days of the great sailing vessels they were fed lemons and limes (excellent sources of vitamin C) to prevent scurvy. A deficiency of vitamin A, on the other hand, can lead to acne and other skin problems and extreme deficiencies of vitamin B2 (riboflavin), B3 (niacin), and B6 are associated with various types of skin inflammations, hair problems, and mucous membrane sores and inflammations. Severe protein malnutrition, as seen in many famine-ridden Third World nations, can result in changes in the color and texture of the skin and hair, and hair loss. Iron depletion from a variety of causes, including improper diet, repeated extra-heavy menstrual bleeding, and nursing, can result in anemia and yellowish, pallid skin.

Excesses of certain nutrients can also cause problems. High iodine ingestion, from the overuse of iodized salt or overconsumption of shellfish and other seafoods or kelp, can result in an acnelike breakout of deep pustules and cysts on the face, chest, and back. Excessive intake of beta-carotene from carrots, certain green leafy vegetables, or capsule supplements can turn skin a deep yellow. Overingestion of vitamin A can lead to extreme dryness and cracking of the skin and mucous membranes. These are just a few of the effects that your diet can have on your skin.

IDEAL WEIGHT AND WEIGHT LOSS

Nowadays almost everybody seems to be concerned about calories and weight reduction. Our national preoccupation with weight is even reflected in the calories-per-serving information on the product labels of many foodstuffs (and not just those intended for dieters). Such a concern is hardly misplaced given that nearly 12 percent of the American population is considered to be obese. In addition to all the other ill effects of being overweight, too much fat in the wrong places can kill the appearance of otherwise super skin. And if you've been extremely overweight for a very long time, losing weight can leave you with sagging skin.

Many dieting books and other health brochures contain tables listing ideal weights for men and women based on height and bone frame (small, medium, large). One well-known weight chart is published by The Metropolitan Life Insurance Company. There's no magic to figuring out how many calories you need each day: simply multiply your ideal weight by 15. For example, if your ideal weight is 125 pounds, to maintain that weight, you should consume a maximum of 125 × 15, or 1,875 calories daily.

On the other hand, if you wish to lose weight, you need to reduce your caloric intake by 500 calories a day in order to lose 1 pound each week, or by 1,000 calories per day to lose 2 pounds each week. If you are 10 pounds overweight and wish to weigh 125 pounds, you would need to consume no more than 1,375 calories per day in order to lose that weight in ten weeks. Gradual weight loss—between 1 and 2 pounds per week—is of course healthier for you than crash dieting; furthermore, weight lost gradually is less likely to be put back on.

A BALANCED DIET

Eating a well-balanced diet supplies your daily nutritional needs plus a surplus of storable nutrients and is the key to staying healthy and avoiding nutrition-related skin problems. To maintain optimal health, you need a diet consisting of plenty of water, proteins, fats, carbohydrates, vitamins, and minerals. Water is essential for all our metabolic processes. Proteins are needed for cell growth and repair. Carbohydrates provide energy. Fats supply storage energy, and vitamins and minerals are of vital assistance in regulating metabolism and normal growth and functioning of the body.

For skin and overall health, therefore, merely watching your calories is obviously not enough; your diet must contain the right balance of nutrients. It should include a variety of foods chosen from the four major food groups: Meat/Protein; Dairy; Fruit/ Vegetable; and Bread/Cereal. Ideally, it should consist of 50 percent carbohydrates, 20 percent protein, and 30 percent fat of which two-thirds should be derived from vegetable sources and one-third from animal sources. (Unfortunately, in this regard, the typical American diet leaves something to be desired. Most of us eat too much fat, and obtain 60 pecent of our fat calories from animal sources and 40 percent from vegetable sources.)

If you need help with nutrition and dieting, seek the counsel of an accredited nutritionist, but beware! There are a lot of nutritional quacks and pseudoscientist diet specialists around. In addition, there are foodstuff manufacturers who barrage you with a multitude of claims. In fact, nearly 3 percent of all advertising contains nutritional and health claims. For help in eating healthy, you might contact the following: the Food and Nutri- tion Board of the National Academy of Sciences, the American Dietetic Association, American Board of Nutrition, American Institute of Nutrition, American Society of Nutrition, American Society of Clinical Nutrition, or the nutrition department of a local medical school.

Most experts agree that a well-balanced diet will also contain all the vitamins and minerals that a normal, healthy person needs. To date, thirteen vitamins and more than sixteen essential minerals have been identified as *requirements* for good health. Iron, calcium, and zinc are examples of three minerals essential for health. Vitamin A is important for maintaining skin smooth- ness and elasticity. B-complex vitamins contribute to a glossy, smooth complexion. Vitamin C is important for the synthesis of collagen and elastin fibers, and vitamin E is believed to play some role in retarding the aging process and preserving cell membranes, but research in this area is still at an early stage.

Despite what some health-food store owners, vitamin and mineral supplement manufacturers, or self-proclaimed "nutri- tionists" would like you to believe, most of us who consume ordinary Western diets (even those of us living on fast food or junk diets) do *not* develop vitamin and mineral deficiencies. People who are on crash reducing diets of fewer than 1,000 calories per day or are following certain fad diets, the elderly, and casual vegetarians may need vitamin and mineral supplementation.

If you do take vitamin and mineral supplements, do not exceed the federal government's Recommended Daily Allowance (RDA) guidelines. *RDA's are not minimum requirements.* They actually indicate higher levels of each nutrient than most people need.

Certain vitamins, such as vitamins A and D, taken in megadoses, can act like drugs and seriously affect your health. It is likewise a mistake to oversupplement with minerals. Since minerals most frequently work in a delicate balance with each other, taking an excess of one mineral may actually interfere with the action of another. Finally, a lot of misleading advertising suggests that your needs for vitamins and minerals are increased by nervous tension. There is simply no scientific basis for these assertions. In general, check with your doctor before you take any kind of supplement, especially in high doses.

EXERCISE

Americans are becoming increasingly fitness conscious. Nearly 70 percent of the population now exercises, 25 million of whom only started to do so in the past couple of years. Exercise makes you feel and look better. It not only improves your muscle tone and posture, it also improves the color and texture of your skin. Vigorous exercise increases blood flow to your skin, supplying it with more oxygen and nutrients. In large measure, this accounts for the "healthy glow" that follows a strenuous workout.

Exercising, unfortunately, is not without its down side for skin. Depending upon which specific exercises or sports you enjoy, as the shield from the outside environment your skin can take a beating from the effects of sun, wind, water, heat, cold, scrapes, bruises, blisters, calluses, and perspiration. Joggers are prone to developing sore, chafed, or tender nipples ("jogger's nipples") and cyclists irritated buttocks and knees.

Fortunately, you can prevent many of these problems by taking a few simple steps. While "'no pain, no gain" has become a popular phrase among exercise enthusiasts, you really do not need to abuse your skin or your body in order to reap the rewards of a sensible exercise program. I tend to be more a believer in "no gain through unnecessary pain."

Sun protection and adequate moisturization are especially important if you exercise regularly. Before swimming in a chlorinated pool, for instance, apply a moisturizer to your skin liberally to protect it against chlorine, which is potentially very drying and irritating. After you come out of the water, rinse yourself thoroughly with tap water as soon as possible and liberally reapply a moisturizer while your skin is still moist. Before skiing, make sure you liberally apply a moisturizing sunscreen both to keep you from chapping and protect you from ultraviolet radiation.

Naturally, for greater safety and comfort, you should always try to wear appropriate clothing and use the proper protective gear for the sport or activity you choose. In general, wear loose, light clothing in warm weather; loose-weave fabrics such as cotton allow for greater sweat evaporation. Avoid synthetics—they are known not to let the skin "breathe." Women joggers should use a sports bra and a moisturizer on their nipples and wear soft T-shirts. Cyclists should use pads to protect their knees and buttocks.

As a rule, all your exercise wear should be laundered after each use to reduce bacteria and odor buildup. Use a gentle soap such as Ivory Snow and avoid the use of harsh soaps, detergents, and fabric softeners; if not completely rinsed out the ingredients in these products can accumulate in your clothing, then be leached out by perspiration during exercise, and thereby cause skin irritation.

Remove makeup and jewelry *before* working out. Heavy makeup, particularly oil-based cosmetics, can block sweat evaporation, and sweating is especially important for temperature regulation when you work out vigorously. Jewelry can get in your way while you exercise, and can also be the source of allergy or irritation. Nickel, to which many people are allergic, is contained in most costume jewelry and even, to varying extents, in the clasps or chains of some more expensive jewelry. When you perspire heavily, small amounts of nickel may be leached out of the jewelry and cause problems for those who are susceptible. (Nickel is also alloyed in gold in 14 carat or higher gold jewelry; in these types of jewelry, however, it is so tightly bound to the gold that it rarely poses a threat.)

EXERCISE ALLERGY

Many sedentary people who hate to exercise often joke that they are "allergic" to exercise. However, it is estimated that nearly 1 million Americans have a serious and potentially life-threatening allergy to exercise. The symptoms include itching, hives, hoarseness, wheezing, difficulty breathing, and a precipitous drop in blood pressure. Doctors are not sure whether these symptoms are triggered by the activity itself or the body heat generated by it. In any event, if you experience any of these symptoms following exercise, see your doctor or an allergist.

STRESS

For many of us, paradise might be defined as a life without stress. Imagine: no cares, no worries, no responsibilities. Alas, real life is just not that way, so the complete elimination of stress is an unrealistic goal. Some stress can even have a favorable effect on your life by helping to motivate you to accomplish your goals. Unfortunately, all of us experience periods of heightened, unhealthy stress from time to time.

According to the National Mental Health Association, "anxiety and tension are essential functions of living." As any experienced traveler on life's road would agree, life is filled with stresses from the small to the big. Everything from changing your job, meeting new people, leaving home, losing a loved one, marriage, and divorce can create stress. Fortunately, most of us have the wherewithal to cope with periods of heightened nervous tension and are able to ride them out.

As though having to deal with stress itself were not enough, many skin problems (as well as certain internal organ conditions) can be triggered or worsened by increased nervous tension. It's been written that while the eyes may mirror the soul, the skin can mirror the mind. In fact, the relationship between the skin and our emotions is so intimate that some people have referred to it as "our emotional skin." Strain shows. Profuse sweating, facial flushing, severe itching, hives, acne, eczema, and psoriasis are just a few of the many conditions known to be triggered or aggravated by nervous tension. In addition, both oral and genital herpes flare-ups can be triggered by stress—a devastating problem for many sufferers.

Emotional stress can have profound effects on hormone secretions and immunity (the ability to fight off infections). Western medical science is just now beginning to appreciate the enormous influence of our minds on disease causation and therapy. The effect of mind over matter is nowhere more apparent or striking than in the case of warts (see chapter 9). Warts are caused by viruses and, as such, may be considered to be "colds" in your skin. In suggestible children (and in some suggestible adults), warts can be made to disappear simply by rubbing a placebo medicine over them, if the patient is convinced that the drug is a potent anti-wart medicine. Before any more satisfactory methods were available, dermatologists and pediatricians for years used harmless liquids to "cure" warts in this fashion. This form of suggestion therapy worked (and continues to work) in many cases.

In more severely troubled people, the skin may actually become a battleground for psychological stress. Certain people under enormous stresses (usually self-generated) seek outlets in scratching, gouging, or tearing at the skin of their faces and bodies. Grotesque scars may result from these self-inflicted wounds. Other severely troubled individuals may compulsively —albeit unconsciously—pull out hair, scratch at pimples, or continuously rub or knead their skin, causing persistent irritation, bumps, and damage. Such patients often meet questioning about whether they might be causing their own skin problems with vigorous denials. Treating these kinds of mind/skin problems requires a combination of intensive dermatological therapy and psychological counseling.

Even for those of us armed with normal coping mechanisms, controlling, reducing, and eliminating stress can still be difficult; learning to live with stress is a lifelong task. One important aspect of coping involves the ability to separate issues that you can do something about from those that you cannot. Regular physical exercise is another means of reducing stress, as is learning relaxation techniques (see pages 88–90). Last, but certainly not least, is learning to draw upon your sense of humor to help you to relieve pressures and reestablish proper perspective.

While certain drugs can reduce anxiety and relieve stress symptoms, they can create their own problems. Unfortunately, nearly 28 percent of the adult population takes such drugs almost all the time. Addiction and drug abuse may result from their long-term use. To prevent psychological or physical addiction to these drugs, doctors usually prefer to prescribe anti-anxiety, anti-stress medications (*anxiolytics*) for only short periods of time, at the same time recommending or instituting other kinds of non-drug therapies. Surprisingly, for many stress-related skin conditions, drug therapies have proven unsuccessful.

There are certain warning signals that suggest stress may be getting out of your control; you should remain alert for them: (1) Feeling thrown for a loop by seemingly minor problems; (2) finding it increasingly hard to relate to people with whom you previously have had good relations; (3) becoming obsessed about your problems; (4) feeling suspicious or distrusting most of the time; (5) feeling trapped in your life; and (6) having persistent, unfounded inferiority feelings. If you recognize these warning signals in yourself, seek help.

Stress management is becoming an increasingly popular concept for preventing illness and rendering a person less susceptible to infection. As a result, many types of relaxation therapies have become popular lately. These are briefly discussed at the end of the chapter.

SMOKING

Every cigarette ad and every carton and package of cigarettes carries warnings of the serious dangers of smoking. Emphysema, lung cancer, and heart disease are among the grave consequences; these are well-known and well publicized. Other illnesses linked to cigarettes include stroke, chronic bronchitis, and cancers of the mouth, throat, and esophagus. Every year approximately 320,000 deaths in the United States alone are smoking related.

"Smoker's face" (Figure 6.1) is a less well known condition. The skin of chronic smokers can look pale and sallow. In addition, the facial skin may appear to be a patchwork of deep creases, wrinkles, and lines that typically radiate from the upper and lower lips and from the corners of the eyes. Nicotine-induced constriction of blood vessels carrying nutrients to the skin is believed to play a role in the development of these unsightly skin changes. Owing to blood vessel constriction, skin temperature may decrease, particularly in the limbs, and fingers and toes may feel cold. Smoking can also stain your fingers and teeth, and leave a stale smell on your breath and in your hair.

Cigarette smoking may also affect healing after plastic surgery. One noted New York plastic surgeon found that smokers have twelve times the risk of developing poor wound healing and skin sloughing (or shedding) after a facelift. Smoking-induced compromise of the skin's capillary circulation is believed to be at fault. In these circumstances sloughing usually occurs near the incision lines in front of and below the ears. Such wound-healing problems may in turn result in permanent loss of skin color and scar formation. Interestingly, stopping smoking several weeks before surgery can reduce the likelihood of these complications, but not to the level seen in nonsmokers. Nevertheless, if you are a smoker and contemplate cosmetic surgery, you should quit smoking at least five weeks before surgery

Quitting smoking is not easy; however, there are a number of different methods to help you. These include group programs sponsored by voluntary health organizations, behavior modification therapy aimed at analyzing why you need to smoke and suggesting activities to help you break the habit, medical therapies such as the use of nicotine chewing gum, individual psychological counseling, and hypnosis. Some people have been able to cut out cigarettes on their own, cold turkey. Others have been able to give them up gradually. If you wish help, consult your family physician or contact the American Cancer Society, American Lung Association, or American Heart Association.

Figure 6.1 Typical "smoker's face"

ALCOHOL

Make no mistake: *Alcohol is a potent drug.* Nearly 70 percent of all adult Americans drink, and it is estimated that about 10 percent of them exhibit some form of alcoholism. Surveys indicate that many drinkers, both "social" and "problem" drinkers, believe that alcohol reduces stress and tension. Furthermore, these same studies indicate that stress reduction is the conscious motive for drinking in many situations. In most cases, light "social" drinking (one or two drinks per day) has not been shown to have harmful effects on skin and overall health. Nevertheless, this should not be understood to be an endorsement of drinking. Drinking has been around for thousands of years, but as yet there are no proven benefits.

Like smoking, alcohol can harm not only your health but your looks. Most people feel a warmth in their skin after drinking; many see a reddish glow to their cheeks. A fair proportion of drinkers, especially those who are fair-complected, flush prominently after drinking. Often these are people who tend to flush easily in tense social situations or after drinking or eating spicy foods or hot beverages. Flushing results from dilation of the small blood vessels in the skin of the face, neck, and chest. The tiny blood vessels subsequently constrict and the flush disappears. For most people, alcohol-related flushing is only temporary and fades in a few hours.

For some people, however, especially those who have been drinking for years or those who have been drinking heavily, the flush may persist; in these cases, it is believed that the blood vessels lose some of their ability to constrict. A dense network of disfiguring, reddish-purplish "broken" blood vessels can appear on the face, neck, and chest. These blood vessels, called *telangiectasias,* are particularly prominent on the sides of the nose and the cheeks.

Alcohol can disfigure in other ways, too. Adult acne is often severely aggravated by drinking. In predisposed individuals, deep, tender, potentially scarring cysts and pustules may form within hours after drinking. Besides "broken" blood vessels, other kinds of unsightly blood-vessel problems can appear elsewhere on the body, especially in persons with long-standing alcohol problems. If liver inflammation occurs, the skin may turn yellow (jaundiced). Nails may also discolor. Finally, being "falling-down drunk" can result in an assortment of bruises, cuts, lacerations, and more severely disfiguring skin and bodily injuries.

DRUGS

Drugs are plant and animal derivatives or synthetic chemicals that can affect your behavior, body, and mind. When prescribed and supervised by a physician, drugs can help to treat or cure diseases and alleviate or reduce pain and suffering. *Drug abuse,* on the other hand, is usually defined as the improper and unsupervised use of one or combinations of five different kinds of drugs. These are (1) *cannabis* derivatives such as marijuana and hashish; (2) *stimulants* such as amphetamines or cocaine; (3) *depressants* such as barbiturates, tranquilizers, and methaqualone; (4) *narcotics* such as opium and its derivatives, heroin and morphine; and (5) *hallucinogens* such as LSD and PCP.

Most drugs with abuse potential can have harmful effects on the skin. For example, marijuana can cause acne flare-ups, trigger hives, and may be responsible for a form of pinkeye. Depressants ("downers"), particularly certain tranquilizers, can cause severe allergic reactions resulting in skin shedding. Stimulants ("uppers"), such as amphetamines ("speed") and cocaine, can cause severely dry, chapped lips and allergic eruptions. Cocaine sniffing, by constricting nasal blood vessels, can lead to nasal sores and perforations of the nasal mucous membranes and cartilage, leaving a hole between the nostrils. Amyl nitrites ("poppers") can interfere with proper oxygenation and can temporarily impart a bluish hue to the skin. Barbiturates are known to cause blistering around the mouth and over the hips and ankles.

Drugs are out there and are readily available. Some are rather cheap, too. For example, one vial of crack (free-base cocaine) costs only about $10. However, the cost in human suffering of a few highs is just too great. In our fun-oriented, fast-paced, high-anxiety society, temptations and excuses to try "recreational" drugs are many. The "It's not going to happen to me" attitude often prevails, but it is wrong, sometimes dead wrong. It can happen to anyone. If you already have a drug problem, seek help right away, before it's too late. If you haven't done drugs, don't start—as with cigarettes and alcohol, if not on account of your health, at least for your looks.

METHODS OF RELAXATION

If strain shows, doing something to reduce it can only help the way you look. Nonstop work or play is unhealthy. You need to relax in order to feel and look your best. Since smoking, alcohol, and drugs do not promote relaxation, what does? Telling yourself to relax, or being told by others, may only serve to increase your anxiety and heighten your sense of frustration and failure. You must learn *how* to relax.

More and more, relaxation techniques are being studied and accepted by various segments of the medical community. Among the more popular ones are biofeedback, yoga, visualization (imaging) exercises, meditation, and hypnosis.

No one relaxation method is right for everyone. The choice depends largely upon the techniques that most appeal to you and seem to work best for you. No matter what methods you choose, however, you probably won't achieve relaxation instantly. Experts say that in the beginning it may take you twenty minutes; after practice, you may be able to reach a relaxed state in less than five minutes. And once learned, these techniques may be called on whenever needed to refresh you.

MASSAGE

The term *massage* encompasses a wide range of manipulative techniques including Shiatsu (acupressure), Swedish massage, and reflexology. Massage for the purpose of promoting relaxation has been practiced for thousands of years. More recently, in the United States, there has been a renewed interest in massage with a therapeutic orientation, particularly in the field of sports medicine.

No one knows for sure the benefits of massage. Those ascribed to it include improved blood circulation, hence improved oxygenation and nutrient transport. Other possible benefits include reducing muscle pain and swelling, stretching tendons, reducing tissue swelling (*edema*), and promoting healing of strained muscles. More research is needed to confirm the benefits. Perhaps most important of all are the psychological benefits. Massage enthusiasts will tell you that a good massage feels wonderful and makes them feel great. One thing is for sure, however—massage cannot break up and knead away unwanted fat or cellulite (see chapter 11).

Warning: Massage should be performed with caution on anyone having underlying skin, circulatory, or heart problems. In addition, acute muscle strains or tears should not be treated by massage within seventy-two hours of the injury. In these instances, a physician should be consulted. However, other than these, I have no major objections to massage. The bottom line: If you have the time and money, a professional massage can be at the very least a relaxing and pampering experience.

SAUNAS, STEAM ROOMS, AND WHIRLPOOLS

Saunas (or Finnish baths) consist basically of exposure to extremely hot (more than 170° F.), relatively dry air (5 percent to 25 percent humidity). Steam baths are similar but use moist air heated to 120° F. and raised to 95 percent humidity. Whirlpool baths are bathtub-size units that produce a single whirling current of hot water. Whirlpool spas are communal units made of acrylic or fiberglass, while hot tubs are simply communal whirlpools made of wood.

Enthusiasm for each of these seems to have increased as people have become more health and fitness conscious. Proponents cite their supposed benefits, including the symptomatic relief of asthma and bronchitis, muscle relaxation, and pain relief. About 150,000 hot tubs and whirlpool baths are sold each year in North America and it's estimated that sales will continue to increase by 15 to 20 percent annually.

Some claims for these treatments stretch credibility. Sauna baths cannot retard or prevent skin aging. While using a steam room certainly can help moisturize your skin, a steamy shower accomplishes the same thing. Anyway, any moisturizing benefits are lost twenty minutes after you leave the steam room unless you thoroughly slather yourself with a moisturizer while your skin is still moist. The heat in saunas and steam rooms can help you shrink away a pound or so of weight, but you gain most of it right back the minute you take a drink of water.

Testimonials notwithstanding, do saunas, steam rooms, and whirlpools really provide any health value? Few would disagree that indulging in them can make you feel better psychologically. Moreover, within a supervised program of rehabilitation, whirlpools can be helpful for promoting improved joint and muscle mobility in people with arthritis and certain other disabilities. And they can help soothe sore muscles, which is why I have no serious objections to their use by otherwise healthy people. However, because they are at higher risk of heat stress, older people and pregnant women should limit their use of saunas, steam rooms, and hot tubs.

Finally, a few precautions are in order. Before entering and after leaving, drink plenty of water to prevent dehydration. Don't stay more than 15 minutes in a sauna, 12 minutes in a steam room, or 10 minutes in a hot tub. Don't use body oils or heavy cosmetics on your skin as they can inhibit sweating. Last, make certain that the public whirlpool at the club or gym is properly cleaned and adequately chlorinated. Not long ago, pimplelike bacterial infections of the thighs and buttocks were seen in people frequenting certain public whirlpool baths (see chapter 9).

PART TWO

COMMON SKIN PROBLEMS

WHO SAYS ACNE IS JUST KID STUFF?

Acne is a familiar, often frustrating, and sometimes permanently disfiguring condition. Don't let anyone try to persuade you otherwise. Millions of dollars are spent each year on over-the-counter (OTC) acne products and treatments, and acne sufferers constitute a substantial portion of the patients seen by most general-practice dermatologists.

A solitary pimple on your face does not necessarily mean acne (it could be the result of allergies, skin infections, or even the rubbing of your collar against your skin), but if that pimple becomes many, it probably *is* acne. Three types of pimple problems can affect adults: *acne vulgaris, acne rosacea,* and *perioral dermatitis.* Although these conditions may resemble each other, they are quite different. Rest assured, however, there is much that can be done to combat and control acne.

This chapter not only identifies the types of acne in detail but explains what you can do for yourself and what your doctor can do for you regarding treatments, therapies, and medications.

ACNE VULGARIS ("TEENAGE ACNE")

Acne vulgaris, or plain pimples, has been plaguing mankind for thousands of years. Although acne is often referred to as "teenage acne," this is misleading, for it is not a sign of maturation, like growing a beard or breast development. While it is true that more than 80 percent of adolescents develop some form of acne, it is also true that nearly 95 percent of the population will suffer from acne at some point in their *adult* lives. In fact, contrary to popular belief, acne is a disease that some people do not outgrow. Moreover, some people reach adulthood before suffering from acne. Regardless of the age of onset, acne is usually treated in the same way.

Acne severity ranges from the occasional appearance of a few isolated pimples, or "zits," to widespread breakouts that may leave scars on face, chest, and back. When persistent or severe, acne can be the source of embarrassment and much needless psychological distress and loss of self-esteem. If improperly treated or left untreated, it can lead to permanent scarring and disfigurement. Even acne scars can—and often do—remain life-long sources of emotional distress.

The cause(s) of acne is unknown, though *genetic (hereditary)* and *hormonal* factors are believed to play significant roles. With the onset of puberty, men and women begin to secrete increased amounts of sex hormones, including male hormones *(androgens)*, which are believed to be important in acne development. Precisely because men secrete greater amounts of male hormones, they tend to have more severe cases of acne than women. This increased hormone production is also believed to be responsible at least in part for the oily skin of which many acne sufferers also complain. And racial factors seem to play a role, too: Whites tend to have more severe acne than blacks.

While stress is not a cause of acne, nervous tension and physical stresses often play important roles in triggering or aggravating it. I always warn my patients that emotional stress, such as boyfriend-girlfriend problems, marital difficulties, illness or

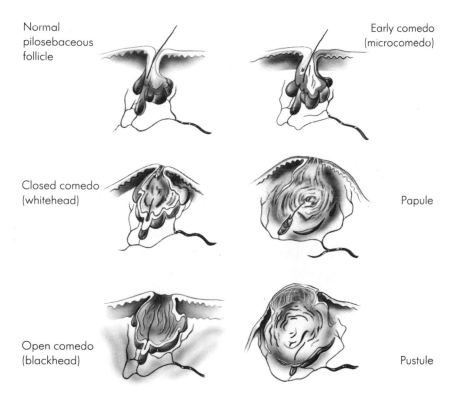

Normal
pilosebaceous
follicle

Early comedo
(microcomedo)

Closed comedo
(whitehead)

Papule

Open comedo
(blackhead)

Pustule

Figure 7.1   The development of acne blemishes

death in the family, or physical stresses, such as menstruation (especially during the week before the period), fevers, sore throats, and hive and allergy attacks, may cause acne to flare up or worsen. At the same time, I reassure my patients that their condition will usually improve once the stressful episode has passed.

Acne vulgaris is quite distinctive. It typically consists of four types of blemishes: *papules* (pimples), *pustules* ("pus-heads"), *closed comedones* (whiteheads), and *open comedones* (blackheads). In more serious cases deep cysts and pock-mark scars can also be seen. The four types of blemishes may not be present at the same time; lesions may occur alone or in combination. Acne vulgaris (see Figure 7.1) differs in a number of ways from acne rosacea, which it may resemble at first glance to the untrained eye.

Acne begins within hair follicles, which everyone has on his or her face, chest, and back. Under ordinary circumstances, secretions from the sebaceous glands within the follicles travel up the follicle and are released onto the surface of the skin through the pores. In acne, a small mass of cells called a *microcomedo* plugs the opening to the pores. A blackhead results when the top of the plug is exposed to the skin surface. (The color of the blackhead is caused by the dark pigment in your skin and oxidation of the exposed plug; it is *not* caused by dirt.)

A whitehead is formed when the plug rests below the skin surface and does not open onto it. Whitehead formation is a crucial step in acne development. Oils and debris accumulate within the clogged pore. Trapped below the surface, they are then broken down into highly irritating substances by otherwise harmless (noninfectious) bacteria known as *propionobacterium acnes.* Finally, like a balloon bursting from overexpansion, the follicle ruptures and spills its irritating contents into the surrounding skin, heightening the inflammation and creating the papules, pustules, and cysts so familiar to the acne sufferer. When the inflammation spreads deep within the skin, cysts are formed. When normal tissue is destroyed, permanent scars result.

Acne can range from mild to severe, and dermatologists use a convenient and more precise way of grading its severity. Grade I (mild acne) consists only of whiteheads and/or blackheads. Grade II (moderate acne) consists of blackheads, whiteheads, and small pimples with minimal inflammation, usually confined to the face; grade III (severe acne) consists of blackheads, whiteheads, and deep, inflamed pimples. Finally, grade IV (very severe acne) is characterized by scarring, deeper cysts, and many pustules on the face, chest, and back.

CONTROLLING ACNE

Unfortunately, there is still no cure for acne. However, many fine treatments are available to control its manifestations. I always tell my acne patients on their first visit that my job is to make them look as though they don't have a problem until a true acne cure is found, or until they "outgrow" this problem. For many people home treatment with a few OTC medications is all that is necessary. For more severe problems, or those that do not respond to simple therapy, I suggest you consult with a dermatologist as soon as possible.

HELPING YOURSELF

Let's begin by exploding a few common myths about acne.

Acne is not a disease of dirt, so *overscrubbing your skin with harsh soaps, acne soaps, or abrasive cleansers is unnecessary.* In fact, it can make your skin worse. Scrubbing may dry it out so much that it will burn or sting when you apply real acne medications. Gentle cleansing with a mild, soapless soap, such as Lowila cake, is all that is usually needed to remove oil, cosmetics, and dirt buildup.

Foods do not cause acne. Acne is neither caused nor made worse by chocolates, fried foods, colas, nuts, potato chips, candy, ice cream, pizza, or other kinds of junk foods. As a rule, I don't recommend eating these foods, which are unhealthy for the rest of your body, particularly your heart and blood vessels, but you need not avoid them for the sake of your skin.

However, foods high in iodine—shellfish, kelp, seaweed, iodized salt, and mineral supplements containing iodine—have been linked to acne flare-ups. If you have an acne problem, you should consume these items in moderation or, if possible, eliminate them entirely from your diet.

The sun is not necessarily your best friend in the war against acne. While it is true that sun exposure "dries up" pimples and that a tan helps to mask persistent blemishes, the sun may also precipitate a flare-up of acne. Ultraviolet rays not only thicken the horny layer of the skin and contribute to plugging the pores, but also can damage the openings of the pores, which leads to blockage. It is then an easy step to the development of whiteheads, which usually appear about four to six weeks after sun exposure.

Although proper skin cleansing was discussed in chapter 3, and moisturizers and cosmetics are covered in chapters 4 and 5, it is important to reemphasize here that vigorous scrubbing, the

GENERAL TIPS FOR SELF-HELP

- Use mild soaps and don't overwash or overscrub your skin.
- Use only oil-free moisturizers, oil-free or gel foundations, and powder or gel blushes.
- Restrict astringents to occasional and sparing use.
- Avoid abrasive sponges or washcloths.
- Don't pick, squeeze, or pop your pimples.
- When in doubt, or if your problem is severe, seek professional help.

use of harsh soaps (and so-called acne soaps), and the use of washcloths or polyester scrub brushes, in a misguided attempt to wash away or dry up acne, leads to dry, chapped, flaking skin—skin that is too dry and tender to withstand the often slightly drying side effects of most antiacne topicals. The notion of scrubbing away at acne is so ingrained in many people that when their skin does grow dry and chapped from overwashing, they choose to give up using their medications rather than cut back on washing.

Without question, certain cosmetics, particularly heavy, oily makeups, aggravate acne by clogging pores. Dermatologists call this condition *acne cosmetica.* At one time, many doctors advised patients with acne to avoid using any makeups at all. Nowadays this need no longer be the case. However, when choosing cosmetics, be sure to look for oil-free or water-based formulations and specifically for products advertised as noncomedogenic (i.e., noncomedone forming, nonacne forming). These have been tested by daily application to the skin of a rabbit's ear for several weeks to determine whether or not they cause acne. Allercreme, Almay, Clinique, Dermage, and Revlon produce noncomedogenic cosmetics for people with oily or acne-prone skin.

HELP FROM OVER THE COUNTER

Four main types of ingredients, alone or in combination, are found in most nonprescription acne creams, gels, or lotions: sulfur, resorcinol, salicylic acid, and benzoyl peroxide. If you have excessively oily or shiny skin, you may find astringents (see chapter 3) occasionally helpful for blotting excess oil between cleansings. Many of my patients have found ordinary witch hazel, or individually prepackaged alcohol towelettes, such as the kind your doctor uses to cleanse your skin before drawing blood, to work satisfactorily. Alternatively, you may use Sebanil, a commercially available astringent/cleanser containing acetone. However, when used too frequently, these astringents can cause excessive dryness and irritation. Instead, you might simply try blotting skin oils with a clean, white facial tissue periodically throughout the day.

Sulfur and resorcinol are *keratolytic* (peeling) as well as antibacterial agents. They are often sold in flesh-tinted lotions that can be used in place of cosmetics for covering blemishes (Rezamid lotion, Clearasil's Adult Care cream). For that reason, men find these products particularly useful. Vlemasque, a sulfur-containing mask useful for more stubborn cases of acne, need only to be left on for twenty minutes and then washed off. Unlike most other topicals, it doesn't have to be left on overnight to be effective—a decided advantage for spouses or lovers.

Salicylic acid also works as a peeling agent to loosen and soften thick, clogged pores. It is particularly helpful for blackheads. Saligel and Keralyt gel are examples of OTC salicylic acid preparations.

Benzoyl peroxide in gel form (rather than cream or lotion) is believed to work most effectively and consistently against acne, for it serves as a peeling and antibacterial agent capable of penetrating the pores. Benzoyl peroxides have proven useful not only for treating existing acne blemishes, but for preventing the appearance of new ones.

Most benzoyl peroxide gels are available by prescription only, and are generally marketed in 2.5, 5, and 10 percent strengths. More important, the lower strengths have been shown to be as effective as the 10 percent formulation and somewhat less drying. Clear By Design and Fostex BPO 5 are two OTC benzoyl peroxide gels. Neutrogena Acne Mask is an effective mask form of benzoyl peroxide that only needs to be left on for about twenty minutes.

HELP FROM YOUR DERMATOLOGIST

If you have a more stubborn case of acne or if a trial of simple therapy has not proven successful, see your dermatologist, who will have available a broad selection of prescription medications and treatments. These include the use of topicals such as benzoyl peroxide; vitamin A acid; a number of different antibiotic creams, lotions, and ointments, and oral medications such as antibiotics and Accutane; and finally, surgical procedures for shrinking or draining acne cysts and correcting scars.

BENZOYL PEROXIDES A wide array of water-, alcohol-, and acetone-based benzoyl peroxide gels is available by prescription. Water-based preparations are generally the least drying, and alcohol-based formulations the most. Your doctor can select the product best suited to your skin. I generally prefer to start with water-based emollient gels, such as Desquam-E 2.5, to prevent excessive dryness.

RETIN-A Many contend that Retin-A *(tretinoin, vitamin A acid)* is one of the most effective antiacne topicals available today. It is believed to penetrate into clogged follicles, and works by making the cells within the plug less sticky, thus speeding the production of new, healthier cells. Retin-A is available in gel, liquid, or cream forms, the cream being the least drying, the gel the most. Here again, I opt to begin with the least drying preparation. **Warning:** Many people notice a slight worsening of their acne within the first two or three weeks of use before noticeable improvement begins.

TOPICAL ANTIBIOTICS Representing a significant advance in acne treatment, topical antibiotics are believed to work by suppressing propionobacterium acnes. It is believed that in some cases they may also play a direct role in suppressing inflammation.

There was a time when only oral (systemic) antibiotics were available. This meant that whenever you needed antibiotics for facial acne, you had to subject your whole system to the effects of the drug. The theoretical advantage of topical antibiotics, then, is that they are applied where they are most needed; the rest of your body needn't suffer. Nowadays, I seldom prescribe an oral antibiotic before giving a patient a trial of a topical one.

Erythromycin, clindamycin, and *tetracycline* are the three most common antibiotics found in topical preparations that are available as lotions, creams, and ointments. Most dermatologists agree that topical tetracycline is not as effective as the other two. T-Stat, Eryderm, and Erymax lotions are popularly prescribed erythromycin preparations, and Cleocin-T is an effective clindamycin topical. Some people find Erycette lotion, an erythromycin solution that comes in easy-to-carry, individually wrapped, sterile foil packets, particularly convenient to use.

Most topical antibiotics are drying. To minimize unnecessary dryness, wash your face gently and not more than twice a day. In general, wait twenty to thirty minutes after washing before applying the medications since their drying effects are enhanced when you apply them to moist skin. And do apply them sparingly. This is especially important when using Retin-A; a pea-sized amount of it is sufficient to cover your entire face. Naturally, if you experience burning, stinging, itching, redness, scaliness, or swelling after using any topical, discontinue its use immediately and seek medical advice, especially if these symptoms persist. In general, all topical antibiotics require between one and four weeks before benefits can be observed.

ORAL ANTIBIOTICS Still considered the mainstays of acne therapy, oral antibiotics are believed to work on the same steps of the acne cycle as their topical counterparts. These days, however, they are often reserved for tougher, more resistant cases of acne.

Tetracycline is widely prescribed and has been used for many years. Minocycline and erythromycin are also frequently prescribed. In contrast to their rapid effect in curing certain bacterial infections (usually in a matter of days), you may be surprised to learn that oral antibiotics usually take from three to six weeks to be effective in controlling acne. Impatient to see results, many sufferers are often frustrated by this delay. Because of this, I usually warn patients that they should not expect to see significant improvement in their condition for several weeks.

To be effective, tetracycline and erythomycin must be taken (quite inconveniently) either one hour before or two hours after eating and certainly never along with dairy products or antacids, which interfere with their effectiveness. For that reason, I prefer to prescribe minocycline (Minocin) or erythromycin ethyl succinate (E.E.S.-400) since these antibiotics may be taken with less regard to mealtime and dairy products—a blessing in the minds of many patients.

While serious side effects from oral antibiotics are rare, you may experience slight discomfort from gastrointestinal upset, queasiness, and diarrhea. Discontinuing the medication for a few days, adjusting the dosage, changing the dosage schedule, or switching to another antibiotic usually will ameliorate these problems. Vaginal yeast infections (candida, monilia) are another common problem associated with taking oral antibiotics. If either of these should occur, and you must be maintained on the oral antibiotic in order to control your acne problem, your doctor may prescribe douching or oral and topical antiyeast medications. Once satisfactory control of the acne is achieved, the dose of antibiotic can be reduced or the drug eliminated altogether.

ACCUTANE A drivative of vitamin A, Accutane is a major breakthrough in the treatment of severe nodulocystic, scarring acne. It is intended for those who have not previously responded to the most aggressive forms of combined topical and oral therapy. While Accutane is not a cure, many acne sufferers have remained free of their condition for several years after using it. Between sixteen and twenty weeks of therapy are usually required, and improvement is usually not seen for about ten to twelve weeks. In fact, some worsening of the condition generally occurs within the first few weeks.

Unfortunately, Accutane has many side effects, both minor and major. These include dry, chapped skin and dry mucous membranes. Moreover, nose bleeds, sore gums, musculoskeletal aches and pains, and increased sun sensitivity are among the other common minor side effects. Fortunately, these problems generally disappear shortly after the drug is stopped.

The more serious side effects include abnormal spine and ligament calcification, diminished night vision, blurred vision, mood changes, hair loss, and abnormal elevations of blood lipid (fat) levels. Some of these problems may be permanent, especially if Accutane is not stopped soon enough after they appear. Finally, and very importantly, *Accutane must not be taken by any woman who is trying to conceive or who is not taking adequate contraceptive precautions.* Human birth defects have been directly attributed to Accutane when used during pregnancy.

Given these side effects, I generally do not agree with the practice of some physicians who prescribe Accutane for people with less severe acne conditions *before* aggressive trials of more conventional therapies have proven unsuccessful. Furthermore, while the benefits of using reduced dosages of Accutane are currently being studied, preliminary findings suggest that such benefis are comparatively short-lived. All these considerations notwithstanding, however, Accutane represents a remarkable advance in the treatment of previously unmanageable severe cystic acne.

ACNE SURGERY This term is another way of describing two very important adjuncts to acne therapy: *comedone extraction* (the opening and removal of blackheads and whiteheads) and *incision and drainage of acne cysts.* In the first, the dermatologist uses the tip of a fine scalpel blade or fine needle to unroof the blackheads or whiteheads and then removes the core with a special instrument called a *comedone extractor.* The procedure, which is usually only minimally uncomfortable, not only makes you look better almost immediately, but also dramatically decreases the population of whiteheads before they turn into inflamed pimples and cysts. When severe inflammation and cysts have already occurred, your doctor may elect to use a fine scalpel blade to incise (open) and drain them in order to speed their healing and reduce the risk of scarring. This procedure, too, is usually only slightly uncomfortable.

THERAPEUTIC INJECTIONS The injection of an anti-inflammatory *steroid*, frequently *triamcinolone acetonide suspension*, is the procedure of choice for shrinking inflamed acne pimples and deep cysts. Some people have reservations about the use of steroids but these concerns are usually unfounded and based on hearsay or misapprehension about the term *steroid*. While it is true that complications may arise in patients with conditions such as rheumatoid arthritis or systemic lupus erythematosus, who require treatment with steroids in high doses (orally or by injection) for long periods of time, they seldom occur when steroids are administered in low doses for short periods (one to three weeks).

An intralesional steroid is injected into the spot where it is needed. Moreover, only small doses need to be injected, so very little of the steroid actually gets absorbed into your system. Acne cysts usually shrink and resolve within twelve to seventy-eight hours following injection. The sooner inflammation is brought under control, the less likely it is that there will be any permanent scarring. Occasionally, a small depression may form at the injection site, but generally this will return to normal by itself within several weeks to several months.

COSMETIC SURGERY FOR ACNE SCARRING Unfortunately, no topical or systemic drug currently available can eliminate acne scars after they have occurred, hence the importance of seeking medical attention early, before irreversible scarring has occurred. However, there are several surgical procedures available to improve scars ranging from the broad, shallow craterlike ones to ice-pick scars (narrow, deeply pitted, tightly bound down) and to make them less noticeable. These include *chemical peels, dermabrasion, excision of ice-pick scars,* and *collagen injections.*

Chemical peels, or the application of a strong acid to the face, are seldom helpful for improving any but the most superficial scars. The acid, usually *trichloracetic acid* or *phenol,* is applied to the skin by cotton-tipped applicators or brushes and destroys the top layer by causing the equivalent of a second-degree burn. Chemical peels may help to make the skin feel more taut. In general, however, the results usually are not as rewarding as those achieved by other cosmetic procedures. And furthermore, overexposure to the sun must be avoided for the first two to three months after chemical peels to prevent the development (often permanent) of blotchy pigmentation.

Dermabrasion (skin planing or skin sanding) has been used for over thirty years to render broad, pock-mark scars shallower, less craterlike (Figure 7.2). This is accomplished with up to three basic cutting tools—diamond fraises, wire brushes, and serrated wheels—that sand down the surrounding skin, the theory being that the shallower the pock mark, the less shadowing within it, and the less obvious the scar.

Fair-skinned people are better candidates for dermabrasion be-

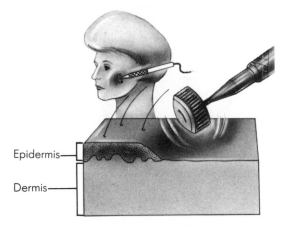

Epidermis

Dermis

Figure 7.2 Dermabrasion. This procedure involves mechanical sanding down of the top layer of skin.

cause they exhibit less color contrast between treated and un-treated skin than most darkly pigmented people. And as with chemical peels, postoperative sun exposure must be minimized for about three months to prevent blotchy discoloration.

Ice-pick scars are deeply pitted, narrow scars with rigid walls. Because they are so deep, ice-pick scars are not significantly improved by chemical peels, dermabrasion, or collagen injections (see below). Three types of corrective surgery are routinely per-formed to improve them. In the *punch-excision* procedure, the pit scar is simply cut out with a cookie-cutterlike instrument known as a *punch,* and the resulting wound closed with ultrafine stitches. In this case a fine line scar replaces the deep circular pit. In a second procedure, known as *punch-elevation,* the scar tissue is elevated to the surface and then sanded down. The pit is replaced by a fine, in most cases, barely visible, round, smooth spot. Finally, in the third technique, *punch-grafting* (Figure 7.3), the plug of scar tissue is removed and replaced by a graft of tissue taken from behind the ear. Here again, a faint round plug may be visible. From a normal distance, however, the rims usually blend in with other skin surface irregularities.

As you know, collagen is the normal supporting protein ma-terial of our skin and other soft tissues. While the collagen found in many expensive moisturizing creams *cannot* be absorbed into

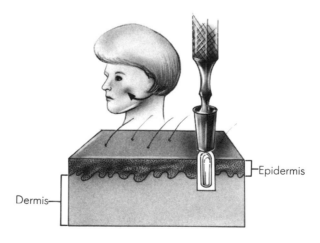

Figure 7.3 Punch graft. Skin from behind the ear is grafted into an "ice-pick" acne scar.

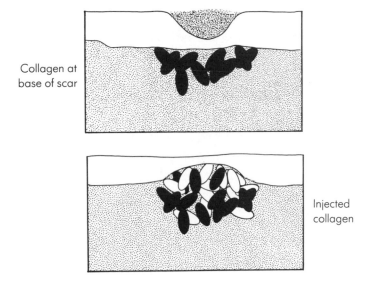

Collagen at base of scar

Injected collagen

Figure 7.4   Injectable collagen for depressed acne scars

your skin, Zyderm is injected right where it is needed—below the scar. The injection of purified bovine collagen (Zyderm, Zyplast) to plump up depressed scars has proven beneficial in many cases (Figure 7.4). Injectable collagen has a number of advantages. The procedure, which consists of a series of injections, takes only a few moments to perform; is usually only minimally uncomfortable; and the patient can usually return to work immediately afterward.

Having received FDA approval a number of years ago, Zyderm collagen has been used in injectable form in over 400,000 people to date. (*Silicone,* with which Zyderm and Zyplast should not be confused, has never received FDA approval for the treatment of acne scars, despite the fact that it has been around for more than thirty years.)

Zyderm is generally reserved for shallow defects, and Zyplast for broader and deeper ones. Unfortunately, the results are temporary with both; some loss of correction occurs between six months and several years after the initial treatments. Subsequent touch-ups, however, generally require fewer treatments than the initial therapy.

A test dose of Zyderm is administered to the forearm about

four weeks before treatment is contemplated to screen for potentially allergic patients. In addition, people with a history (not a family history) of autoimmune diseases (such as lupus erthematosus, polyarteritis, polmyositis, rheumatoid arthritis, and psoriatic arthritis, in which the body manifests allergies to its own proteins) are not candidates for Zyderm injections. About 3 percent of otherwise healthy people are allergic to injectable collagen, and about half of them manifest their allergy *after* the actual treatment has begun. Once the allergy develops, further treatments are no longer possible for these people. Instead, they must await the development of other injectable materials. Fibril is one type currently under investigation.

ACNE ROSACEA

Acne rosacea, or more simply, rosacea, is adult acne. The age of onset ranges from twenty to fifty, and the problem can be life-long. While men are much more likely to develop severe rosacea, women are three times more often affected by this condition. In addition, people with fair complexions are more prone to rosacea.

The pimples, pustules, and cysts that occur in rosacea may look like typical acne, but closer scrutiny reveals the absence of whiteheads and blackheads—a very helpful sign for differentiating the two conditions. Further, in rosacea, pimples and cysts rarely appear on the chest and back.

Since both types of acne give you pimple problems, you might be thinking: What difference does it make which type I have? However, it is important for treatment purposes to make the distinction. Rosacea is a complex inflammatory condition of unknown cause, and it frequently consists of more than just pimples. People with rosacea may be prone to prolonged episodes of facial flushing and tend to develop numerous "broken" blood vessels *(telangiectasias),* and overgrown oil glands on the face and neck *(sebaceous hyperplasia).* In more advanced cases, the overgrown oil glands may merge on the nose to give a W.C. Fields–type nose *(rhinophyma).* Eyelid irritations *(blepharitis),* as well as other types of eye problems, are also associated with rosacea.

As with ordinary acne, stress and excessive sun exposure can aggravate rosacea. On the other hand, diet may actually play a role in many cases of rosacea. Alcohol, beverages containing caffeine, such as coffee, tea, and colas, hot beverages, spicy foods, and pork products have been associated with flare-ups of rosacea in certain people. Extremes of heat and cold may do so as well. If you have rosacea, it would be useful to keep a diary of your attacks to see whether any can be traced to the ingestion of a particular food item.

The treatment of rosacea depends upon which problems are present. The acne can be treated in much the same way as common acne. "Broken" blood vessels can be closed off by subjecting them to a mild electric current *(electrolysis of telangiectasias)*. Overgrown oil glands can be flattened by the use of other electrical devices *(electrosurgery)*. And eye problems may require consultation with an ophthalmologist.

PERIORAL DERMATITIS

Perioral dermatitis consists of a cluster of tiny pimples and pustules in the so-called muzzle region of the face—around the mouth, sides of the nose, and on the chin. Inexplicably, the skin of the upper lip is characteristically spared. Perioral dermatitis typically affects women in their twenties and thirties.

The cause of perioral dermatitis is unknown, but the *presumed* causes include the prolonged use of corticosteroid creams, fluorinated toothpastes, fragranced cosmetics, and the Pill. In many cases, however, no cause or association can be found. Happily, therapy for this condition is more satisfactory than our knowledge of what causes it or why it is limited to the perioral area. Oral tetracycline or minocycline is quite effective, and resolution usually occurs in two to eight weeks. For some people, however, a second course of oral antibiotic therapy may be required. Also, topical sulfur and salicylic acid preparations may be prescribed in place of or in conjunction with oral therapy. With perioral dermatitis there is no scarring.

COMMON SKIN RASHES

*T*hroughout your life, your skin may play host to a wide variety of rashes. Often rashes are not only uncomfortable, especially when widespread, they can also be unsightly and can pose a big obstacle to achieving good skin. Few rashes, however, are the result of inadequate hygiene.

Dermatologists frequently refer to skin rashes as *eruptions* because they appear to erupt or break out on your skin. (Your dictionary may define them as "an eruption of red spots on the skin" or "a sudden appearance of bumps or discolorations.") Many of these eruptions are caused by agents such as bacteria, fungi, and viruses (these are covered in chapter 9), but a number of others are believed to be noninfectious in origin. Frequently, the precise causes of noninfectious eruptions remain unknown.

Most noninfectious rashes are not serious and can be treated at home or in the dermatologist's office. (Acne, discussed in chapter 7, is one example of a noninfectious eruption.) On the other hand, some can be quite debilitating and occasionally require hospitalization.

This chapter, which is devoted to the causes, prevention, and treatments of several of the more common noninfectious rashes, identifies stumbling blocks along the road to good skin and what you and your doctor can do about them.

ECZEMA (DERMATITIS)

The terms *eczema* and *dermatitis* are interchangeable and cover a group of several similar skin conditions, although *dermatitis* (*derm* means *skin,* and *itis* means *inflammation*) best describes our current understanding of these conditions. To the naked eye, these conditions strongly resemble each other under the microscope. In general, they tend to be extremely itchy conditions that exhibit the following skin changes during their course: redness, swelling, blistering, oozing, crusting, scabbing, thickening, peeling, and discoloration. *Since they are not caused by germs, eczemas are not contagious.* Furthermore, although some highly allergic people seem more prone to eczema, eczemas per se are not truly allergies.

Four main types of dermatitis are discussed in this section: *atopic dermatitis, nummular dermatitis, contact dermatitis,* and *seborrhea* and *seborrheic dermatitis.*

Regardless of their causes, eczemas may progress through three distinctive stages—*acute, subacute,* and *chronic.* Some forms exhibit all three stages, while others only one or two.

Hallmarks of acute eczema typically consist of intense itching, redness, and swelling; however, scratch marks and the formation of blisters and oozing also characterize this stage. Poison ivy rash is an example of an acute eczema.

Subacute eczema exhibits fewer blisters and less oozing than acute eczema. Scaliness and peeling are often present in this stage, and redness and scratch marks continue to be prominent. Nummular dermatitis and seborrheic dermatitis are examples of common subacute eczemas.

Chronic eczema is characterized by thick, leathery, and often painfully cracked skin. Depigmented or abnormally dark skin is common in the affected areas. The skin changes are largely the result of persistent scratching and rubbing by the sufferer. Redness, blisters, and oozing are not typically present in this stage. Atopic dermatitis is a common example of chronic eczema.

ATOPIC DERMATITIS

Atopic dermatitis is a widespread condition, affecting about 3 percent of the American population. It is one of the most common conditions of childhood; 2 percent of infants and 5 percent of children are estimated to experience symptoms at some time. While the exact cause of this condition is unknown, atopic dermatitis tends to run in families having histories of eczema, asthma, hay fever, and hives. Also, people with atopic dermatitis usually have excessively dry, sensitive skin. About one in every five sufferers, however, do not have such a family background. Fortunately, more than half of all infants recover from atopic dermatitis by the age of two, and more than two-thirds of all sufferers outgrow their condition somewhere between the ages of five and twenty-five. The remainder, however, continue to be troubled by the condition throughout their adult lives.

Atopic dermatitis may pass through all three of the eczema stages. In infancy, the acute and subacute stages are more commonly encountered. In adulthood, the eruption characteristically involves the bends of the elbows and the backs of the knees. Other areas, including the face, may also be involved in more severe cases. Severe adult atopic dermatitis typically includes generally dry, lackluster skin; intense, unrelenting itching, especially at nighttime; thickened, brownish skin with accentuated skin markings; scratch marks; and crusts.

People with atopic dermatitis experience many ups and downs; they may seesaw between being entirely clear and in real misery from the relentless itching. Nervous tension and physical illnesses (major ones as well as minor ones such as colds, fevers, sore throats, and ear infections) may trigger flare-ups. The overzealous use of soap and water and rapid shifts in temperature and humidity can also prompt an outbreak. Contrary to popular wisdom, foods rarely play a triggering role in atopic dermatitis, except in some small children. In these instances, citrus fruits, eggs, fish, artificial coloring, or milk may precipitate a flare-up. Interestingly, there is scientific evidence that breast-fed infants are less likely to develop atopic dermatitis than their bottle-fed counterparts.

Allergy skin testing to determine any specific food allergies is far less reliable than simple observation. For example, upon testing you may exhibit an allergy to a particular food yet have no symptoms when you actually eat that food. Conversely, you may not react to a specific food when tested, but respond strongly when you eat it. Moreover, desensitization shots, such as those used to treat hay fever–type allergies, are seldom useful in treating atopic dermatitis and even may worsen the condition.

Unfortunately, we are still unable to cure atopic dermatitis. However, once the condition has been diagnosed, your dermatologist can advise you and prescribe a variety of medications to alleviate symptoms and clear up the eruptions. Therapy for most sufferers generally consists of the combined use of topical corticosteroid creams or ointments and oral antihistamines *and* following a few commensense rules.

Topical corticosteroid creams and *ointments* (e.g., Maxivate, Temovate, and Diprolene), which are anti-inflammatory, prescription cortisone derivatives, have become the mainstays of eczema treatment. In fact, they are the preparations most widely used in dermatology today. Depending upon the severity of the eruption, your doctor may prescribe high-, medium-, or low-potency topical steroids. In general, these ointments are applied to the skin one or more times daily and usually bring about relief of symptoms and clearing up of abnormal skin changes within a matter of days. They are extremely effective for reducing itching. Topical corticosteroids may look and feel like cold cream when applied to your skin, but they are not. If used daily for several weeks, the more potent topical steroids can cause irreversible, premature thinning of the skin, and development of "broken" blood vessels, permanent stretch marks, skin pigment loss, and increased skin fragility. Therefore, they must be used with extreme caution and only under the strict supervision of a physician.

Antihistamines (anti-itch and sedative pills) can also be helpful. More than seven different classes of antihistamines are currently available. Effective alone or in combination to control symptoms, they are believed to work by blocking the inflammatory effects of histamines (a chemical mediator that is responsible for the known manifestations of allergy) and raising the itch threshold. *Hydroxyzine* (Durrax and Atarax) is an effective, commonly prescribed antihistamine. Unfortunately, most antihistamines make people groggy, so driving while taking them is ill-advised. For the same reason, they should not be combined with alcohol or other sedatives. Recently, a new, nonsedating antihistamine, Seldane *(terfenedine),* was introduced, but it remains to be seen what place, if any, this drug will have in our anti-itch, anti-eczema armamentarium.

A number of simple rules that apply to choice of clothing and to regulating the household environment may also be helpful in controlling atopic dermatitis. Where possible, street clothing should be made of cotton, instead of wool, which tends to be highly irritating to atopic skin. All intimate apparel that rests directly upon the skin should also be made of cotton. For the same reason, loose-fitting clothing is preferable to tight, constricting garments.

While the role of the common house-dust mite in triggering or aggravating atopic dermatitis is still being investigated, some dermatologists and allergists feel that, at least for the time being, attempts should be made to reduce exposure to it. Although an allergen-free environment outside of a laboratory is impractical, at the very least, the bedroom, where much time is ordinarily spent, usually can be made more dust-free. Rugs and carpeting should be avoided, and furnishings and coverings made preferably from plastic, nylon, or cotton. Headboards and shelving above the bed are dust traps and also should be avoided. Mattresses and pillows should be made of synthetic foam or foam rubber and covered with plastic mattress covers.

Finally, dryness must be actively avoided. The use of synthetic soapless soaps; gentle, nonabrasive cleansings; and the liberal use of moisturizers should help to prevent recurrences. Cold-air humidifiers or the use of shallow pans of water near radiators can reduce room dryness and, consequently, itching.

NUMMULAR DERMATITIS

Nummular dermatitis is a relatively common form of eczema. The word *nummular* means coin-shaped and describes the patches of eczema that most often affect the upper and lower extremities, and upper back and buttocks regions. Nummular dermatitis appears most often in older people, and in those with very dry skin. For the most part, it is considered a subacute form of eczema. Patches of nummular dermatitis are red, round, weepy, or crusty. These patches may range from the size of a dime to a silver dollar. Itching can be severe.

Nummular dermatitis typically improves during the summertime and worsens during periods of heightened emotional stress. In children, it has been linked with atopic dermatitis. In others, it has been linked to contact with irritating substances (see below). Nummular dermatitis typically exhibits periods of clearing and flaring up, or may persist for years.

Treating nummular dermatitis consists of eliminating contact with any known irritants or aggravating environmental factors, such as dryness. In full-blown cases, the use of topical steroids and oral antihistamines may be necessary to control symptoms. When itchy patches are few in number, the dermatologist may choose to treat them by instilling a small amount of a cortisone derivative, using triamcinolone acetonide, directly into the spots (intralesional injections) in addition to, or in place of, other therapies. Keeping the skin moist and well-lubricated at all times is a must.

CONTACT DERMATITIS

As the name implies, contact dermatitis is a rash that results from the contact of an irritating or allergenic substance with your skin. The substance that causes the problem is often referred to as the *contactant*. When contact dermatitis results from a true allergic reaction to a substance, it is called *allergic contact dermatitis*. (In general, an allergy is a sensitivity or overreaction of your body to a substance that for most people causes no problems.) When it results from simple irritation by a harsh substance or from rubbing or some other direct mechanical irritation, it is referred to as *irritant contact dermatitis*.

Irritant contact dermatitis is far more common than its allergic counterpart; nearly 80 out of every 100 instances of contact dermatitis are irritant. Unlike atopic dermatitis, neither type of contact dermatitis has been linked to heredity nor are they triggered or aggravated by emotional stresses or physical illness. Irritant dermatitis typically occurs on one's very first exposure to the contactant. By contrast, an allergic dermatitis does not occur upon first exposure. In fact, when you first develop a skin allergy to a particular substance, e.g., poison ivy, it may be the second, hundredth, or thousandth time you have been in contact with it.

Hand dermatitis, once referred to as *housewives' eczema,* is a common example of irritant contact dermatitis (although occasionally, hand dermatitis may also be allergic in nature). Besides housewives and house cleaners, it affects many people, such as food handlers, bartenders, certain industrial workers, nurses, surgeons, and dentists. The irritating effects of overusing soap and water, and contact with raw foods, detergents, waxes, spray cleansers, abrasives, solvents, urine (from diaper changing), oven cleaners, scouring cleansers, bleaches, ammonia, polishes, paints, and other harsh chemicals in the home or workplace are frequently responsible for this problem. Rashes under rings are another example of irritant hand dermatitis, resulting from the entrapment of water or irritants under the ring.

Irritant dermatitis, by no means limited to the hands, may affect any area of your skin where contact has been made. Redness and tiny blisters are typical of acute irritant dermititis, while scaling and deep painful cracks indicate prolonged, repeated exposure.

Poison ivy (also *poison oak* and *poison sumac*) *dermatitis* is a well-known example of allergic contact dermatitis. The word *poison* is a misnomer in this instance, since the reaction is a true allergy and has nothing to do with being poisoned. Poison ivy allergy usually follows within one to seven days of contact of the poison ivy resin with the skin. Interestingly, many people are afraid of "catching" poison ivy by contact with blister fluid. In reality, the blister fluid is not contagious, unless it has become secondarily contaminated by bacteria. This means that sterile blister fluid can neither spread eczema to nonaffected parts of the body or to other people. However, contact with resin-contaminated clothing, even long after the original exposure, can retrigger the allergy.

Nickel allergy is another common example of allergic contact dermatitis. Because nickel is found in so many common items— medallions, zippers, necklaces, costume jewelry, hairpins, curlers, thimbles, needles, scissors, coins, etc.—nickel allergy can be a source of considerable inconvenience and annoyance. Other substances known to cause contact allergy include rubber products, hair dyes, hair sprays, shampoos, cosmetics, glues, and topical medications. In general, allergic contact dermatitis is an acute eczema and produces redness, blistering, oozing, and weeping at contact sites. If a skin-allergy-sensitive person has repeated contact with the allergen, subacute and chronic eczema may dominate.

Finding the cause of an irritant dermatitis is usually not difficult, since the eruption characteristically appears shortly after the use of some new material or product. On the other hand, discovering the precise cause of contact dermatitis, particularly allergic contact dermatitis, sometimes requires a bit of detective work. Contact allergies generally occur after use of a relatively new material or product, but may also follow the use of a product that has been used without any problem for many years. If you develop a rash and suspect that you have a contact allergy to some item, stop using that item for several days to see if the rash clears up. If it does, you have your answer, though you may want to use the substance again to see if there is a reaction.

If you and your doctor have trouble pinpointing the culprit, your doctor may suggest *patch testing,* a quick, safe, and painless way to find out what you are allergic to. Usually the dermatologist will begin by patch testing you to a *screening* tray of chemicals commonly found in many commercial products and known to cause contact allergies in many people. Your doctor may also test you directly with the products you suspect may be at the root of your allergy. A small amount of each chemical is placed on an adhesive-backed gauze pad and taped in place on your back or inner arm for forty-eight hours. If a reaction occurs, your doctor can then tell you which substance(s) you are allergic to, what common products contain them, and what substitutes you can use. Patch tests should *not* be confused with *scratch tests* or intradermal tests used by allergists, where the skin is actually pierced and a substance containing the suspected allergen is injected.

In principle, treating contact dermatitis of any kind is quite simple. An ounce of prevention is worth a pound of cure. First and foremost, avoid contact with anything to which you have been found sensitive. Once irritant or allergic dermatitis has developed, however, medical treatments are largely the same as those for atopic dermatitis, namely the use of topical steroids and antihistamines.

In the case of hand dermatitis, the use of thick vinyl gloves (e.g., Allergerm) in combination with washable white cotton glove liners can be extremely helpful for wet work, such as doing dishes or gardening. Certainly they should be used when you are working with acids, alkalis, and solvents. In addition, the plain cotton gloves can be used to protect your hands when doing dry work such as dusting. Purchase several pairs of cotton gloves and launder them frequently to prevent a buildup of grease and perspiraton, which themselves can contribute to skin irritation.

SEBORRHEA AND SEBORRHEIC DERMATITIS

Seborrhea (plain dandruff) and its more severe form, seborrheic dermatitis, are extremely common conditions. (*Cradle cap* is the lay term for seborrheic dermatitis in infancy and early childhood.) It has been estimated that dandruff or flaking scalp affects somewhere between 36 and 70 percent of the American population and occurs at all ages. These figures translate into millions of sufferers. Although dandruff is not a serious condition, its presence can be quite embarrassing and socially compromising. Those regions of the body having the highest concentrations of sebaceous glands—the face, central chest and back, armpits, navel, and groin—are the most affected.

The precise cause(s) of seborrhea and seborrheic dermatitis is not known. Heredity may play some role; the tendency to develop dandruff problems seems to run in families. Emotional factors may also play an aggravating or triggering role. Likewise, physical stresses, such as colds, fevers, sore throats, or allergy attacks, may precipitate flare-ups in susceptible individuals. Finally, there is some evidence linking a scalp yeast, *pityrosporon orbiculare,* with seborrheic dermatitis.

From time to time, predisposed people will experience rapid increases in the number of horny cells produced and the rates at which these cells are shed. In fact, they may have a rate of dead cell production and loss that is *twice* that of a person without the condition (Figure 8.1). In seborrheic dermatitis, dead cells also tend to be larger than normal. In general, dandruff is most noticeable in adolescents and adults and least noticeable in children and the elderly. It is also seasonal, being most severe in winter and mildest in summer.

While seborrhea is characterized largely by itching and unsightly flaking, seborrheic dermatitis is characterized by larger patches of redness and fuzzy borders, greasy, yellow-red scales, and thick crusting. These patches may appear on the scalp, behind and within the ears, between and within the eyebrows, and on eyelid margins. Because of their scaliness, patches of seborrheic dermatitis are often confused with patches of dry skin. The misguided use of heavy moisturizers to treat a presumed dry-skin condition frequently results in worsening of seborrheic dermatitis.

A cure for seborrhea and seborrheic dermatitis is not yet avail-

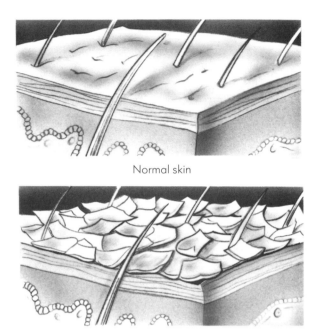

Normal skin

Increased cellular turnover rate in seborrheic dermatitis

Figure 8.1 Seborrheic dermatitis

able, but the condition is usually easy to control. Most cases involving the scalp may be controlled by more frequent shampooing or the use of commercial, over-the-counter antidandruff shampoos, which are usually composed of one or more of the following five active ingredients: *zinc pyrithione* (Sebulon), *sulfur* and/or *salicylic acid* (Sebulex, Ionil), *selenium sulfide* (Selsun Blue) and *tars* (Sebutone, T-Gel). For best results, leave the medicated shampoo on your scalp for between five and ten minutes before rinsing it off; it will have little effect if it is given insufficient contact time with your scalp.

When seborrheic dermatitis does not respond to the use of medicated shampoos, you should see your dermatologist. Other conditions, such as psoriasis (see below) and fungal infections (chapter 9) may mimic seborrheic dermatitis and need to be excluded. Once this has been done, your doctor may begin by recommending more potent prescription shampoos, such as Exsel Lotion. In addition, topical corticosteroid lotions or gels may be prescribed (Maxivate Lotion, Topicort Gel). In general, gels and lotions penetrate more easily and are more cosmetically acceptable in hairy areas than creams. If yeasts are believed to play a role, an antiyeast lotion such as Mycelex solution or Lotrimin lotion may also be prescribed. Topical corticosteroids and antiyeast medications are usually stopped once complete clearing is achieved. At that point, adequate control can usually be maintained by the regular use of shampoos.

PSORIASIS

Psoriasis vulgaris, or psoriasis, is a chronic, noncontagious inflammation of the skin that affects an estimated six to eight million Americans and approximately 3 percent of the world's population. It ranges in severity from very mild to potentially life-threatening. To give you an idea of its impact, approximately ten thousand psoriasis sufferers are hospitalized each year in the United States at a cost of over $100 million.

In general, psoriasis first appears in early adulthood, although it may begin in infancy or late in life. Men and women are affected equally. The precise cause(s) of this widespread disease is unknown, but heredity plays an important role in many cases. In terms of probability, it has been estimated that a person having one parent with psoriasis has about a 10 percent chance of developing it, while having two parents with the condition increases the risk to nearly 40 percent. Where a hereditary predisposition exists, heightened emotional stresses and physical illness may aggravate or trigger the eruption. Other aggravating factors include excessively dry skin, sunburn, sore throats, and cuts and scrapes of the skin. Although psoriasis may occasionally resemble eczema, it is an entirely unrelated condition.

While psoriasis may affect any area of the skin, the elbows, knees, arms, legs, scalp, nails, and genital regions are most often involved. Dermatologists are usually able to diagnose psoriasis by its appearance alone. For reasons that remain unknown, the lesions are often symmetrically oriented; that is, they appear simultaneously on both sides of the body in mirror image. Sometimes, however, to confirm their suspicions, doctors may need to take a biopsy—a small sample of skin tissue—to look at under the microscope.

A very disfiguring condition, particularly when widespread, psoriasis in its most common form starts out as small red patches that enlarge and become covered with thick, silvery scales. These scales are sometimes referred to as *micaceous* scales, since they resemble the scaly mineral mica. In most cases of psoriasis, itching is absent or only mild. Cracking of the skin *(fissuring)*, which may also occur, can be extremely painful. About 5 percent of psoriasis sufferers also develop *psoriatic arthritis*, a destructive, painful, and disabling form of arthritis resembling rheumatoid arthritis.

In psoriasis, skin cells are produced two to seven times faster than in normal skin. Dead cells within the horny layer, instead of being shed rapidly, stick together to form abnormal silvery scales typical of this condition. Flaking can be so severe that psoriasis is often confused with seborrheic dermatitis, although these conditions are utterly different. In general, flaking from psoriasis is much more severe than with simple dandruff or seborrheic dermatitis, and it is also generally more resistant to treatment with commercial antidandruff shampoos.

Unfortunately, psoriasis remains an incurable condition, but active research continues and many satisfactory therapies have been devised to clear up or control the condition. However, *treatment of all but the mildest forms should be under the supervision of a dermatologist experienced in treating psoriasis.*

Effective antipsoriatic therapies include the use of topical corticosteroid creams and ointments, intralesional injections of cortisone derivatives, and antihistamines when itching occurs. Other therapies include the use of tars, anthralin, and ultraviolet-light therapy. More severe cases may require potent drugs such as Methotrexate and Etretinate, which have serious side effects.

For more than 100 years, coal tar and its derivatives have been used to treat psoriasis. They may be used in baths (Balnetar), applied in lotion form directly to the body (T-Derm lotion) or the scalp (T-Gel lotion), or shampooed in as mentioned earlier. Coal-tar derivatives can help to reduce plaque size, redness, and itching. Tars soothe the skin and are believed to work by decreasing the rapidity of cell production and turnover.

Anthralin, another petroleum derivative, has also been used for many years, though it fell into disfavor for a long time because it tended to stain the skin and clothing a reddish brown. Recently, cosmetically more acceptable vanishing cream preparations, such as Dritho-Creme and Lasan's Cream, have become available. And such preparations may be helpful when applied for only twenty to thirty minutes at a time instead of overnight (so-called short-contact anthralin therapy).

For more stubborn or widespread cases of psoriasis, coal-tar lotions are often used in conjunction with ultraviolet light B (UVB) therapy. Developed more than sixty years ago, this is known as the *Goeckerman regimen,* named after its Mayo Clinic originator. Goeckerman therapy is often used in a hospital setting and is quite effective for alleviating symptoms and clearing up psoriasis. On an average, about forty treatments, taken either daily or several times per week, are needed for clearing up the symptoms.

Under the strict supervision of a dermatologist, Goeckerman therapy may also be taken at home, using a home ultraviolet-light unit. These units can be purchased with a doctor's prescription through National Biological Corporation, Twinsberg, Ohio, or Atlantic Ultraviolet Light, 250 North Fehrway, Bayshore, New York. Alternatively, people who live in sunny climates year round can use natural sunlight.

Psoralen plus high-intensity ultraviolet light A (PUVA) is another form of ultraviolet light therapy usually reserved for individuals who have failed to respond to conventional therapies. Psoralen is a drug that when taken orally two hours prior to UVA exposure enhances the beneficial effects of ultraviolet light. Approximately twenty-five treatments are required to achieve total clearing up. Thereafter, a monthly maintenance therapy of two to three treatments is required to maintain clearing up.

It should be noted that when treating psoriasis with either Goeckerman or PUVA therapies, the doctor and patient must weigh the immediate benefits of therapy versus the long-term risks for the development of ultraviolet-light–related premature aging of the skin and skin cancers.

Methotrexate, an anticancer drug that must be used under the strict supervison of a physician, is occasionally prescribed for intractable psoriasis, either alone or in combination with other therapies. Administered orally or by intramuscular injection once a week, methotrexate can be helpful to carefully selected people when other therapies have not worked. Close monitoring is required to prevent damage to the liver, which is the most serious potential side effect of this medication.

Finally, an oral drug recently approved by the FDA, Tegison (etretinate), a vitamin A derivative, has been found to clear many cases of previously resistant psoriasis. Unfortunately, many side effects, both major and minor, may result from the use of this drug, including severe dryness and chapping of the lips, musculoskeletal aches and pains, calcification of the spine and ligaments, and elevations in blood lipid levels. Furthermore, Tegison can cause birth defects in the fetus of a woman who conceives while on the drug. For that reason, strict attention to birth control is essential for any women of childbearing age under therapy and for about two years thereafter. Tegison is stored in the body, so it is recommended that you wait two years after stopping it before trying to get pregnant. To enhance its beneficial effects and to reduce the total dose required, Tegison therapy may be combined with PUVA treatments. Needless to say, Tegison must be used only under strict supervision of a physician.

PRICKLY HAIR FOLLICLES

Prickly hair follicles, or *keratosis pilaris,* is a condition that is so common it is generally regarded as a variation of normal skin. It appears as numerous reddish, rough, spiny little bumps situated at the openings of the pores on the upper outer arms and upper outer thighs, and gives the skin a coarse, sandpaper or graterlike appearance and feel. However, in more severe cases, legions of keratosis pilaris can involve the entire chest and back. Some people confuse them with pimples. Seen most commonly during the teens and twenties, the condition spontaneously disappears in most people by their thirties.

Treatment of keratosis pilaris is usually unnecessary. Most people are relieved to hear that the condition is harmless. The use of an all-purpose moisturizer such as Moisturel, to keep the skin soft and soften the spiny bumps, is generally all that is necessary. For more severe or widespread cases, which pose significant cosmetic problems or engender psychological problems, the dermatologist can prescribe Lac-Hydrin Lotion, a high-potency moisturizer available by prescription only. Lac-Hydrin has been demonstrated to be safe, even for use on children, and effective for softening and reducing the unsightly bumps of keratosis pilaris. For most people, though, benign neglect is the best form of therapy.

HIVES

Hives (urticaria) or *welts* are pinkish swellings of the skin and mucous membranes. (Sometimes they are called *wheals.*) Approximately twenty percent of us are affected by hives at some time in our lives. They are usually very itchy and generally last no more than thirty-six hours, often fading somewhere between one and six hours after developing. Hives vary in size from ½ to 12 inches in diameter. Severe swelling is known as *angioedema.* In most instances, hives are related to the release of a natural chemical called *histamine,* which is responsible for the itching, redness, and swelling.

When a hive attack lasts for less than six weeks, doctors call the episode *acute* urticaria; when it extends beyond six weeks, it is termed *chronic* urticaria. Acute urticaria usually results from an allergic reaction to foods (especially shellfish, nuts, berries, to-matoes, eggs, citrus fruits, and pork), drugs (particularly aspirin, penicillin, sulfa, and codeine), insect bites, and emotional stress. Chronic hives may be caused by these same factors, but also may be associated with exposure to heat, cold, and sunshine, or the presence of infection or other serious internal illnesses. Unfortunately, in the overwhelming majority of cases of chronic hives, allergens or other specific causes cannot be identified.

The ideal treatment of hives consists of finding the cause and eliminating it. This is usually easier with acute urticaria; chronic urticaria generally requires an extensive investigation, including detailed history, blood tests, urine and stool tests, and X-rays when indicated. Cool compresses, lotions, and the use of antihistamines are front-line therapy for hives. Oral steroids (cortisone derivatives) such as *prednisone* are sometimes needed to control severe acute attacks. When swelling is widespread or, more important, when it involves the mucous membranes of the throat, where breathing may be compromised, an injection of Adrenalin (*epinephrine*) is given.

COMMON SKIN INFECTIONS

Your skin is a playground for germs. No matter how attentive to cleanliness and personal hygiene you may be, you are nonetheless covered from head to toe with a variety of fungi, viruses, and bacteria. Under normal circumstances, these germs cause few problems, and by and large, they merely colonize (or harmlessly reside upon) the surface of your skin.

Different areas of your body house different populations of germs in vastly different numbers. For example, on your arm each square inch may be home to only a few hundred bacteria, yet every square inch of your armpit teems with close to a million of these organisms. The more damp and dark an area of your skin, the greater the number of germs to be found there. For that reason, the genital, anal, and armpit areas make marvelous "greenhouses" for the growth of germs.

Ordinarily a delicate—that is, easily disturbed—balance exists in which the various types of germs on your skin (as well as elsewhere within your body) keep each other in check. When this balance is disrupted for any reason, infection may result. Some of these infections amount to little more than minor annoyances, while others, if neglected or improperly treated, can lead to more serious, occasionally even life-threatening, illness. This chapter covers the causes, prevention, and treatment of a variety of infectious bacterial, fungal, and viral rashes.

COMMON FUNGAL RASHES

RINGWORM

Ringworm is the common name for a skin infection that is not caused by a worm at all but by a *fungus* (a microscopic, plantlike organism). Several different types of fungi can cause ringworm infections. Characteristically, ringworm appears as reddish, scaly rings with clear centers (hence the name). Frequently they may exhibit blistering, oozing, scaliness, and cracking of the skin. In persistent cases, fungi can attack the fingernails and toenails, leading to the development of yellowed, thickened, distorted, crumbling, and loose nails. Fungal infections often cause itching and burning that, along with the concern about nail disfigurement, are usually the primary reasons that people seek medical attention.

Dermatologists refer to ringworm infections as *tineas.* Ringworm of the feet and toes (athlete's foot) is known as *tinea pedis;* ringworm of the groin (jock itch), *tinea cruris;* ringworm of the scalp, *tinea capitis;* and ringworm of the entire body, *tinea corporis.*

The fungi of ringworm are found just about everywhere in our environment. Nevertheless, the infection is most often picked up from other infected humans, and occasionally from dogs, cats, or other domestic animals. Jock itch is common in certain predisposed people because of the moist, humid environment of the groin. Men are especially prone to it because of the occlusion between the scrotum and the inner thighs. Communal showers, locker room floors, and sweaty socks and shoes are potential sources for spread of athlete's foot. Finally, the shared use of combs, brushes, and hats, particularly among children, contributes to the spread of scalp infections.

Because the appearances of these infections frequently mimic eczemas or psoriasis, a dermatologist's help is frequently needed to diagnose tineas. In addition to examining the involved areas, your doctor may use the microscope to examine skin scrapings from the affected areas. If he finds slender fungal filaments called *hyphae,* an immediate diagnosis can be made and appropriate therapy started. A fungal culture is usually taken, although this requires an incubation period of two to three weeks. In certain cases, particularly in suspected scalp infections, the dermatologist may expose the affected area to a special ultraviolet-light source *(Wood's light),* looking for the blue-green fluorescence characteristic of some types of tinea infections.

Fortunately, most tinea infections are caused by a handful of related fungal organisms and may be cured in much the same manner. Most infections respond to the simple use of broad-spectrum antifungal creams and lotions, such as Spectazole, Loprox, and Nizoral creams. Scalp and nail problems generally require the use of oral antifungal agents, such as *griseofulvin* (Fulvicin P/G 330) or *ketoconazole* (Nizoral). As a rule, fingernail infections may take six to twelve months to cure and toenail infections, which are especially difficult to cure, considerably longer, frequently twelve to eighteen months. Unfortunately, not all fungal infections of the nails respond to either form of therapy.

Griseofulvin, one form of oral antifungal antibiotic, has been used successfully for more than thirty years, even in infants. Queasiness and headaches are its most common side effects, but they tend to pass within a few days of starting the drug, so therapy usually need not be stopped. Temporary liver or kidney irritations are rare side effects of griseofulvin. In most cases, such irritation clears up quickly once the drug is discontinued.

Nizoral, a recently introduced oral antifungal agent, is usually reserved for more stubborn cases of fungal infection, i.e., those that have not responded to a combination of conventional topical therapies and griseofulvin. For unknown reasons, chemical irritation of the liver occurs in approximately one out of every fifteen thousand users. Because of their potential for side effects, both griseofulvin and particularly Nizoral should be used only under strict medical supervision. To monitor their patients during long-term therapy with either drug, most physicians order periodic blood and urine screening tests.

Antifungal therapy, whether topical or oral, should be continued until all fungal invaders have been eradicated. It is not good enough for your skin simply to feel better or for it to look completely cleared. In this instance, overkill has its benefits. To reduce the possibility of recurrence, your doctor may recommend that you treat yourself for a short time past the point where you are completely clear. For further insurance, he may wish to repeat a fungal culture examination of the previously affected area to ensure that no fungal organisms remain. Unfortunately, even with these additional measures, there is no guarantee that reinfection will not occur.

Finally, there are a few simple measures you can follow to reduce your chances of contracting or spreading ringworm infections: (1) Avoid trading combs, brushes, hats, or other headgear with anyone else. (2) If you have a pet with a skin problem, have the pet examined and treated promptly by a veterinarian. (3) To prevent athlete's foot, keep your feet clean and dry. Dry your feet thoroughly after bathing and exercising and remove any debris that accumulates between your toes. (4) Use cotton socks, rather than moisture-trapping woolen ones. (5) Wear sandals whenever possible during hot, humid weather. (6) Lightly dust your feet, socks, and shoes daily with an antifungal dusting powder such as ZeaSorb-AF, Desenex, or Tinactin.

TINEA VERSICOLOR

Tinea versicolor, another type of common fungal infection, is found worldwide and accounts for approximately 5 percent of all fungal infections. Although it is sometimes confused with ringworm, tinea versicolor is unrelated. It is caused by an overgrowth of an organism, pityrosporon orbiculare, a normal resident of your skin. For reasons that are unclear, infection begins when the organism converts from a docile inhabitant to an aggressive attacker.

When the rash of tinea versicolor is widespread, it can be quite noticeable, especially during the sunny summer months, because the presence of the fungus interferes with your skin's ability to tan normally. Thus, normal tanning of the surrounding skin serves to highlight the infected spots. In fact, some people mistakenly attribute the lesions of tinea versicolor to sun exposure, referring to them as "sunspots." Even after complete cure, it may take several months for your skin color to even out.

Tinea versicolor ordinarily involves the neck, trunk, and arms, and owes its name to the various shades of white, pink, or brown that typify its appearance. The face is seldom involved. Lesions are characteristically oval and covered with fine scales. The infection rarely causes any symptoms, and itching is infrequent.

As a rule, tinea versicolor is harmless, so people usually seek medical attention for cosmetic reasons. In many cases, the dermatologist can exclude the presence of other fungi by examining skin scrapings under the microscope. Since tinea versicolor often fluoresces an orange-gold color when exposed to a Wood's light, this test can be especially helpful in confirming the diagnosis. In addition, a Wood's light examination can also be helpful *after* treatment has been completed to ensure that the organism is no longer present. Since washing away the surface scales of the lesions can interfere with fluorescence, you should avoid washing or bathing the affected areas for twelve to twenty-four hours before a Wood's light exam.

Tinea versicolor infection often can be readily eradicated. Your doctor may prescribe topical broad-spectrum antifungal creams, such as those used to treat ringworm infections. The repeated application of selenium sulfide shampoos or sodium thiosulfate lotions (Exsel, Selsun, Tinver) has also proven helpful. Unfortunately, infection frequently recurs in susceptible individuals. The prescription of oral Nizoral, which has been shown very effective for curing and preventing recurrences of tinea versicolor, is generally reserved for the most stubborn or widespread cases.

YEAST

Skin and mucous membrane infections caused by the yeast fungus, *Candida albicans*, are quite common. Candida is a normal inhabitant of the mouth, vagina, and large intestine. Here again, the precise factors that trigger candida to convert from inhabitant to invader are unknown. What *is* known is that the infection is more common in diabetics, obese individuals, and those taking antibiotics, oral steroids, or birth control pills.

These yeasts are responsible for sores and cracking at the corners of the mouth *(angular cheilitis);* whitish patches on the inside of the cheeks (thrush); "cheesy" discharges from the vagina; redness, itching, and swelling of the vagina; and damp, red eruptions under the breasts, under the penile foreskin, and within the body folds of overweight individuals *(monilial intertrigo)*. Candida are also responsible for certain cases of redness, swelling, and tenderness around the nails *(Candida paronychia)*. Recently, candida has been blamed by some for causing a whole constellation of conditions ranging from general tiredness and depression to psoriasis, but scientific evidence is not convincing.

Diagnosis can usually be made by history and clinical appearance alone, although fungal scrapings and culture may be ordered for confirmation. Candida infections usually respond to topical broad-spectrum antifungal creams, such as those used to treat ringworm infections, or to specific antiyeast preparations such as Mycolog *(nystatin)* ointment. In stubborn cases or in the face of repeated infections, the use of the medication in tablet form (Mycostatin) may be prescribed to clear the intestine of yeasts. For some intractable cases, oral Nizoral has been found to be extremely effective. However, as mentioned earlier, this drug must be used under strict medical supervision to monitor closely for side effects.

VIRAL SKIN INFECTIONS

Common warts, herpes zoster, herpes genitalis, molluscum contagiosum, and *genital warts* are now the most common viral infections of the skin. Although genital herpes, molluscum, and genital warts may be spread by nonsexual means, nowadays the spread of these germs occurs so commonly through sexual contact that they are frequently categorized as sexually transmitted diseases. For that reason, these three infections are discussed in chapter 15, Sex and Your Skin. The focus in this section is on *common warts, herpes zoster (shingles),* and *pityriasis rosea.*

WARTS

Veruccae is the technical name for warts, of which there are several different types. In general, warts are named for either their outward appearance or their location on the body. For example, *verucca plana,* or flat wart, takes its name from its smooth, flat-top appearance, while *filiform veruccae* are so named because of the threadlike (filiform) projections from their surfaces. *Verucca plantaris (plantar wart)* is located on the plantar (bottom) surface of the foot. (The word *plantar* is often mistaken for *planter,* but these warts have nothing to do with planters or farming.) *Periungual veruccae* are located around the nails, and finally, *verucca vulgaris* (common wart) is the familiar, rough-surfaced variety often found in children. All warts contain little black specks, which represent tiny wart blood vessels.

Warts are caused by a virus known as the *human papilomavirus (HPV).* To date, more than thirty-six types of closely related HPVs are known to exist, and researchers seem to be finding more each year. A wart may be thought of as a kind of "cold" in the skin; just as some people seem to be more susceptible to colds than others, certain people seem to be more susceptible to wart infections.

Although they typically involve the hands and feet, wart viruses can infect any part of the skin. They usually cause no symptoms, except when they infect the area around the nails or over the pressure points of the heels and soles. On exposed areas, they can be quite disfiguring.

Prior trauma to the skin plays an important role in the development of warts, and this is believed to be the reason why the hands and feet, areas subjected to much wear and tear, are such frequent sites of attack. Children and teenagers are most often affected, but adults are by no means immune to attack. Warts are contagious and may be spread from one part of an infected person's skin to another and, though it is less likely, to other individuals.

Wart infections can follow one of three routes. They may persist unchanged for many years; they may disappear spontaneously as the body's immune system finally fights them off; and they may spread to other areas and become numerous. Some recurrences, if not most, are believed to result from the fact that warts can "seed" the surrounding normal skin with virus before they are removed, allowing the new wart colonies to sprout later. Interestingly, the spontaneous disappearance of warts probably accounts for so many people believing in folk remedies; for hundreds of years, people have been "witching" away warts by rubbing them with stones, potatoes, ear wax—or so they thought!

Home therapy for warts, wherein an acid is used to dissolve infected tissue, is sometimes successful. Lotions containing salicylic acid and/or lactic acid (Occlusal and Viranol) or adhesive plasters (Mediplast) may be useful. Alas, these treatments do not always work, and even when they are effective, complete destruction of wart tissue often requires six to twelve weeks, sometimes longer.

To maximize your chances for success, you need to be attentive to details when using wart remedies. Unless your physician directs you otherwise, you should follow these basic instructions: Soak wart for fifteen to twenty minutes; dry thoroughly; abrade with pumice stone; apply medication; allow medication to dry and cover with a waterproof bandage. When using wart plasters, cut out a little cardboard template exactly the shape and dimensions of the wart. The template may then be used to cut out exact "fits" from the adhesive plaster. This will allow you to precut a number of applications in advance and will ensure more accurate coverage of the wart. Plasters may be changed daily or left in place for about a week. As with antiwart lotions, your routine should be "soak, pumice, and apply."

Dermatologists may use more caustic substances *(cantharidin* and *trichloroacetic acid)* to treat your warts. They may also use freezing liquids *(cryotherapy)* such as *liquid nitrogen* to destroy them. Don't expect miracles. Several treatment sessions are usually required to effect a cure.

I find the use of *electrocautery,* i.e., the use of a heat-producing electric current, the most satisfactory and consistently successful means of eliminating unsightly or painful warts with the least chance of recurrence. Performed under local anesthesia, electrosurgical removal of warts takes about five minutes, and is virtually painless.

SHINGLES

After an outbreak of chicken pox has cleared up, the causative virus, *varicella/zoster,* does not leave the body. Instead, the chicken pox virus enters a state of dormancy within nerve tissue near the spinal cord. Herpes zoster, or shingles, results from localized reactivation of the chicken pox virus usually many years after the original outbreak of chicken pox. The reasons for reactivation are unclear. Although occasionally it occurs in people with serious underlying conditions, most often it occurs in otherwise completely healthy people over the age of forty.

Shingles typically appears as a cluster of blisters on a reddish base. The blisters usually erupt on only one side of the body or face along the area supplied by the reactivated nerve tissue. The reason for this is not known. The blistering eruption is often preceded by sensations of itching, tingling, burning, or numbness within the affected area. Symptoms range from none to all of the above and extreme pain. In fact, the pain can be so severe that it mimics that of a severe heart attack or acute appendicitis, depending upon the location of the pain.

Milder cases clear up without further problems, while in more severe cases, scarring may mark the outbreak site. Unfortunately, in some cases, *post-herpetic neuralgia* (nerve pain) can persist for weeks, months, or years after the episode. About 50 percent of patients over age sixty develop post-herpetic neuralgia. On the other hand, unlike other types of herpes infections, an outbreak of shingles usually occurs only once in a lifetime.

There is no cure for shingles. Plain tap water or Burow's solution compresses may be used to dry up weeping or oozing lesions. Topical antibiotics such as Silvadene Cream may be prescribed to prevent bacterial contamination. In addition, pain medications and antihistamines may be prescribed where appropriate. In severe cases, especially in persons over the age of sixty, a short course of oral anti-inflammatory steroids such as *prednisone* may be prescribed to prevent post-herpetic neuralgia. Recently, a new cream, Zostrix (capsaicin), was introduced; when applied five times a day for ten days, it has been purported to alleviate post-herpetic pain. The long-term effectiveness of this cream awaits further testing.

PITYRIASIS ROSEA

Pityriasis rosea is an outbreak that begins as a large single pinkish patch on the skin, usually on the chest or back. Within one to two weeks smaller patches, similar in appearance to the original "mother" or "herald" patch, typically crop up in a fir tree or Christmas tree pattern over the remainder of the trunk and extremities. Itching occurs in approximately one-fourth to one-half of all patients. There are usually no other symptoms, and the person generally feels well. The cause of pityriasis rosea is not known, but some believe it is viral in origin, hence its inclusion in this section.

The condition occurs commonly in young adults during the spring or autumn months. New patches frequently appear in waves throughout the course of the illness, which usually lasts for two to six weeks. It may persist for as long as six months, but this is rare.

Generally, diagnosis is readily made from the history and appearance of the lesions, although occasionally pityriasis rosea may be confused with ringworm infections. Most often, simple reassurance is the best prescription for this condition. When itching is severe, however, topical steroids and oral antihistamines may be prescribed. Sometimes, especially if there is extensive involvement of the face (which seldom occurs), a short course of oral steroids may be initiated. Response to treatment is generally quite rapid.

BACTERIAL SKIN INFECTIONS

Bacterial infections of the skin, or *pyodermas,* may be caused by a wide variety of bacterial organisms, but the overwhelming majority are caused by two organisms, *staphylococci* and *streptococci* (*staph* and *strep,* for short).

Bacterial infections of the skin are usually named according to the level of the skin infected. For example, *impetigo,* the most common of all the bacterial skin infections, is a highly contagious infection limited to the uppermost layers of the skin. Lesions of impetigo are typically extremely itchy, reddish, blistering, weeping patches, and the development of honey-colored crusts is highly characteristic of this type of infection. Children are frequently affected. Although impetigo is most often caused by staph organisms, if it is caused by certain strains of streptococci, a serious allergic kidney inflammation known as *poststreptococcal glomerulonephritis* may result weeks after the infection has passed. This condition remains the most dreaded complication of untreated or inadequately treated impetigo.

If an infection is located high up near the opening of the hair follicles (pores), it is referred to as folliculitis. Often itchy and resembling small pustules of acne, folliculitis is generally caused by staph. If left untreated, it may spread.

Folliculitis often follows repeated trauma to an area, such as shaving. During the disco craze, folliculitis of the buttocks and thighs, resulting from the constant rubbing of tight jeans against the skin during dancing, was seen so frequently by dermatologists that it was nicknamed "disco dermatitis." More recently, a form of folliculitis attributable to contamination of communal

USING MEDICATIONS PROPERLY

Few people will argue that the cost of drugs these days is extremely high. This is especially true when it comes to the cost of topical corticosteroid creams and ointments. Small tubes may cost $10 while larger tubes may run as high as $40. For people with persistent conditions, this may translate into thousands of dollars each year. Even pills, particularly the newer antibiotics and anti-inflammatory drugs, may cost more than a dollar per capsule. Therefore, it is important to know the proper way to use these medications so that you get the most benefit from them for the least money and waste.

TOPICAL CORTICOSTEROIDS

Topical steroids are the most widely used skin medications. For some reason, many people who use them seem to operate on the principle that "if a little is good, a lot must be better." With most of these creams, this is just not so. In fact, the principle should be "a little goes a long way."

As a rule, apply topical creams and ointments very sparingly in a thin layer. Gently rub them into your skin slightly past the borders of the affected area, avoiding smearing large areas of normal skin. A rule of thumb: 2 grams of cream will cover your hand, head, face or anogenital area; 3 grams will cover an arm, chest, or back; 4 grams one leg; and between 30 and 60 grams your entire body.

PILLS

Believe it or not, many adults do not know how to swallow a pill properly. Many people swallow pills while sitting or lying down in bed and some do so without water. In one recent report, it was found that pills taken sitting down, without fluid, did not make it to the stomach 50 percent of the time. Moreover, when taken lying down, some pills were found to stick in the esophagus, the tube leading to the stomach, for up to two hours. Beyond the fact that they then can't possibly do you any good, they may irritate the sensitive lining there and cause serious problems. This is particularly true of aspirin. Interestingly, even if you think you feel a pill going down, you may be being deceived.

For best results, take your pills standing up, or at least sitting erect so that gravity can help. Take a sip of fluid before swallowing the pill, wash it down with 3 or 4 ounces of fluid, and then again with an additional 3 or 4 ounces as a "safety flushing." Stay on your feet or sit erect for a least two or three minutes (preferably thirty minutes) after swallowing the pills. Finally, avoid breaking tablets, since the ragged edges increase the likelihood of having them stick in your esophagus.

If you forget to take your pills at the right time, take them as soon as possible thereafter. However, if it is close to the time for your next dose, just take the regular dose at the next regular time. Don't yield to the common temptation to double up, for this could seriously harm you. Naturally, you should check with your doctor if you have any questions about any of your medications.

hot tubs and whirlpool baths is being seen in increasing numbers.

Furuncles (boils) develop when bacteria invade more deeply into the pores and cause inflammation within the surrounding skin. Hot, red, and tender, boils are often mistaken for highly inflamed pimples. Boils most often appear on the face, scalp, underarms, and buttocks. The familar *sty* is simply a boil of the eyelid. When severe, furunculosis may be accompanied by weakness and fever.

Carbuncles, which are larger and deeper than boils, are *abscesses* filled with pus, debris, dead skin cells, and bacteria. They are red hot and exquisitely painful. Unlike furuncles, carbuncles involve extensively many hair follicles and their surrounding tissue.

Do not attempt to squeeze boils or carbuncles, especially if they have not come to a head. You risk making the infection much worse by squeezing germs into your bloodstream and causing a serious complication, *septicemia* (blood poisoning). Even your doctor may not lance them until they have come to a head.

Cellulitis is a common, although more serious, form of strep infection of the skin. Cellulitis most often affects the legs, although it can involve any area of the body. This infection is accompanied by the early appearance of high fever, weakness, shaking, chills, pain, and infection of the lymph glands. The skin of the affected region is typically red and swollen. When deep swellings develop on the face and are associated with severe headache and blistering, the condition is known as *erysipelas (St. Anthony's fire)*. Erysipelas is potentially fatal if not treated promptly. Extreme cases require hospitalization and the use of intravenous antibiotic therapy.

DIAGNOSING AND TREATING BACTERIAL SKIN INFECTIONS

Diagnosing bacterial infections of the skin is usually not difficult and is based upon a careful assessment of the history and appearance of the lesions. A *bacterial culture and sensitivity test* is often ordered to determine which organisms are responsible for the infection and which antibiotics will best eliminate them. Occasionally bacteria other than staph and strep are responsible for skin infections. For example, whirlpool bath folliculitis is caused by the organism *pseudomonas,* rather than by staph or strep. It is important for your doctor to know this so that the appropriate antibiotic can be selected.

As a group, pyodermas generally respond quite rapidly to oral antibiotic therapy. However, while strep infections respond rapidly to penicillin, some staph infections do not. Certain staph organisms produce a specific enzyme that inactivates regular penicillin. As a result, for staph infections doctors now routinely prescribe enzyme-resistant penicillin derivatives such as *dicloxacillin* or *erythromycin* (e.g., E.E.S. 400). Topical antibiotics are often prescribed to supplement oral therapy. Regardless of the causative germ, a ten-day course of antibiotics is usually required for complete cure. Happily, however, most people are rendered noncontagious to others within two days of beginning antibiotics.

Topical therapy usually consists of applying warm tap water or Burow's solution compresses to the affected area or soaking it in warm water several times a day to help circulation and speed healing. Frequently, it also means the use of topical, nonprescription antibiotics such as Polysporin or Bacitracin ointments. Since a fair number of people may develop an allergy to antibiotics containing neomycin, I generally do not recommend them. In more troublesome infections, your doctor may prefer to prescribe a more potent topical antibiotic, such as Garamycin cream or ointment.

SKIN GROWTHS: THE HARMLESS AND THE BAD

*G*rowth. The very word is enough to send a tremor through most people. And it is no wonder. Daily we are bombarded with bulletins containing bad news about cancer. So when people see the words *skin cancer,* they all but ignore the first and fasten on the last. At first glance, the statistics *are* alarming. According to the American Cancer Society and the Skin Cancer Foundation, skin cancer is estimated to affect one in every seven Americans each year. More than 500,000 new cases will be diagnosed this year. But there is encouraging news in all this. Few people die from the most common form of skin cancer, *basal cell carcinoma,* and cure rates exceed 95 percent. *Malignant melanoma,* about which there is so much talk today because of the relationship between sun damage and skin cancer, is the most serious, but the least common. And not every growth means cancer.

Doctors generally refer to good and bad skin growths as *benign* and *malignant tumors.* A tumor simply means any large growth.

Another commonly used medical word, *lesion,* means any kind of abnormal spot. Lesions may be benign or malignant.

Contrary to what you may think, the word *tumor* doesn't necessarily imply a serious growth. Many tumors, in fact, are quite harmless. Others may merely be unsightly or esthetically disfiguring. A benign tumor is one that does not seriously affect your overall health. On the other hand, some benign tumors can cause problems of their own. If a benign tumor grows too large, for example, it may begin to press on sensitive surrounding structures and cause pain or damage, occasionally even extensive damage.

By contrast, a malignant tumor, or cancer, not only possesses the potential for local growth and tissue destruction, but in some cases may spread through the blood and lymph system and threaten life. Finally, when dermatologists talk of *premalignant* lesions, they're referring to certain growths that are harmless by themselves, but have the *potential* to progress to malignancies.

Before discussing the various kinds of benign and malignant growths that can affect your skin, I will describe in general terms a few of the more common methods for diagnosing and treating them. With this basic information in mind, you will find the discussions that follow more meaningful. Interestingly, some of the techniques used to diagnose or treat various types of skin growths are those used at other times for cosmetic surgery. For example, a chemical application for the treatment of premalignancies of the skin is fundamentally the same as a chemical peel for wrinkles. And a shave biopsy, the procedure used to diagnose a skin growth, is often used for the removal of a beauty mark.

BIOPSY

Because your skin is so accessible to examination by the naked eye, dermatologists often are able to make a diagnosis through the time-honored means of taking a history and performing a thorough examination of the skin with the naked eye or with the aid of a magnifying glass. Unfortunately, a definite diagnosis cannot always be made this way. To establish a diagnosis or confirm his clinical impression, your dermatologist may elect to perform a *biopsy*. When doctors use the word *biopsy*, many patients immediately think cancer. This is by no means always the case. Biopsies are only a means for establishing or confirming a suspected diagnosis.

Simply defined, a biopsy is the removal of a small piece of tissue to be examined under the microscope by a *pathologist*, a physician who specializes in recognizing diseased tissue under the microscope. Since a biopsy is only a small tissue sample, should a skin growth on your body prove to be malignant, your dermatologist usually will have to remove completely any remaining abnormal tissue. By contrast, should a lesion prove benign, further surgery is usually unnecessary. When growths are small, the entire growth may be removed as part of the biopsy procedure, satisfying the dual purposes of diagnosis and complete removal.

Skin biopsies are performed in a number of ways, depending upon a number of factors, including the size, shape, location, and type of growth. In general, dermatologists refer to a biopsy procedure by the manner in which it is performed or by the instruments used to perform it. Specifically, there are *shave, curet, scissor, punch,* and *excisional* biopsies (Figures 10.1–10.5).

Regardless of which procedure is chosen, the area to be sampled is first numbed with a local anesthetic, usually a *lidocaine (Xylocaine)*. *Adrenalin (epinephrine)*, which constricts blood vessels, is usually coupled with Xylocaine to prolong the anesthetic effect and reduce bleeding. An ultrafine needle, which causes minimal discomfort, is used to administer the anesthetic. I usually warn my patients that they will feel a little pinch as the needle enters their skin and then a little burning sensation as the anesthetic spreads around. Occasionally, particularly for more anxious patients, your doctor may supplement local anesthesia with the use of nitrous oxide gas (laughing gas, or sweet air) such as dentists often use to sedate patients. Sometimes, especially for removing very small growths, your doctor may not inject anesthetic at all and instead may choose simply to freeze the biopsy site momentarily with *ethyl chloride* or *flurethyl spray.*

In a shave biopsy (Figure 10.1), one of the most common diagnostic procedures performed by dermatologists, tissue to be examined is "sculpted" away from the skin surface with a scalpel. A horizontal cut is made through the surface of the growth, and only enough material is removed to enable the pathologist to confirm the diagnosis. Because a deep cut is not made in the skin, the risk of scar formation is reduced. This technique is often used for the cosmetic removal of certain growths such as moles.

Curettage, another popular biopsy technique, involves the use

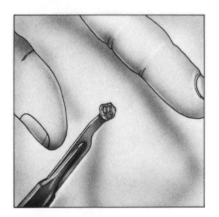

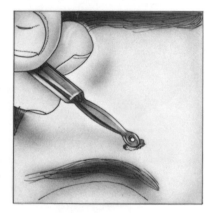

Figure 10.1   Shave biopsy   Figure 10.2   Curet biopsy

of a special instrument known as a *curet* (Figure 10.2), a scooplike surgical instrument with a circular cutting edge. Curets are available in several sizes and are used for "scraping" or scooping tissue off the skin. Curettage is used not only for biopsies but, even more frequently, for completely removing certain types of malignant growths after biopsy confirmation has been obtained.

Scissor biopsies are used primarily for growths that protrude above the skin surface on stalks. Specially tapered scissors (Figure 10.3), known as *iris* or *gradle* scissors, are generally used for this purpose and are particularly useful for removing growths from the surface of hairless areas, such as the eyelid, sides of the neck, and penis. Scissor removals are quick and relatively painless to perform, even without local anesthesia; wounds heal nicely on their own and usually require no stitches. Very small growths, such as skin tags, are especially amenable to scissor removal.

Punch biopsies get their name from the use of a cylindrical cookie-cutter-like instrument. To cut tissue, the dermatologist exerts a firm downward pressure on the skin while rotating the handle of the punch between the thumb and index finger (Figure 10.4). Punch biopsies are used to sample very small lesions in their entirety or portions of very large lesions. Stitches *(sutures)* are generally used to close larger punch biopsy wounds, although small ones are frequently left to heal spontaneously.

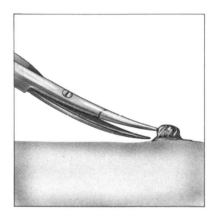

Figure 10.3   Scissor biopsy

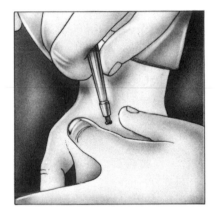

Figure 10.4   Punch biopsy

As a rule, excisional biopsies are performed when large or deep specimens are needed. A scalpel is used to cut vertically and deeply into the skin to remove an elliptical piece of lesional tissue, as well as some surrounding normal tissue (Figure 10.5). Because of the generally larger size of excisional biopsy wounds, sutures are required for closing them. An excisional biopsy allows the best assessment of the depth of a growth and thus is used commonly when dealing with certain types of suspected malignancies where assessing lesion depth is needed to determine *prognosis* (outcome). When only a small portion of a growth is removed by this technique, the biopsy is referred to as *incisional.*

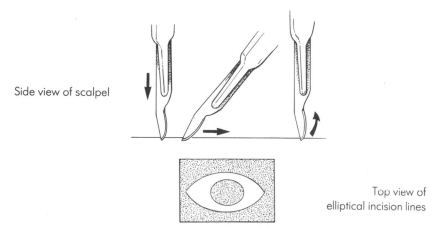

Side view of scalpel

Top view of
elliptical incision lines

Figure 10.5   Excisional biopsy using a scalpel

As a rule, cosmetic surgeons plan excisional procedures to take advantage of your skin's natural lines so that surgical scars may be concealed. To do this, they orient the final line of the scar and stitch lines to fall within the skin's natural tension and wrinkle lines (Figure 10.6). Natural tension lines tend to be the result of muscle movements beneath the skin; wrinkle lines are primarily due to years of accumulated sun damage.

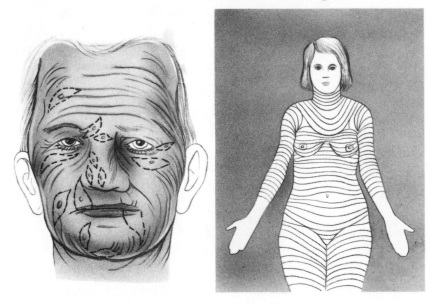

Figure 10.6   Skin tension and wrinkle lines of the face and body

ELIMINATING SKIN GROWTHS

Dermatologists routinely employ several methods for removing or destroying unwanted skin growths. The choice of procedure in a particular case depends not only on the type, size, location, and depth of the growth to be removed, but upon the age and general health of the patient.

As mentioned earlier, lesions are sometimes completely removed as part of the biopsy procedure. In such cases, no further treatments are needed. At other times, most especially when dealing with skin cancers, more involved procedures, such as *curettage* and *electrosurgery, Moh's chemosurgery, radiation therapy,* or *cryotherapy,* are needed to completely eradicate the malignancy.

Electrosurgery refers to several different methods for using electrical devices to destroy or remove unwanted tissue (see Figure 10.7, page 159). It is commonly combined with curettage in the treatment of proven skin cancers, especially basal cell and squamous cell cancers, and the cure rate exceeds 95 percent. In general, each type of electrosurgery requires prior numbing of the skin with a local anesthetic. Electrosurgical wounds heal quite satisfactorily on their own and require no stitching.

Electrodessication, in which the electric needle is held either in contact with the tissue or a short distance away, relies upon the use of electric sparks to dehydrate unwanted tissue. It is very frequently combined with curettage for treating certain types of skin cancers and is referred to as a D&C. Through a different mechanism, *electrocoagulation* destroys diseased tissue by delivering an intensely hot electric current directly to the lesion to coagulate ("boil") it. *Electrocautery* uses an electrically heated wire, rather than an electric current, to damage tissue. Finally, a fourth type of electrosurgery, *electrolysis,* is used primarily for removing unwanted hair or "broken" blood vessels (and is discussed in chapters 11 and 17). By and large, electrosurgery is safe, but care must be exercised when performing certain types of electrosurgery on patients with cardiac pacemakers because the electric current may interfere with proper functioning of the pacemaker device.

Radiation therapy (or *radiotherapy*) is the use of X-rays to eradicate certain growths and malignancies. For some basal cell and squamous cell cancers, radiation therapy may be used as an alternative to surgery, particularly in older or debilitated individuals. Although at one time it was used to treat a variety of inflammatory and benign conditions, radiation is now generally reserved for malignant conditions. Radiation treatments for skin cancers, which may number between five and twenty, depending upon the circumstances, take only a few minutes to administer and require no anesthesia. X-rays cause damage to the genetic material within cancerous cells, leading to their death and destruction. A wound forms at the radiation site and later heals spontaneously without stitches.

Although the site of radiation treatment generally heals satisfactorily, after a number of years the skin in the treatment area may grow thinner, more fragile, discolored, display "broken" blood vessels, and may even develop open sores (radiation ulcers). Because of these potential postradiation effects, I do not usually advise radiation therapy for young, healthy people.

Moh's chemosurgery is probably the single most effective technique available for curing skin cancer. It is especially valuable for removing very large skin cancers and those that have recurred following treatment by other methods. In Moh's chemosurgery, a detailed three-dimensional map is made of all quadrants of the tumor tissue. The cancer is then repeatedly sliced away and each slice immediately examined under the microscope. The procedure is continued until all diseased tissue has been removed. Naturally, in cases of large or neglected tumors, the wounds that result from Moh's chemosurgery tend to be large. Nevertheless, they usually heal satisfactorily when they are left to heal spontaneously without stitching. However, if the cosmetic result is not satisfactory, additional corrective procedures may be performed at a much later date. Cure rates with Moh's chemosurgery for even the largest and most difficult skin cancers are approximately 96 percent.

Cryotherapy, or the application of freezing solutions, is another frequently used form of treatment. Liquid nitrogen, which is capable of freezing skin lesions down to $-176°F.$, is the freezing agent most commonly used. Dry ice may be used for this purpose, but this is rare.

Liquid nitrogen can be applied by a cotton-tipped applicator or may be delivered through a hand-held or larger, stationary spray device. One or more cycles of freezing and thawing are often needed to destroy tumor cells adequately. A blister and sore at the treatment site form within hours and usually heal spontaneously within two weeks. Since the extreme cold acts as an anesthetic, no additional anesthesia is required for cryotherapy. Unfortunately, temporary or permanent loss of skin pigmentation occasionally occurs at the treatment site, and there may also be prominent scars.

Sometimes dermatologists bypass surgery and instead select certain anticancer creams or potent acids to treat various kinds of precancers of the skin. One such chemical, 5-fluorouracil (5-FU, Efudex), is applied twice daily to affected areas for about six weeks. While normal skin remains unaffected, precancers of the skin are preferentially destroyed by this chemical. By directly interfering with the genetic material in precancerous cells, this chemical inhibits precancer-cell reproduction and growth, which leads ultimately to their destruction.

Efudex is particularly useful when numerous precancerous lesions are present and surgery is therefore less practical. After about two weeks of daily application, affected spots become intensely red, inflamed, itchy, painful, blistered, and crusted. Generally this reaction fades gradually over a three-week period. The advantage of Efudex therapy is that the chemical hunts out not only those precancers that can be seen by the naked eye, but also those that are in the process of forming. Smoother, less mottled skin results and scar formation seldom occurs. Nevertheless, because of the intensity and discomfort of the inflammatory reaction, many people opt for other forms of treatment.

More recently, the antiacne, anti-wrinkle medication Retin-A has been used to treat certain premalignant lesions of the skin, and preliminary investigations have thus far been encouraging.

Application of this drug two times a day for two or three months leads to thinning or elimination of many lesions. Improper use or overuse of this drug can lead to excessive dryness and irritation. The final place of this versatile drug in the treatment of premalignancies of the skin awaits further study.

When many premalignancies are present, potent acids such as trichloroacetic acid may be applied to the skin in an effort to "resurface" it. The acid, which is usually applied with a cotton-tipped applicator, causes the equivalent of a second-degree burn. Since chemical application takes only moments to perform, no anesthesia is ordinarily required. Isolated lesions or large areas containing many lesions may be treated in this fashion.

Within minutes of application, patients experience a temporary, intense burning sensation. Soon after, a chalk white "frost" appears over the treatment area. Redness and swelling follow shortly thereafter. Within one to two weeks the frost scales off the skin, leaving a smoother surface. Exposure to the sun must be assiduously avoided for two to three months following treatment to prevent the development of mottled skin discolorations within the treatment areas.

COMMON BENIGN SKIN GROWTHS

CYSTS

Cysts are harmless growths containing keratin, cellular debris, and oil gland secretions. Located largely within the deeper layers of the skin, cysts are filled with a whitish-brown cheesy material that occasionally oozes out onto the skin surface. Cysts can appear almost anywhere on the body, including the scalp and even the feet, though this is rare. Unfortunately, nobody knows why cysts appear or how to prevent them. However, certain people seem to demonstrate a familial trait for developing them.

Milia and *sebaceous cysts* are two very common forms of cyst. Milia look like large whiteheads and are common on the face, particularly in older persons. In contrast, under ordinary circumstances the skin surface overlying a sebaceous cyst is usually either normal in appearance or may show a small blackheadlike pore opening. Frequently more than one cyst can be found on close examination of the entire skin surface.

True cysts form within hair follicles and possess saclike walls. In fact, pathologists name cysts according to the specific types of cells that compose the sac wall. As a rule, cysts by themselves are merely nuisances. They do not turn into cancer. On the other hand, they may occasionally become irritated or infected and cause pain, tenderness, redness, and swelling, especially when large. When infected, cysts strongly resemble boils or acne cysts, and it is sometimes hard even for the doctor to tell the difference. Rarely does blood poisoning result from severely infected or improperly or inadequately treated cysts.

TREATMENT   Treating cysts is simple. Milia are removed by opening them with an ultrafine needle or fine scalpel and expressing their cores. When numerous, they may be obliterated by electrodessication. Larger cysts can be excised or opened and drained under local anesthesia. To minimize the chance of recurrence, the entire sac must be dissected from the surrounding skin with which it may be tightly bound and then completely removed. Regrowth of a cyst may occur when even minute fragments of the sac wall remain. Accompanying infection is treated by appropriate antibiotic therapy. Inflamed sebaceous cysts, like acne cysts, may be quieted down by the use of intralesional corticosteroid injections (chapter 11). Biopsying a cyst is seldom necessary.

SEBACEOUS GLAND HYPERPLASIA

Overgrown oil glands, or *sebaceous gland hyperplasia,* are a common problem for people of middle and older age. Often they appear as part of the full-blown picture of acne rosacea (chapter 7). The growths are yellow to ivory colored, lobe-surfaced, waxy-looking bumps on the face. While there may be only one, most often spots are found all over the face. Overgrown oil glands are harmless and do not turn into cancer, but they can be cosmetically troubling, especially when there are a lot of them.

TREATMENT   Electrosurgery performed under local anesthesia can be quite helpful for flattening overgrown oil glands. However, the treatment does nothing to prevent new growths from developing; new ones often continue to appear throughout life. In addition, since the base of the oil glands extends deeply into the skin, electrosurgically flattening their surfaces serves only to improve their appearance temporarily. Touch-ups are usually necessary anywhere from several months to several years later. Cryotherapy has been helpful in some cases, while excision surgery to remove the affected glands once and for all leaves a small scar—hardly a worthwhile trade. For that reason, excision of sebaceous hyperplasia is seldom performed.

SOLAR LENTIGINES

Solar lentigines (singular: *lentigo*) are flat age spots, often called "liver spots." Liver spots have nothing at all to do with your liver and probably got the name because they tend to be light- or dark-brown in color and are sometimes shaped like a liver. Solar lentigines range in size from a quarter of an inch to several inches. Largely a product of accumulated sun damage, they typically involve the exposed areas of the face, backs of hands, and arms.

While they are cosmetically disfiguring and considered age's mark of Cain by some, solar lentigines are otherwise harmless and possess no malignant potential. For the most part they are diagnosed by their clinical appearance alone. Sometimes, however, particularly on the face, they may be confused with more serious brown marks, especially malignant melanoma. In those cases, a biopsy may be necessary to establish or confirm the diagnosis.

TREATMENT   For cosmetic considerations only, solar lentigines can be removed by either electrosurgery, chemical applications, or cryotherapy. I prefer electrosurgery, since I find that chemical applications and cryosurgery entail a greater risk of subsequent, occasionally permanent, discoloration of the treated areas.

SEBORRHEIC KERATOSES

Seborrheic keratoses are heaped-up liver spots. They typically appear as thick, "stuck on," scaly, greasy-looking growths. In addition to all shades of brown, they may exhibit a variety of shades of yellow. On the lower extremities, they may sometimes be whitish-gray in color and because of their resemblance to stucco, are nicknamed "stucco" keratoses.

Seborrheic keratoses may be found almost anywhere on the body and range in size from a quarter of an inch to many inches in diameter. In fact, it is not uncommon to see many seborrheic keratoses that have grown to the size of a quarter or half dollar on the same person.

The appearance of seborrheic keratoses is usually so characteristic that a biopsy is seldom necessary. However, on occasion, they may mimic more serious skin tumors, such as basal cell skin cancer or malignant melanoma. In such cases, biopsy is essential to ensure correct diagnosis.

TREATMENT Since seborrheic keratoses are harmless growths and rarely exhibit malignant change, removing them is largely a matter of esthetic considerations. They are located very superficially in the skin, so they can be quite easily removed under local anesthesia by simple curettage. Electrosurgery, cryotherapy, and chemical applications (especially for thinner keratoses) may also be used. In general, I prefer curettage to these other methods because in my experience it yields the most consistently satisfactory cosmetic results and scar formation is rare. Because of their superficial location in the skin, deep excision is never warranted owing to the considerable risk of scar formation from this procedure.

SKIN TAGS

Skin tags, *papillomas* or *acrochorda* (singular: *acrochordon*), are harmless, flesh-colored or light- to dark-brown redundancies of skin that hang on fine stalks. Some people mistakenly refer to them as skin *tabs*. Skin tags usually appear on the eyelids, neck, shoulders, armpits, and groin of people over forty years old. Diabetics, postmenopausal women, and pregnant women are particularly predisposed to develop them. The tendency to develop skin tags seems to run in families. Many lesions, sometimes twenty or more, may be present at the same time. Interestingly, several recent studies have shown a high association between the presence of skin tags and intestinal polyps. If you have many skin tags, and especially if you are experiencing any gastrointestinal symptoms, I suggest that you consult your physician about this. While smaller skin tags and those with broad stalks seldom cause problems, larger ones and those with long narrow stalks often twist. When this happens bleeding and infection may result. For that reason, I generally advise the preventive removal of these kinds of skin tags.

TREATMENT Scissor removal, electrosurgery, and cryosurgery are all successful methods for removing skin tags. With any of these techniques, many—if not all—of these growths can be removed quickly in one session. Because skin tag removals are usually so rapid, local anesthesia is often unnecessary. For the more anxious person, however, nitrous oxide may be used. Numerous tiny skin tags can be removed by electrosurgery alone. Larger ones respond to scissor removal with electrosurgery of the base. Individual growths seldom recur after removal. However, new ones often crop up periodically and removals generally need to be repeated every two to five years.

LIPOMAS

Lipomas, another common form of benign skin tumor, result from an overproduction of fat cells within the deep fatty layer of the skin. Given their situation, the overlying skin usually appears perfectly normal. When compressed, however, they have a characteristic spongy feel to them, which may cause them to be confused with sebaceous cysts. In general, lipomas are harmless tumors that cause no symptoms, although they can be quite painful.

TREATMENT   If they cause no symptoms or cosmetic embarrassment, lipomas may be ignored. When indicated, excisional surgery is the preferred means for removing them, particularly large ones. Smaller lipomas are sometimes removed by a method known as *piezosurgery*. While the patient is under local anesthesia, a small incision is made over the top of the lipoma and the contents extruded through the incision. By "delivering" the lipoma through a small incision in this fashion, fewer sutures are needed and the resulting scar is smaller and less visible. More recently, *liposuction* (chapter 11) has been used successfully in a few cases to remove very large lipomas.

SKIN CANCERS

Like other forms of cancer, skin cancers are believed to arise from cells that have become abnormal and have lost their ability for controlled growth and reproduction. The reasons for such transformations are not yet entirely understood. Cancer growth is characterized by a wild, unrestrained overproduction of abnormal cells.

PREVENTING SKIN CANCERS

Skin cancer is almost always preventable. In most cases, it is also completely curable when treated in the earliest stages. For that reason it behooves every one of you to know the warning signs of cancer and the ABCDs for detecting melanomas. Early warning signs of skin cancer include the appearance of a new growth, or a change in size, shape, or color of a preexisting growth. Other signs include the development of sores, crusts, scabs, or bleeding within a supposed mole, wart, liver spot, or freckle, or the development of itching or pain in such spots.

The American Academy of Dermatology in conjunction with the American Cancer Society has developed the ABCD rule for melanoma detection. A stands for Asymmetry; that is, one side of an abnormal mole does not match the other side in appearance. Normal moles are generally symmetrical. B stands for Border Irregularities; the edges of a mole may be jagged like the coast of Maine or the Gulf of Mexico. Normal moles have smooth borders. C stands for Color. The presence of mixtures of red, white, blue, brown, and black are particularly suspect. Ordinary moles are fairly uniformly pigmented. Finally, D stands for Diameter. Growths greater than ¼ inch and those that demonstrate a rapid or continuing increase in size should be brought to the attention of a dermatologist.

BASAL CELL CANCERS

Basal cell carcinoma (BCC), or *basal cell epitheliomas (BCE)* as they are sometimes called, are by far the most common form of skin cancer. For that matter, they are the most common form of cancer affecting humans. Typically, basal cell cancers appear as raised, translucent, pearly bumps on sun-exposed skin. In addition, if left untreated, basal cell cancers may ulcerate, bleed, and crust. Many people initially confuse them with ordinary pimples and try to scratch or wash them away.

Four hundred thousand new cases of basal cell skin cancer are reported annually, and 90 percent of these are clearly related to accumulated sun damage. BCCs received a good deal of media attention recently when President and Mrs. Reagan and Ted Koppel were diagnosed and treated for them.

Fortunately, basal cell cancers have little potential to *metastasize* (spread by way of the lymph and blood systems), and few people die from them. Nevertheless, they are capable of causing extensive destruction of surrounding normal skin and underlying tissues. Consequently, they should not be ignored and viewed as harmless "little nothings." As a rule, the longer a person waits before seeking medical attention, the more damage the tumor does. Tissue destruction by these tumors can also be responsible for bleeding and infection. Biopsy confirmation is important when BCC is suspected.

TREATMENT   Common forms of skin cancer treatment include curettage, with or without electrodessication, surgical excision, cryosurgery, Moh's chemosurgery, and radiation therapy. As mentioned earlier, Moh's chemosurgery is particularly valuable for treating cancers that have recurred following treatment by other means. Curative skin cancer surgery is most often performed in the office setting and completed in one session. Cure rates generally exceed 95 percent. However, since individuals with proven skin cancer have a greater than 50 percent chance of developing a new skin cancer at a different location within two years following treatment, annual complete skin check-ups make good sense for anyone with a history of skin cancer.

SQUAMOUS CELL CARCINOMA

Squamous cell carcinomas (SCCs) are the second most common form of skin cancer. Between 80,000 and 100,000 new cases are diagnosed each year. SCCs appear as elevated, pink, opaque bumps or wartlike or mushroomlike growths on the skin. They tend to ulcerate and bleed and may become infected. The rim of the ears, the face, lips, and hands are particularly susceptible sites of involvement. Like BCCs, SCCs are widely believed to be the result of chronic sun damage. They may also arise within areas of prior X-ray radiation damage, nonhealing wounds, ulcerations, and infections. As a rule, squamous cell cancers that result from sun damage seldom metastasize. By contrast, those linked to other causes have a greater potential for metastasis. SCCs are responsible for more than 2,000 deaths each year, so biopsy confirmation is very important.

The methods for treating SCCs differ little from those used for BCCs. When squamous cell skin cancer has already metastasized throughout the body, consultation with an *oncologist* (an internal cancer specialist) is usually sought.

MALIGNANT MELANOMA

Malignant melanoma is by far the least common of the three main types of skin cancer. On the other hand, it is by far the most serious. Malignant melanoma is a potentially fatal form of malignancy capable of metastasizing by way of the blood and lymph systems. Lesions of melanoma usually begin as flat, molelike growths having somewhat irregular or indistinct borders. As they continue to grow, they may turn various shades of red, white, blue, brown, or black. The upper head, neck, upper trunk, and lower extremities are common locations for their development, but malignant melanomas may involve any area of the body (see Figure 10.7).

Current statistics point to a virtual epidemic of malignant melanoma: 25,000 new cases are diagnosed each year. The incidence of malignant melanoma has been rising alarmingly in our society, at a faster rate than any other cancer except for lung

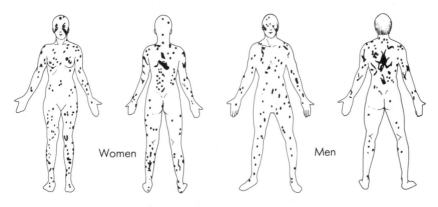

Women   Men

Figure 10.7   Anatomical locations of malignant melanomas

cancer in women. Its incidence has been doubling every ten years since 1950 and has increased by 340 percent within the past decade alone in the sun-drenched American Southwest. Melanoma mortality figures have also been doubling each decade since 1950; it is responsible for nearly 8,000 deaths each year.

While no one is immune, not even black people, some people are at particularly high risk, namely those with fair skin, freckles, blond hair, blue, green, or gray eyes, who sunburn easily and tan poorly, have a family history of skin cancer, live in sunbelt areas, spend short but intense periods of time in the sun, have a large number of regular moles on their body, or have dysplastic nevi (see pages 161–63).

Diagnosis of malignant melanoma is usually made by excisional biopsy when a suspected lesion is small. An incisional or punch biopsy may be performed when the tumor is very large.

TREATMENT　Malignant melanoma can be cured by wide excisional surgery when it is caught at a stage where it is still entirely restricted to the upper levels of the skin. It is generally excised along with a margin of surrounding normal tissue and sent to a pathologist to determine that all diseased tissue has been removed. As a rule, the deeper the invasion of the tumor at the time it is discovered, the poorer the prognosis. Once melanoma has already metastasized, the services of an oncologist are needed.

Cryosurgery, electrosurgery, and curettage are not performed on melanoma-containing tissue, since the destruction of such tissue by these procedures would not permit the pathologist to determine whether the surgery was complete and adequate. Radiotherapy is ineffective for melanoma.

PRECANCERS OF THE SKIN

Millions of people are affected by precancerous lesions. In terms of sheer numbers alone, they represent no small problem. Precancerous growths lie somewhere on the spectrum between normal tissue and cancers. In general, while precancers are not true cancers and are themselves usually harmless, *they are important because they retain the potential to progress to cancers.* Four common types of precancers concern us here: *actinic keratoses,* which are forerunners of squamous cell skin cancer; and *dysplastic nevi, congenital nevi,* and *Hutchinson's melanotic freckles,* which are forerunners of malignant melanoma.

ACTINIC KERATOSES

Often called *solar keratoses,* actinic keratoses are precancers leading to squamous cell skin cancer. The overwhelming majority of cases result from years of accumulated sun damage. (Not surprisingly, the words *actinic* and *solar* both mean sun-related.) Initially, actinic keratoses may be smooth and flat. With time, they typically appear as irregular, scaly, red or reddish-brown rough spots. When numerous, as they sometimes are, especially in people with fair skin, they can be quite disfiguring cosmetically. In most cases, the diagnosis can be easily made on appearance alone. When a question exists, a curet biopsy usually provides sufficient tissue to confirm the diagnosis.

TREATMENT Actinic keratoses may be treated by any of several methods, including curettage, chemical application, cryosurgery, and Efudex therapy. Each method is curative. However, the use of topical 5-fluorouracil cream has the additional advantage of seeking out precancers in the making, before they become visible to the naked eye. As mentioned earlier, many people dislike the intense inflammation that such therapy causes. Accordingly, most opt for one of the other methods of removal.

DYSPLASTIC NEVI

The word *dysplastic* means faulty, and *nevi* (singular: *nevus*) means moles. Dysplastic nevi, therefore, are faulty or, more correctly, atypical moles. Somewhere between 5 percent and 9 percent of the adult white population of the United States have them, which translates into 9 to 16 million people. The tendency to form dysplastic nevi often runs in families, although some affected individuals know of no others in their family who have them. (Such individuals are considered instances of *nonfamilial* or *sporadic* dysplastic nevi.)

Dysplastic nevi are believed to possess the potential to progress to malignant melanoma. Moreover, the presence of dysplastic nevi anywhere on the skin is a marker for a person who is at increased risk of developing malignant melanoma even within areas with currently normal (nondysplastic) skin. In general, the overall risk of developing malignant melanoma is believed to be relatively low in sporadic cases of dysplastic nevi. However, the risk may be extremely high (exceeding 97 percent) in persons with dysplastic nevi who have close blood relatives with dysplastic nevi and histories of malignant melanoma.

If your dermatologist suspects that you have dysplastic nevi, one or more suspicious nevi may be biopsied to confirm the diagnosis. Once diagnosed, photographs of additional lesions may be used for periodic comparison. However, I believe that a dysplastic nevus should be removed entirely so that it will never have the opportunity to turn into melanoma. When a few are present, this is feasible. When there are many of them, I recommend that only the most suspicious lesions be biopsied and removed. Persons with proven dysplastic nevi should perform periodic self-examination of their complete skin surface (see Figure 10.8) on a monthly basis. You should direct particular attention to the appearance of new moles or changes in any preexisting

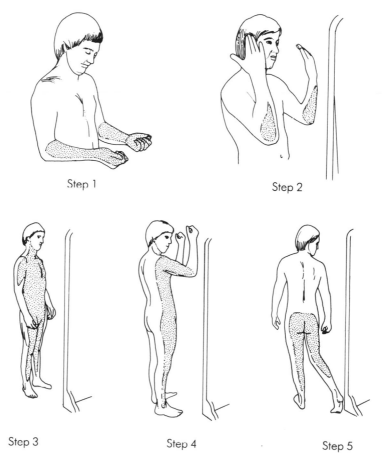

Step 1 Step 2

Step 3 Step 4 Step 5

Figure 10.8 Skin self-examination

ones. In addition, periodic examination by a dermatologist—
every six to twelve months for those in low-risk groups, and
every three to six months for high-risk groups—is strongly advised. At those times, additional biopsies of suspicious lesions
may be warranted.

CONGENITAL NEVI

Congenital nevi are moles with which you were born (birthmarks). They may or may not have hair in them, but this is
unimportant. Size, however, is important. Individuals with congenital moles larger than 9 inches in diameter have a nearly nine
times higher chance of developing malignant melanoma than

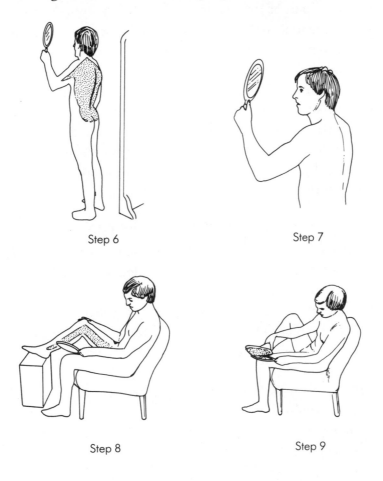

Step 6

Step 7

Step 8

Step 9

persons in the population at large. Although the precise risk for developing malignant melanoma in individuals with small or medium-size congenital moles is not precisely known, it is also believed to be higher than the risk within the general population.

TREATMENT Complete surgical excision is the only recommended treatment for large congenital moles. When they are so large that complete surgery is not feasible, cryosurgery or dermabrasion may be tried. However, because the cells of congenital moles are typically located deeper in the skin, more superficial methods of removal such as dermabrasion and cryosurgery remain of limited value. Some dermatologists prefer to follow congenital moles periodically with the aid of measurements, diagrams, or photographs. However, until we learn otherwise, I generally recommend the removal of all congenital moles measuring over 1½ inches in diameter. Since the cosmetic result of excising these moles is usually quite satisfactory (in many cases, the small surgical scar that results is an improvement over the original mole), I believe that any benefits of following these potentially troublesome growths by measurements, etc., are not worth the risk of developing melanoma.

HUTCHINSON'S MELANOTIC FRECKLES

Named for its original describer, Hutchinson's freckle or *lentigo maligna* is a dark-colored, often large, frecklelike patch. It occurs most often on the cheeks of elderly individuals and may progress to malignant melanoma in as many as one third of all cases. Initially tan in color, Hutchinson's freckles continue to enlarge and darken slowly over several years.

TREATMENT Complete excision is the treatment of choice. Cryosurgery has also been tried with some success owing to the peculiar increased sensitivity of pigment cells to destruction by cold temperatures.

MAKING A GOOD THING BETTER

HELPING NATURE: COSMETIC SURGERY

*B*eauty is in the eyes of the beholder, we've been told. Beauty *is* a relative concept and represents the inherent quality of a person or object to be pleasing to the eye or the mind. Although many people may not be able to describe precisely which features make a person beautiful, most of us have our own preconceived notions of what beauty is, and these notions are most often dictated or shaped by cultural influences.

Attractiveness studies of young people clearly indicate that good-looking individuals possess many school, business, and social advantages over their less attractive peers. A recent study showed that many job interviewers make up their minds about applicants within the first thirty seconds of the interview—that is, in only enough time to respond to the applicant's appearance. Based upon appearance alone, attractive people are judged to be more capable, warm, kind, sensitive, and extroverted than less attractive people. Social scientists refer to this phenomenon as the "what is beautiful is good" philosophy.

Attractiveness studies with older people have only recently been undertaken. Not surprisingly, these have yielded the same results as the studies of young people: More attractive older people are socially more advantaged and more likely to enjoy a richer and fuller quality of life. A recent University of Pennsylvania study about how physical appearance affects self-perception in older women found that "the physically attractive perceived themselves to be healthier, to have a greater feeling of well-being and a more positive outlook on life . . . to be more cheerful, less depressed, and better adjusted. They registered greater satisfaction with their lives, were more socially outgoing, and more realistic. The attractive women perceived themselves as having less sickness and indeed were in better health."

Even more surprisingly, a major study, this time of men, actually found that those who looked old for their age were in fact older in terms of the physiologic functioning of such organs as the heart, lungs, kidneys, etc., and generally less healthy than those who looked younger than their years. Dramatically, in follow-up studies it was found that attractive men lived longer, too. The weight of scientific evidence seems clear: Good looks contribute to better health and longer life.

Because good looks have been shown to be so important to social and business success, scientists have been trying for years to capture the essence of—or more precisely—the equation for human beauty. Figure 11.1 is an artist's rendering of "ideal" beauty. This standard of beauty is based on what a sample of male American college students found most attractive in women when asked to judge a series of photographs. The basic elements of this "ideal" woman include wide cheekbones, their width about six-tenths of the length of the face from the hairline to the chin; eyes high and wide, with a width of about one-third of the face at eye level; high eyebrows and large pupils; a smile about half the width of the face at mouth level; small chin; and a nose area smaller than 5 percent of the area of the entire face.

Unquestionably, more goes into the making of beauty than simple mathematics. Figure 11.1 does not take into account such

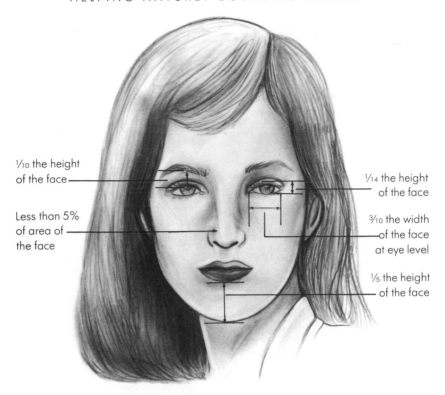

1/10 the height
of the face

1/14 the height
of the face

Less than 5%
of area of
the face

3/10 the width
of the face
at eye level

1/5 the height
of the face

Figure 11.1   Ideal beauty

important qualities as style, grace, refinement, elegance, inner energy, and so forth. Nevertheless, in pursuit of beauty and of helping nature, increasing numbers of people are seeking the benefits of cosmetic surgery. You might be surprised to learn, however, that there is nothing new about this. The *Susruta,* an Indian text dating from about 600 B.C., describes ancient surgical techniques for reconstructive nasal surgery.

Cosmetic surgery, now a $250-million-a-year business, is no longer the privilege of the rich and famous. Nearly 600,000 operations are performed each year, and this number is still climbing. By 1984, statistics showed that the demand for cosmetic surgery was up more than 60 percent over the previous three-year period and that men constituted nearly 20 percent of that demand. Moreover, cosmetic surgery is not just the province of the young or middle-aged; increasing numbers of women and men are having their initial cosmetic surgery *after* age sixty-five.

Cosmetic, or *plastic,* surgery covers a wide variety of medical and surgical methods for changing your appearance. The term *plastic surgery* is derived from the Greek word *plassein,* which means to mold, form, or restore. Some cosmetic procedures consist of nothing more than simple injections; other procedures involve complicated or delicate surgery and require days to weeks of recuperation.

A number of cosmetic procedures have been described elsewhere in the book, specifically the use of injectable collagen, dermabrasion, and chemical peels for acne scars and the excision of ice-pick scars (chapter 7); and the removal of many kinds of unsightly growths, such as moles, liver spots, age spots, skin tags, fat tumors, sebaceous cysts, and overgrown oil glands (chapter 10). This chapter deals with a variety of other increasingly popular cosmetic procedures, including wrinkle and scar removal, fat suction surgery, fat transplantation, the removal of unwanted blood vessels, breast surgery, and abdomen tightening.

KNOW THYSELF

Bear in mind Socrates's motto—"know thyself"—when considering cosmetic surgery. Before you decide upon cosmetic surgery, it is essential that you clarify your motives for wanting a certain procedure performed. Experience has taught us that you can almost guarantee yourself dissatisfaction and disappointment with the results of any cosmetic surgery if you start off unsure about whether you are ready for it in the first place. It has to be something *you* want and not because someone else has told you to do it. Having surgery done because your boyfriend, husband, or some other friend or relative wants you to can lay the groundwork for considerable postoperative disappointment, friction, and conflict. In such cases, I usually discourage my patients from having the procedure and advise them to go home, think about it carefully, and discuss their feelings openly with the other people involved.

To avoid disappointment, not only must you *want* a certain procedure, but your expectations for the outcome must also be realistic. Some people search for a miracle that no scalpel could possibly create. Disappointment almost certainly lurks close by if you mistake a cosmetic surgeon for a miracle worker capable of turning you into a stunning movie star with the wave of a scalpel. Disappointment is also likely if you believe that changing your appearance will automatically or necessarily win you more friends or respect, or provide a shortcut to a better sex life, for example. This is not to say that looking better and feeling better about yourself will not increase your self-confidence and sociability. It may, but there are no guarantees.

The ideal candidate for cosmetic surgery has been described as one who wants one or two specific things done and has no expectations that such changes will radically affect his or her life. By contrast, the less-than-ideal patient has been characterized as a picky, overly critical person who basically doesn't like himself. Another less-than-ideal candidate is someone who comes into the office carrying a high-fashion magazine and says, "Make me look like this."

One final source of considerable unnecessary disappointment and aggravation is the failure to realize that even when the results are satisfactory, they are not instantaneous. A scalpel is not a magic wand. It takes time, often weeks to months, for swelling, discoloration, and scarring to become less obvious or disappear entirely. Be prepared for this and expect to use cover-up cosmetics or clothing until healing is complete.

CHOOSING THE RIGHT DOCTOR

No doctor is right for everyone. Sometimes you have to do quite a bit of searching to find the best one for your needs. And even if you are careful about choosing, finding the right cosmetic surgeon can be quite complicated these days. In the past, if you wanted any kind of cosmetic work done, you went to a plastic surgeon. Today, many fields of medicine have subspecialties that are devoted to cosmetic surgery. For example, many training programs in *otolaryngology* (ear, nose, and throat), *ophthalmology* (eye), *oral surgery* (advanced dental surgery), and dermatology regularly include cosmetic surgery as part of their residency training programs. So if you are considering fat suction surgery or fat transplantation, for example, you could consult a dermatologic or plastic surgeon. If you wanted nose surgery, you could consult a plastic or otolaryngologic surgeon.

Although a well-trained and experienced surgeon in any of these specialties is technically capable of performing the desired procedure, some suggestions for selecting a cosmetic surgeon are in order. Probably the best way to choose a surgeon is to see some of his work. If you have any friends or relatives who have had cosmetic surgery, ask them whether they were satisfied with the care they received and the results. Alternatively, you might ask a trusted family physician or internist for a recommendation. These doctors frequently know the reputations—if not the work—of several local cosmetic surgeons. Finally, as a last resort, you can contact your local County Medical Society and ask for a board-certified, university-affiliated physician who performs the kind of surgery you wish.

Naturally, it goes without saying that you should choose a doctor with whom you feel comfortable. In general, this means one who takes the time to explain what each procedure will involve and how much discomfort, if any, there is during and after the procedure, how much it will cost, how much time you will be out of work, what complications to expect, and what results you can realistically expect. Above all, you should feel comfortable talking with the doctor and feel that you are able to communicate your concerns and fears with him. These are the essential elements of any good doctor-patient relationship.

Finally, a word to the wise. There has been a recent upsurge of television, radio, and print advertising for large cosmetic surgery clinics. Some of these clinics have offices nationwide. Many of them offer free consultations, early appointments, same-day service, free limousine pickup, and bargain fees. *Caveat emptor:*

Be wary of any place that guarantees results or downplays the risks. No one can tell you exactly how you will look after surgery, even with the most expensive computer imaging systems. Don't let yourself be talked into any cosmetic procedure you don't really want or think you need. Furthermore, check the fees; they may not really be such bargains after all. Remember, undergoing cosmetic surgery is not like buying a trinket at a rummage sale. After all the advertising glitz is gone and the surgery done, you have to live with the way you look for the rest of your life.

WRINKLE REMOVAL

In chapter 10, you learned that certain potent acids, such as *trichloroacetic acid,* in varying concentrations can be used to remove age spots and other growths. *Phenol* is another potent acid often used for chemical peels or *skin peels,* as they are also called. A chemical peel is useful for "freshening" and making more glowing skin that otherwise appears dull. They are also used to even out skin tone irregularities and to lessen or eliminate fine, cross-hatched wrinkles. Wrinkles around the mouth (the kind that cause lipsticks to "bleed") and crow's-feet at the corners of the eyes respond especially well to chemical peels. Chemical peels are believed to work by destroying the surface proteins of the skin, allowing new, fresher skin to replace the sloughed-off skin.

The acids sting and burn for about fifteen to thirty seconds immediately following application, then a white "frost" develops over the treated areas. At that point, the surgeon neutralizes the acid with either water or alcohol. A scab forms at the treatment site, then falls off about ten days later. Treated areas appear red or reddish brown initially, but skin color returns to normal, usually within six weeks to six months. Patients tend to be quite satisfied with the results, which may last for several years before retreatment is required.

To deepen the peel, your doctor may either apply more acid

or cover the treated area with adhesive tape to enhance the penetration of the acid. The tape is usually left in place for twenty-four hours. While chemical peels generally have few complications, deeper peels entail a somewhat increased risk. Possible complications include the development of hypertrophic scars (see pages 176–77) and mottled skin discoloration. In general, the deeper the peel and the larger the area treated, the more post-treatment discomfort and swelling. After a full-face peel, most people are able to return to work in about two weeks.

People with fair skin are better candidates for chemical peels because they generally show less color contrast between treated and untreated sites. You should avoid unprotected sun exposure for about two to three months after a chemical peel to lessen the likelihood of developing mottled discoloration or overpigmentation of the treatment sites. Approximate cost of a full-face chemical peel ranges from $500 to $1,000.

In chapter 7, the use of injectable collagen implants for correcting depressed acne scars was discussed. However, collagen implants are used at least as often to treat facial wrinkles. Those around the nose, mouth, eyes, and forehead respond quite well to this form of treatment. (Injectable collagen is not used to treat jowls and skin sagging; a facelift procedure must handle these problems.)

Depending upon the depth and number of wrinkles being treated with injectable collagen, several treatment sessions may be required. Since corrections usually subside gradually with time, future retreatments are generally necessary. How soon this occurs depends upon how much you laugh, cry, eat, drink, smoke, and expose yourself to the sun. In general, when used to treat shallow wrinkles, a Zyderm correction may last from six months to one or two years. When used for deeper wrinkles and depressions, a Zyplast correction may last from one to several years. As a rule, less collagen is needed for retreatment sessions than is needed to establish the original correction.

To treat wrinkles, most cosmetic surgeons choose the *serial puncture technique* (Figure 11.2). This consists of using a series of

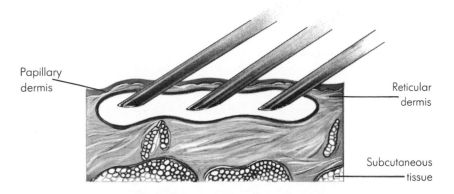

Papillary
dermis

Reticular
dermis

Subcutaneous
tissue

Figure 11.2   Serial puncture technique

needles to inject small amounts of collagen in a row under each wrinkle line. For Zyderm collagen a mosquito-bite-like welt must be raised at each injection site (Figure 11.3). This overcorrection eventually settles down to being flush with the skin in a matter of eight to seventy-two hours. For Zyplast, overcorrection is not desirable. Instead, immediately after injection, the surgeon vigorously kneads and molds the material into the desired correction through the overlying skin with his fingers. Advantages of collagen therapy for wrinkles are that it can be performed in the office in a matter of moments, it engenders no postinjection discomfort, and in most cases, it allows you the added luxury of returning to work immediately. The approximate cost of each Zyderm collagen treatment session is $275 to $400; the approximate cost of Zyplast per session is $375 to $500.

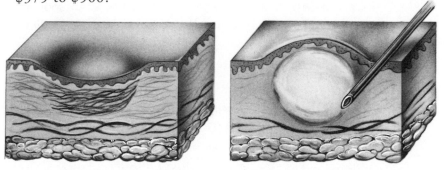

Figure 11.3   Initial overcorrection is necessary with Zyderm collagen.

KELOIDS AND "PROUD FLESH" SCARS

Severe, uncontrolled, or poorly controlled cystic acne may result in the development of depressed "pock" scars. However, severe acne may also result in the development of raised scars known as *keloids* and *hypertrophic scars ("proud flesh")*. Such scars may occasionally also follow surgery or some other form of injury to the skin.

Hypertrophic scars basically represent a complication of wound healing in which healing skin overshoots its mark and produces excess tissue. This excess scar tissue typically protrudes above the skin surface, hence the name "proud" flesh. Fortunately, hypertrophic scars usually do not grow very large. They are generally pink, pinkish red, or purplish red and very firm or rubbery to the touch. They may also be the source of itching and slight discomfort. Frequently, after many months, sometimes even after more than a year, a proud flesh scar spontaneously sinks back to a level flush with the surrounding normal skin, and with time, its color fades to off-white or ivory. However, when this does not occur on its own, the dermatologist can inject a small amount of an anti-inflammatory corticosteroid solution directly into it to promote shrinkage and fading. These intralesional steroid injections may need to be repeated several times at two- to four-week intervals in order to achieve satisfactory cosmetic results.

Keloids are hard scars, ranging in color from flesh to ivory. They also may follow injury, burns, or surgery to the skin. Like hypertrophic scars, keloids generally pose no health problems and are only of cosmetic importance. Unlike hypertrophic scars, however, keloids can grow quite large and become disfiguring.

The tendency to form keloids appears to have a racial and genetic predisposition. Although whites are by no means exempt, keloids more commonly occur in blacks and East Asians. Moreover, certain body locations, such as between the breasts, central upper chest, and between the shoulder blades appear more prone to developing keloids even in whites.

Whereas hypertrophic scars tend to remain confined to the site of prior skin injury or surgery, keloids often extend well *beyond* the confines of the original damage or injury. As a rule, keloids do not shrink by themselves; removal requires medical intervention. Like hypertrophic scars, keloids may be shrunk through the repeated injection of corticosteroid solutions. Some physicians claim to get better results by prefreezing keloids with liquid nitrogen (cryotherapy) to soften them before they are injected. Another procedure for reducing keloids involves excising them, injecting corticosteroid solution into the base, and compressing the wound with elastic bandages to reduce the chance of recurrence.

LIPOSUCTION SURGERY

Liposuction surgery, also called *suction lipectomy* or *fat suction surgery,* is a surgical procedure for removal of unwanted or excess fat cells from the body. It was developed in Europe in the 1970s and was introduced to the United States in the early 1980s. Currently it is the fastest-growing category among cosmetic procedures.

In general, liposuction surgery may be performed in the office or outpatient ambulatory setting under local anesthesia. When more than 1 quart of fat is to be removed, the procedure may be performed in a hospital setting under general anesthesia. Liposuction surgery is not a substitute for dieting and exercise nor is it a procedure designed to correct obesity. It has been especially touted for removing *cellulite.*

Cellulite is the word used to describe the bulged, or orange-peel-like, appearance of fat at the hips, buttocks, and thighs. The exact nature of cellulite is still poorly understood, but Madison Avenue makes good use of it to sell diet programs and fat-reduction devices. The typical bumpy appearance of cellulite is believed to be due to the presence of fibrous bands that course through the fat deposits, separating them into bulging compartments. Because their skin is thinner and their fat deposits generally larger, women complain more often of cellulite. Older people seem to have more of it, too, owing to progressive thinning and loss of flexibility in their skin. Unfortunately, because of genetic differences in how much and where fat is distributed in the body, it is possible to be lean and still have cellulite in some locations.

Liposuction surgery is designed to remove excess fat deposits from the cheeks, jowls, chin, neck, arms, hips, inner and outer thighs ("saddlebags"), abdomen, buttocks, and knees. Currently, the vast majority of lipo-surgical procedures are performed on the thighs, and to a lesser extent on the hips, abdomen, and buttocks. The ideal candidate is a person in otherwise good general health with good skin elasticity.

The procedure consists of making a ½-inch incision beside the area to be treated and inserting a small tube. The tube is attached to a high-pressure vacuum suction and a crisscrossed pattern of suctioning is used to systematically remove the unwanted fat (Figure 11.4). Abdomens and thighs may require from thirty to sixty minutes to treat, necks about twenty minutes, and facial sites from five to ten minutes.

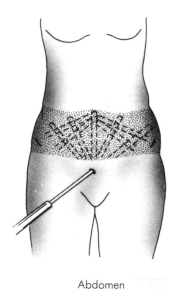 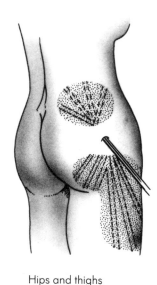

Abdomen   Hips and thighs

Figure 11.4   Liposuction surgery

Generally, the results of liposuction are quite satisfactory. Because the incisions are small, pain and scarring are ordinarily minimal and healing rapid. Most people are up and about immediately after surgery and can usually resume normal activities in a week or so.

Complications have been reported to occur in only 1 to 3 percent of cases. These include postoperative swelling, bleeding, discoloration, the development of a dimpled or "cottage-cheese-like" surface appearance, particularly on the buttocks and abdomen, and diminished sensation within the treatment areas. The problem of diminished sensation is usually temporary and generally lasts for only a few months. The approximate cost of liposuction surgery is $1,500 to $3,000.

MICROLIPOINJECTION

Microlipoinjection autologous fat transplantation, or *fat transfer surgery,* is a relatively new procedure for the correction of deep facial grooves, scars, and other contour deformities. Developed in France, the procedure has only recently been available in the United States. At present, it is practiced by only a handful of American cosmetic surgeons, some of whom are now using the technique for cheek, chin, and even breast augmentation.

Fat transplantation is usually performed in the physician's office, under local anesthesia. The actual procedure consists of suctioning fat tissue from the abdomen or thigh through a needle and replanting it through the same needle into the face or neck to smooth out scars and wrinkles. Both donor and recipient sites require anesthesia. The process is repeated until the desired correction is achieved and then a pressure dressing is applied to prevent blood accumulation and excessive swelling. Since no incisions are made into the skin, no scars result. There are only tiny puncture wounds that quickly disappear within a few days. Patients are generally up and about the day of the procedure.

Because the person's own fat tissue is being transplanted, there is essentially no risk of allergy or rejection of the injected material. However, the long-term risks and complications of this procedure are still unknown. In addition, since no drug or foreign implant material is used, the procedure did not require FDA approval, as compared, for example, to injectable collagen, which required years of safety and efficacy investigations before the FDA approved its use for the general public. More needs to be learned about this promising procedure.

ELIMINATING UNWANTED BLOOD VESSELS

Telangiectasias is the medical term for superficial, unwanted "broken" blood vessels. When telangiectasias occur on the lower extremities, doctors often refer to them as *spider veins,* or *sunburst* or *starburst* varicosities because of their appearance. When numerous on the face, telangiectasias merge together to form a reddish-bluish fishnet pattern that adds a distinct ruddiness to the face.

Spider veins are more common in women. Unlike varicose veins (chapters 16, 17), which are dilations of the larger, deep veins of the legs, sunburst varicosities are dilations of the tiny veins located high up within the skin. These vessels supply neither oxygen nor nutrition to your skin and basically represent cosmetic nuisances.

The precise reasons why these abnormal blood vessels develop is not yet completely understood. However, a hereditary predisposition seems to exist for the development of both facial telangiectasias and spider veins of the legs. Sun damage, excessive alcohol intake, and acne rosacea are known to contribute to the development of facial telangiectasias (chapter 7). Prolonged periods of standing or sitting and injury to the leg from a blow or fall are also believed to be causative factors in the development of spider veins.

Facial telangiectasias are commonly treated by electrolysis. The procedure consists of delivering a tiny electric current through a very fine needle directly to the blood vessels to close them off. Your skin, not being "aware" that the dermatologist is only attempting to do it a cosmetic favor, responds to the treatment by making an effort to re-form or rechannelize the damaged blood vessels. As a result, each treatment site may require one to four treatments spaced at two- to four-week intervals to achieve the desired cosmetic results. The cosmetic results in most cases are quite gratifying. Most people can expect a 75 to 80 percent overall improvement.

Many people find the electric current slightly uncomfortable, but it is administered for only a fraction of a second at a time. Occasionally, tiny pit scars form at some treatment sites, but this is generally minimized by using the smallest amount of current necessary to do the job. The development of slight redness, swelling, and small crusts at the treatment sites are the most common aftermath of treatment and these are generally temporary, lasting no more than a few days. The approximate cost per treatment session is $150 to $300.

Electrolysis is unsuccessful for treating spider veins of the legs. For these vessels, *sclerotherapy* is the treatment of choice. Sclerotherapy is a surgical procedure that involves the use of a syringe with an extremely fine needle through which a tiny amount of *sclerosing* (scar-inducing) solution is injected into the unwanted vessels. Superconcentrated salt solutions are the only liquids approved for this use in the United States. In Europe, however, a variety of other sclerosing solutions have been used successfully. Individuals with a history of blood clots in the legs or lungs are not candidates for this therapy, and sclerotherapy is *not* recommended for facial telangiectasias.

Immediately following injection, the sclerosing solution displaces the blood within the vein, causing it to turn white. Next, it causes irritation to the blood vessel walls, which ultimately leads to closing them off through clot and, later, scar formation within the treated vessels. During the procedure and for a few moments afterward, most people complain of slight discomfort, burning, or a cramping sensation. An ice pack may be applied to the treatment sites and sometimes a pressure bandage.

The majority of spider veins disappear two to eight weeks

after sclerotherapy. As with electrolysis of facial telangiectasias, several treatment sessions spaced at two- to four-week intervals are usually required to achieve satisfactory cosmetic improvement. Here, too, most people can look forward to a 75 to 80 percent overall improvement in appearance. The approximate cost per session is $100 to $350.

Complications of sclerotherapy include the development of small blisters that occur when small amounts of the injected solution leak into the surrounding skin around the injection sites. Fortunately, these blisters generally dry up quickly. Temporary bruising and swelling may also occur. Occasionally, blotchy dark frecklelike pigmentation develops at a treatment site. While such pigmentation often fades with time, it may take several months.

It is important to be aware that successfully eliminating facial telangiectasias or spider viens by either technique doesn't prevent the appearance of new ones. A need for future treatments, several months or several years later, is the rule. Nevertheless, until we learn ways to prevent the formation of these abnormal blood vessels, these techniques provide significant cosmetic relief for many people.

SUPPLEMENTARY PROCEDURES

BREAST SURGERY

Breast surgery generally refers to two kinds of cosmetic breast surgery: *augmentation mammaplasty* and *reduction mammaplasty*. As their names suggest, augmentation mammaplasty is a surgical procedure to enlarge breasts, and reduction mammaplasty is an operation for reducing breast size.

AUGMENTATION MAMMAPLASTY This procedure is designed to improve the appearance and contour of the breasts in women who are troubled by small, underdeveloped or asymetrical breasts. Today it is the most common cosmetic procedure performed on a single area of the body. Some 94,000 women had breast enlargement surgery in 1986. Performed under local or general anesthesia in a hospital or outpatient surgical clinic, breast augmentation surgery consists of implanting special materials within the breast. The incision may be made around the areola, the pink area surrounding the nipple, in the lower portion of the breast, or more rarely, in the armpit area. A pocket is then created, either under the chest muscles or directly under the breast tissue itself. Next, a saclike implant containing either a liquid solution, a silicone gel, or a combination of both is inserted into the newly created pocket (Figure 11.5). Finally, tiny stitches are used to close the incision, which generally heals to a nearly imperceptible scar. The operation takes about 1½ hours. (The direct injection of foreign materials or liquid silicone into the breast caused many serious complications in the past and is no longer performed.)

Postoperative discoloration, swelling, tenderness, and pain are common for several days following breast surgery. Special bandages may be needed initially, and often special bras must be worn for several weeks after surgery. Vigorous exercising, stretching, and lifting are interdicted for several weeks until healing is complete. Some women complain of numbness around

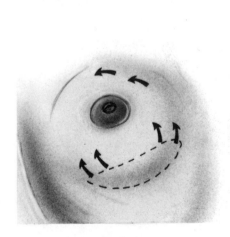
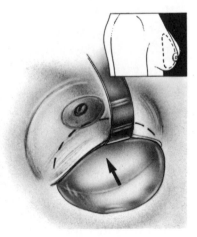

Incision under breast
to create pocket

Inserting the implant

Figure 11.5   Breast augmentation surgery

the incision lines, but this problem is usually temporary. Scar formation around the implants causes others to complain of an abnormal sense of hardness to the breasts. This usually necessitates the surgical removal of the surrounding scar tissue or performing an *enclosed capsulotomy,* a technique for breaking up the scar tissue from the outside.

One attempt to avoid these difficulties is the use of the so-called Même implant, a silicone implant covered by a spongy polyurethane layer. By forcing scar tissue to grow in and around it, the outer polyurethane layer is supposed to prevent the formation of a firm, continuous scar capsule. However, the jury is not yet in on the overall benefits of the Même implant over the others currently used.

Complications of breast surgery have been estimated to occur in as many as 20 to 25 percent of all patients. These include the development of infections and abscesses, bleeding, slow wound healing, wound separation, hardening of the tissues around the implant, and inflammation of the breast blood vessels (*thrombophlebitis*).

REDUCTION MAMMAPLASTY While thousands of women seek cosmetic surgery to enlarge their breasts, thousands more are plagued by overly large breasts. Not only are such women troubled by their physical appearance, but because they must constantly carry the weight of their breasts, they may even suffer back and neck problems, shoulder discomfort, and pain from tight-pulling or cutting brassiere straps. For such women, reduction mammaplasty means not only an improved body contour, but freedom from pain and less restricted physical activity. A complete breast examination, which may include mammography, is performed before surgery to ensure that no underlying problems coexist.

Breast reduction surgery is usually performed in a hospital or outpatient ambulatory surgery setting under general anesthesia. The most common surgical technique chosen is referred to as a *brassiere pattern skin reduction.* In this procedure both horizontal and vertical incisions are made around the areola. Next, through these incisions, excess amounts of fat, fibrous tissue, and skin are removed. Afterward, the areola and nipple, while still attached to underlying tissue, are recentered on the breast. Surgeons usually avoid completely detaching the areola and nipple, since a detached nipple permanently loses all sensation. Occasionally, however, in women with extremely large breasts, the areola and nipple must be detached completely from the underlying tissue and recentered. In this case, loss of nipple sensitivity becomes a trade-off. Following either technique, the wound is closed with fine sutures. The entire operation takes about three hours.

The postoperative course, potential risks, and complications of breast reduction surgery are about the same as those already described for augmentation surgery. The approximate cost of breast surgery is $1,000 to $2,500.

ABDOMINOPLASTY

Abdominoplasty or *abdomen tightening* is a procedure used to cosmetically improve a protruding or pendulous abdomen. Weak abdominal muscles, overweight, and pregnancy contribute to this condition that distresses many people. This procedure is designed to improve the contour of the body by narrowing and flattening the abdomen. It is by no means a substitute for weight loss and it is best reserved for those instances where strict dieting and regular exercise have not been helpful. The ideal candidate for abdominoplasty is a person of normal weight who has weak abdominal muscles and excess skin and fat.

Abdominoplasty is usually performed in the hospital under general anesthesia. While several procedures are available, the most commonly used one involves a U- or W-shaped incision that allows an "apron" of redundant tissue to be removed. One incision is made across the pubic area from one hip bone to the other. A second incision is made around the belly button. Next, the skin of the abdomen is lifted up as far as the bottom of the breast bone and separated from the underlying abdominal wall. Excess fat and fibrous tissue covering the underlying muscles, and excess skin are then cut away. The remaining skin is pulled down tightly and stitched into place to give a taut abdomen. Finally, the navel is repositioned and sutured in place, and elastic pressure bandages are applied.

Patients can usually return home after four days in the hospital. Support garments must be worn for several weeks. Heavy lifting, straining, and vigorous physical activity have to be avoided during that period. Scars remain where the incisions were made, but these become increasingly less noticeable with time, and most people are quite satisfied with the trade-off. The extent of cosmetic improvement depends upon such factors as the individual's innate body build and general skin tone.

The complication rate for this procedure remains quite high, occurring in more than one-third of those undergoing the procedure. Complications include infection, bleeding, death of normal skin tissue at the suture sites, delayed wound closure, and wound separation. However, in most cases, these complications are mild and the ultimate cosmetic result quite satisfactory. The approximate cost of abdominoplasty is $1,500 to $2,500.

HAIR—TOO MUCH OR NOT ENOUGH

*C*urrently available evidence suggests that since the appearance of mammals on the earth, body hair and sexual attraction have been inextricably linked to breeding and preservation of the species. Given the apparent evolutionary link between hair and sexual attraction, it is not entirely surprising that attractive hair continues to be admired. Today's mating rituals, if you will, include hair dyeing, perming, straightening, conditioning, thickening, and blow-drying, to name but a few. Precisely because of this continued preoccupation with hair, too little of it in some places and too much in others can be the source of much embarrassment and emotional distress.

The purpose of this chapter is twofold: to focus on the more common causes of hair loss *(alopecia)* and what can be done about it, and to discuss the causes and management of the often no less vexing problem of excess facial and body hair *(hirsutism)*. A dermatologist should be consulted if you suffer from either of these problems. Depending upon the specific causes, satisfactory treatments are currently available for many hair problems.

NORMAL HAIR

Hair is made of a nonliving fibrous protein, keratin. (You may recall that keratin composes the nonliving, horny layer of your skin.) The *root,* the only living and reproducing region of the hair unit, lies deep below the skin surface, at the base of each hair follicle. Living cells within the root produce the nonliving hair shafts. Because your hair is no more alive than the clothing you wear, no hair-care product can "make your hair come alive," or "rejuvenate," "nourish," or "feed" it.

Each strand of hair, regardless of which portion of the body it is from, is composed of two primary layers (Figure 12.1). The outer layer, which is actually composed of a number of overlapping layers, is known as the *cuticle* and serves to protect the inner layer, the *cortex,* from splitting and fraying. The cortex provides the support for the hair shaft.

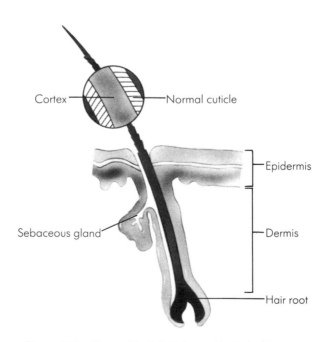

Figure 12.1 Normal hair follicle and hair shaft

Virtually the entire surface of the human body is covered by hair. The only places truly devoid of hair are the palms and soles, the tips of the fingers and toes, the glans penis, and the mucous membranes. All other apparently hairless regions of the body actually contain *vellus* hairs, which are ultrasoft, uncolored, very short hairs. They resemble the *lanugo* hairs that cover the fetus during most of intrauterine development. *Terminal* hairs are the long, thick, coarse, pigmented hairs typical of the scalp, face, armpit, eyebrow, eyelid, extremities, and pubic regions.

Hair growth occurs in cycles. Each cycle contains three phases: a growing phase, a resting phase, and a falling-out phase, known respectively as the *anagen, telogen,* and *catagen phases* (Figure 12.2). Generally speaking, at any one time, approximately 85 percent of hairs are in the anagen (growing) phase, 11 percent in the telogen (resting) phase, and 4 percent in the catagen (intermediate) phase. On a yearly basis, you lose most hair in November, and the least in May. Between 50 and 100 hairs are normally shed from the scalp each day.

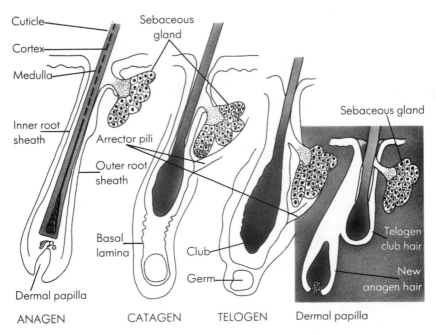

Figure 12.2   Phases of the normal hair cycle

The average growing phase of scalp hairs lasts two to six years, the average resting phase one to two weeks, and the average falling out phase about two to three months. On average, hair grows about ½ to ¾ inch each month. Hairs are shed at the end of the resting phase and replaced by new anagen hairs from the same follicles. No new follicles are made after birth.

Scalp hair varies in color, shape, curl, and thickness even on the same person. These differences are largely attributable to genetics, i.e., inheritance. Blonds tend to have more but thinner hairs—about 130,000 hairs in a normal scalp. Redheads have fewer but thicker hairs—approximately 80,000 hairs; and brunettes are somewhere in between in number and caliber—about 100,000 hairs.

In addition, racial genetics also play a role. Whites tend to have thinner, more elliptically shaped hairs, blacks flattened and curly hairs, and East Asians thick and straight hairs. However, East Asians and blacks tend to have less overall body and facial hair than whites.

In terms of chemical structure, two types of chemical bonds are responsible for how curly, wavy, or straight your hair is. *Hydrogen bonds* are very weak bonds. You can break them temporarily by merely wetting your hair with water. This is why wet hair can be styled easily. *Sulfur bonds,* on the other hand, are strong chemical bonds not easily weakened. They must be broken to create more lasting hair styles, which the chemicals in perming and straightening products are formulated to do.

FRAGILE OR THIN HAIR

There are two kinds of hair-loss problems that do not actually involve any abnormal loss of hair: naturally thin hair and fragile hair.

The thickness of individual hairs is an inherited trait. Some people have naturally very fine hair and others coarser hair. I mentioned earlier that blonds typically have very fine hair and Orientals very thick hair. In general, given the same hair density, that is, the same number of hairs in every square inch of scalp, people with blond hair will usually look as though they have less hair than, for example, their redheaded counterparts. This can sometimes be confused with true hair loss.

While there are as yet no ways to thicken naturally fine hair permanently, temporary thickening of individual hairs can be achieved in a number of ways. The regular use of protein-containing conditioners and body builders can help create the impression of thicker hair. Hydrolyzed proteins and henna are ingredients that have been found to be most useful as thickeners. These ingredients can temporarily bind to the hairshaft, making hair appear less sparse.

The use of hair dyes is another means for thickening naturally fine hair. Hair dyes not only coat the hairs, but also alter their permeability and cause them to swell. If you have thin hair and were already considering dyeing it another shade, you could accomplish both your goals in one step. You must be careful, however, not to overbleach your hair to prevent excess hair fragility. If you don't wish to change your hair color, and would simply like to thicken your hair, choose a hair dye that exactly matches your natural hair color.

Fragile hair also mimics true hair loss. Excessively bleached, permed, or straightened hair tends to be extremely fragile, while excessive sun exposure, the use of overly harsh detergents, and overzealous combing, brushing, or blow-drying can worsen the problem. Individuals, particularly children, who habitually bite, chew, or twirl their hair also damage their hair and promote fragility. Some emotionally disturbed adults, usually women, suffer from a condition known as *trichotillomania,* a compulsion to continually pluck out their hairs.

Fractured hairs create the false impression of a hair-loss problem by exposing patches of scalp; short, broken hairs simply do not cover well. One quick and easy way to determine whether your hair is actually falling out or simply breaking is to examine the ends of your hairs. If a white bulb (the remnant of the root) is present, the hair has fallen out. If no white bulb can be found and you feel stubble when running your fingers over your scalp, it is likely that your hairs are breaking off.

A breakage problem need not be permanent, however. Discontinuing bleaching and perming or refraining from habitual manipulation of the hair is all that is usually necessary to permit hair to regrow normally. In addition, the use of conditioners can be especially helpful for keeping bleached or permed hair more supple and less breakable.

TRACTION ALOPECIA

Traction alopecia refers to hair loss or balding due to prolonged or excessive tension on the hair (more precisely, upon the roots of the hairs). Traction alopecia is a frequent problem among black women, where styling practices such as "corn-rowing," braiding, and hair plaiting are common. Hair loss, most pronounced over the temple regions, is typical of this condition. However, white women are by no means immune to traction. Pigtails and ponytails, or the excessive use of tight rollers, have made traction alopecia everyone's problem. As you might expect, hair breakage and fracturing also occur and add to the traction problem, making the overall picture appear even worse than it is.

The remedy for traction alopecia is easy. If the culprit styling practices are stopped before permanent destruction to the roots has occurred, most, if not all, of the lost hair will usually begin to regrow normally within several months. On the other hand, if these styling practices are continued, permanent alopecia can result.

STRESS-INDUCED HAIR LOSS

It may sound like a mouthful, but *telogen effluvium* simply means stress-induced hair loss. A variety of physical and emotional stresses on the body are known to be responsible for this condition, including serious illnesses, episodes of prolonged high fever, surgery (occasionally even minor surgery), pregnancy, delivery, the cessation of birth control pills, crash dieting, psychiatric illness, divorce, and loss of a loved one. Postpartum hair loss is probably the best-known example of telogen effluvium.

Certain stresses are believed to affect the hair growth cycle so that in some cases as many as 40 percent of the hairs are shifted prematurely from the growing phase into the falling-out phase.

(Interestingly, this abnormal shifting parallels the seasonal molting pattern characteristic of many other mammals.) Telogen hair loss may not be apparent at first. However, stress-induced alopecia can cause considerable hair loss, and when more than 40 percent of the hairs are lost at one time, the alopecia is apparent and distressing.

In full-blown cases, hairs typically fall out in batches on clothing, pillows, etc., which often prompts an emergency visit to the dermatologist. Because telogen effluvium typically begins from one to three months after the onset of the stress, many people fail to make the association. Happily, in most instances, telogen effluvium is not permanent. Once the stress is past, hair usually regrows normally without treatment within several months. If the stress is ongoing, however, the problem may be prolonged.

The diagnosis is usually made from the patient's history. In addition, the dermatologist may pluck some hairs (hair pluck analysis) to confirm the overabundance of telogen hairs and to look for other hair shaft abnormalities. In general, individual hairs are best examined close to the root rather than at their free ends to avoid confusing a true abnormality with the effects of hair shaft weathering. Weathering may be caused by a variety of environmental assaults, including excessive washing and styling, friction, and exposure to sun, wind, or chlorinated swimming water.

Your physician may also order a variety of blood tests to exclude other causes of hair loss. Finally, you may be advised to make a collection of hairs that have fallen out over several weeks in order to determine whether the hair loss is still in an active phase or tapering off. In general, the best form of therapy for telogen effluvium is simple reassurance of the temporary nature of the problem.

ALOPECIA AREATA

Alopecia areata is a common hair-loss condition affecting people of any age, particularly young adults. A familial predisposition can be found in as many as one-fifth of all cases. Round, stark, hairless patches are typical of alopecia areata, which may affect any or all areas of the body. Isolated patches do occur, but usually several appear simultaneously or in tandem. Fractured hairs resembling exclamation points—they taper, then widen at their bases—are characteristically observed along the periphery of the hairless patches and are a helpful diagnostic sign.

The precise cause of alopecia areata is not known, but there is evidence to support the belief that it is a kind of "allergy to self"; that is, a condition in which the body's germ-fighting system *(immune system)* malfunctions and begins attacking the roots of the hairs instead of germs. Doctors refer to such conditions as *autoimmune diseases.* And, while the exact role of stress in alopecia areata is unknown, it is believed to trigger or worsen alopecia areata in some cases.

Alopecia areata can range from mild to severe, and total hair loss can occur. As in the case of stress-induced alopecia, hairs are shifted en masse to the telogen stage and fall out in clumps. When the entire scalp is involved, the condition is known as *alopecia totalis.* When the entire body is involved, the condition is aptly called *alopecia universalis;* in its most severe form, the eyelashes, eyebrows, and pubic hair are also lost.

The diagnosis of alopecia areata and its variants is usually straightforward. In less clear-cut cases, other laboratory tests such as blood tests, fungal scrapings, and Wood's light examination may be ordered to exclude other conditions. Occasionally a small punch biopsy of the scalp is needed to confirm the diagnosis. Other autoimmune conditions that are known to be associated with alopecia areata must also be looked for and excluded. These include *Hashimoto's thyroiditis, Addison's disease, pernicious anemia, juvenile-onset diabetes mellitus,* and *vitiligo.*

In general, the older the individual at the time alopecia areata first appears, the better the prognosis, and the smaller the area of involvement, the better the outcome.

A number of treatments are currently available. Small patches may be treated by the application of high-potency topical corticosteroid creams, particularly with children. In many cases, individual patches are best treated by periodic intralesional injections of anti-inflammatory corticosteroids. Response to therapy is often seen after three or four sessions spaced at three- to four-week intervals. Oral steroids are sometimes used with limited success.

The application of topical *minoxidil,* an antihypertensive drug that has been found to stimulate hair growth, has been found preliminarily to be effective in stimulating regrowth in one-third to one-half of patients with alopecia areata. The use of physical irritants and allergens, such as DNCB, anthralin, and poison ivy resin, for reasons that are not entirely clear, also occasionally stimulate hair regrowth. Finally, the use of PUVA (chapter 8) has likewise been demonstrated to work in selected individuals.

ANAGEN EFFLUVIUM AND OTHER CAUSES OF REVERSIBLE ALOPECIA

Just as physical and emotional stresses can precipitate telogen hair loss, certain frequently prescribed drugs can precipitate hair loss in the anagen (growing) phase. Interference with hair growth in the anagen phase generally leads to narrowing of the hair shafts, hair shaft fragility, or complete failure of hair formation. Drugs that have been associated with anagen hair loss include the antigout medication, *colchicine;* blood thinning agents *(anticoagulants)* such as *heparin* and Coumadin; anticancer drugs such as Cytoxan, Imuran, and Daunomycin; and certain *cholesterol-*

lowering drugs. Normal hair growth is restored once the offending drugs are stopped.

A number of infections, metabolic and endocrine conditions, and drugs have also been linked to various forms of alopecia. These include *superficial fungus infection, syphilis, hypothyroidism* (low thyroid output), *iron-deficiency anemia,* and *malnutrition* (uncommon in the United States). Common drugs known to produce alopecia in certain individuals include the antiacne agent Accutane, the antiarrhythmic and antihypertensive agent Inderal, and the anti-Parkinson drugs *L-Dopa* and *bromocriptine.* Fortunately, in most of these cases, treating the underlying condition, or eliminating the causative drug, leads to complete regrowth of hair.

HEREDITARY HAIR LOSS

No chapter about hair problems would be complete without a discussion of *androgenetic alopecia* or hereditary hair loss. Two popular misconceptions that need to be dispelled immediately are that only men suffer from balding and that the tendency for balding is inherited from the father. Women most certainly do suffer from hereditary hair loss, and the trait for balding can be inherited from either parent. Both men and women normally produce *androgens* (male hormones) and a key factor in hereditary balding is believed to be a heightened sensitivity of scalp hair follicles to these male hormones.

The pattern of hair loss differs between men and women. In male pattern alopecia, the progression of hair loss often begins with recession at the temples and/or the crown of the head. If the condition progresses, only a small fringe of hair may remain on the back and sides of the head. In women, hair loss is typically gradual and is most conspicuous toward the top center of the head. While hair loss in women can diffusely expose large areas of the scalp, complete balding is exceedingly rare. Consequently, most women with this problem can be reassured that they are unlikely to "become bald like a man."

Diagnosing male/female pattern alopecia is usually easy. However, other, potentially remediable causes usually need to be excluded before the diagnosis can be made conclusively. Where some doubt about the diagnosis exists, the dermatologist may order additional tests and perform a scalp biopsy.

A cure for baldness has been sought for centuries, and today potions, magic elixirs, creams, and dreams abound. Nevertheless, since we are currently unable to perform genetic engineering, there is still no cure for androgenetic alopecia.

In the meantime, two forms of therapy have proven beneficial in managing selected cases of androgenetic alopecia: *minoxidil* and *hair transplantation.* Minoxidil (Loniten) is an antihypertensive drug. When orally administered to control high blood pressure, it was serendipitously observed to cause facial and scalp hair growth in many patients. When tested in topical form for treating baldness, between 5 and 10 percent of individuals demonstrated cosmetically acceptable hair regrowth. In still others it was believed that the progression of hair loss may have been halted.

More recently, topical minoxidil has been combined with topical Retin-A cream to treat alopecia. The initial data are encouraging. To date, preliminary studies have demonstrated a 30 to 50 percent cosmetically acceptable hair growth with this combination; however, further studies are needed to corroborate these findings. Another antihypertension agent capable of stimulating hair growth, *viprostil,* is being tested, but the results are not in yet.

Since male hormones are believed to be central to both male and female pattern alopecia, antiandrogen medications known to block the effects of these hormones have been tried with some success. These include Cyproteron *(cyproterone acetate),* the diuretic Aldactone *(spironolactone),* and the antiulcer drug Tagamet *(cimetidine).* In one study of Aldactone, 54 percent of patients with female pattern androgenetic alopecia reported definite improvement in their condition. However, since these drugs are taken orally, are not without adverse side effects, and need to be used indefinitely to maintain their beneficial effects on hair growth, they must be administered cautiously and taken only under strict medical supervision.

Hair transplantation has been performed for nearly thirty years. Although it is not a cure for baldness, it is a means for utilizing the hair that you have remaining to best advantage. Using local anesthesia, small plugs of hair-bearing scalp tissue are removed, usually from the back of the head, and transplanted into the bald areas. Each plug may contain six to twelve hair follicles, and anywhere from forty to one hundred donor plugs are transplanted during one session. Several sessions are usually required to cover a large area. In the properly selected candidate, results can be quite gratifying.

Scalp reduction, a surgical procedure that is often coupled with hair transplantation, is most often performed when large areas of balding preclude the successful use of hair transplantation alone. As its name implies, scalp reduction involves the removal of significant portions of the bald areas, so that fewer donor plugs are needed to cover the remaining area. Occasionally, scalp reduction may be performed by itself to remove an isolated patch of baldness.

HIRSUTISM

Hirsutism, the medical term for excess hair, is defined as excessive terminal hair in women on the upper lip, chin, sideburns, chest, upper back, abdomen, and thighs. Such hairs tend to be coarser and darker than normal hairs. Hirsutism is believed to result from either or both an overproduction of androgens or an increased sensitivity of the hair follicles to normal levels of androgens.

Unwanted or excessive hair can be the source of enormous cosmetic embarrassment and psychological distress. To make matters worse, our culture and folklore has long stigmatized women with this problem.

For the purposes of diagnosis and therapy, dermatologists generally divide hirsutism into two main groups: endocrine gland causes and nonendocrine gland causes. Hirsutism may be related to benign or malignant tumors of the adrenal gland, ovary, and occasionally the pituitary gland. It may also arise from subtle disorders in the function of these glands (functional disorders), in which androgens are overproduced.

When overproduced, androgens can cause serious skin and health problems. If untreated, androgen overproduction may lead to *virilization (masculinization)*. This could include deepening of the voice; the onset of severe, stubborn acne; increase in muscle mass; changes in the distribution of body fat; shrinkage of the breasts; menstrual irregularities; male pattern hair loss; enlargement of the clitoris; and the appearance of the typical diamond-shaped male pattern of pubic hair distribution (the so-called *male escutcheon*). When any of these signs are present, medical attention should be sought as soon as possible.

Nonendocrine causes of hirsutism include racial or familial tendencies for excessive hairiness. In certain racial and ethnic groups, the production of excess body hair is a normal part of growth and development. Among Mediterranean and Middle Eastern peoples, for example, hirsutism is quite typical and normal. In others with this condition, a family trait for excess hair development may be evident. Finally, various medications, among them the anticonvulsant Dilantin and the antihypertensives Loniten and Hyperstat, may cause excess hair production to occur.

Most women with excess, unwanted hair are usually motivated to consult a dermatologist for cosmetic reasons and understandably are often impatient to begin therapy for their problem. Nevertheless, it is important to be absolutely certain that no serious underlying causes for hirsutism are overlooked. A careful history, physical examination, and special blood tests usually clinch the diagnosis. When indicated, endocrinologic and gynecologic consultations may be needed. In most cases of hirsutism, no glandular abnormalities are found and the focus can safely shift to the cosmetic problem of eliminating the unwanted hair.

ELIMINATING UNWANTED HAIR

MECHANICAL METHODS OF HAIR REMOVAL

PUMICING AND TWEEZING   Two inexpensive ways of temporarily removing unwanted hair are pumicing and tweezing. *Pumice stones,* made from volcanic rock, are abrasive materials that can be used to rub and wear away fine unwanted hairs. Hairs removed in this way grow back and pumicing ordinarily must be repeated every few days. For some people, pumicing is a satisfactory means of hair removal. Abrasive methods are not without their drawbacks, however. They are generally time-consuming and often irritating to the skin. A rich, nonacnegenic, all-purpose moisturizing cream or lotion, such as Moisturel lotion, should be used afterward to lessen irritation.

Depilatory gloves are a variation of pumicing. They look like mittens and are generally made of very fine sandpaper. With circular movement and without applying pressure, they can smooth troublesome stubble away. The main advantages of depilatory gloves are that they are easy to use, work quickly, and can be conveniently used several times a day, even at work.

Tweezing or plucking is an old but extremely cheap, quick, and effective means for temporary hair removal. Each pluck generally starts a new growth cycle within the hair root. Occasionally, and fortuitously, repeated tweezing of the same hairs can damage the hair root so much that hair removal at those sites may be permanent. In most cases, however, tweezing needs to be repeated every six to eight weeks. Unfortunately, tweezing tends to be very uncomfortable, and sometimes even very painful. As a result, few hairs are usually plucked at one time. In addition, pimples, pustules, and ingrown hairs often form at tweezed sites. When this occurs, your dermatologist might prescribe an antibiotic astringent, such as T-Stat or Eryderm lotions, for use afterward.

WAXING   Although it may be performed at home, most waxing is done in professional salons. Waxing consists of applying a hot, melted wax to the site of the unwanted hairs. As the wax cools, it solidifies, and the unwanted hairs become embedded in it. Then the wax is stripped away from the skin, carrying with it the embedded hairs down to their roots and leaving the skin quite smooth. In general, waxing must be repeated every six weeks. Cold waxing actually differs little from hot waxing except for the addition of an adhesive strip to the wax application. Overall, waxing is one of the best methods of hair removal, and some contend that is the best method for home use.

Waxing has several drawbacks, however. It may be painful and irritating to your skin, a severe burn could occur if it's applied before the wax has cooled sufficiently, and unwanted hairs must be allowed to grow to an unsightly length of approximately ¼ to ½ inch *above* the skin surface before they can be waxed again.

SHAVING Shaving is the fastest, easiest, and one of the least expensive methods for removing hair from large areas, and it has the added advantage of being painless. While shaving usually must be repeated every one to two days to prevent stubble from becoming obvious, shaved hairs *do not* regrow faster or thicker or darker thereafter. Although most women regularly shave their underarms and legs, many women with excess facial hair dislike the masculine connotation of shaving their faces and choose other methods instead.

For shaving, the choice of electric razor or safety razor is largely one of personal preference. Electric razors are generally less irritating to the skin and less likely to cause nicks and cuts. On the other hand, they usually don't give as smooth a shave as safety razors. Before using a safety razor, your skin should be thoroughly moistened with water and richly lathered with shaving cream. By contrast, if you choose to use an electric shaver, your skin should be completely dry before shaving.

CHEMICAL METHODS OF HAIR REMOVAL

BLEACHING Although bleaching is not a means of removing hair, it is a simple and common means for dealing with unwanted facial hair. Bleaching is cheap, easy to perform, and leaves no stubble or roughness. In general, the less striking the contrast between the bleached hairs and your normal skin color, the more satisfying the cosmetic result. It follows, then, that bleaching usually works best if you have a light complexion. The effects of bleaching generally last one to four weeks. You can buy commercially available bleaches, such as Jolen, or you can make your own with 20 percent hydrogen peroxide to which a few drops of household ammonia have been added.

On the down side, bleaching is time-consuming, and if the bleach is not left on long enough, hairs become reddish in color, rather than blond. Unfortunately, a number of people are sensitive or develop sensitivities to the peroxide and ammonia ingredients contained in home or commercial bleaches. To minimize skin irritation, avoid wetting your skin and always apply a good moisturizer after bleaching. In addition, before bleaching a large area of skin, you should apply a small amount of bleach to a tiny test area of your skin. If no irritation results after about thirty minutes of contact with your skin, you may proceed to bleach the desired area.

CHEMICAL DEPILATORIES (HAIR REMOVERS) Available in cream, lotion, and foam formulas, chemical hair removers are inexpensive and simple to use. Calcium thioglycollate, a chemical used in certain permanent waving and hair straightening products, is the most common ingredient found in today's hair removing creams. It works by disrupting the strong sulfur bonds in hair.

Commercially available as creams, chemical depilatories remove unwanted hairs by reducing them to a jellylike mass that can be easily wiped away. Since they work above and below the surface, chemical depilatories leave your skin smooth, although it tends not to be quite as smooth as after waxing. Like bleaches, however, they have the potential for irritating the skin; a test application before first using them is advisable. In addition, they tend to be expensive to use, time-consuming, and may leave a residual odor on your skin. A good moisturizer should be used afterward to minimize irritation.

ELECTROLYSIS

Electrolysis is the only well-established, *permanent* means of hair removal, and this remains its primary advantage over other methods. Electrolysis consists of sliding a small electric needle, called an *epilating needle,* down the hair shaft to the base of the hair follicle and destroying the hair root at the base with an electric current. In general, an experienced electrologist may be able to treat as many as several hundred hairs in one session, which usually lasts about forty-five minutes.

Unfortunately, professional electrolysis tends to be expensive, often painful, and requires many treatment sessions as regrowth occurs approximately 40 percent of the time. In many cases of extensive facial hair, a year or more of frequent, periodic treatments may be required to achieve satisfactory cosmetic results. Pimples, ingrown hairs, and scarring are occasional complications of electrolysis. The services of an experienced, licensed electrologist should be sought. In general, your local dermatologist is the best source for referral to a competent electrologist(s) in your area.

For women with fewer unwanted hairs, home electrolysis units are available. These tend to work slowly and require patience; only about fifty hairs can be done per hour. Permatweez, a battery-powered unit produced by General Medical Company in Los Angeles, claims to have a self-correcting, protective spring-action mechanism that allows the rounded needle to spring right down to the hair root *only* when the needle has been *properly* inserted into the opening of the pore. After only a few practice sessions, most people can become quite proficient at using these devices.

Finally, a relatively new method of hair removal, employing radiofrequency waves, is now available for home use. Radio waves are transmitted down to the hair roots through a specially designed tweezer. The manufacturer of one such product claims that their device is safe, effective, easy to use, and free of any of the drawbacks of electrolysis. According to the manufacturer, hairs treated by this method tend to grow back less coarse, and after repeated treatments eventually do not regrow at all. Whether this method will live up to its manufacturer's claims remains to be seen.

MEDICAL TREATMENTS FOR HIRSUTISM

Oral agents, which either suppress androgen secretion or block its effects (antiandrogens), are occasionally prescribed in select cases of hirsutism. (Because of their antiandrogen effects, they are also used to treat cases of severe acne vulgaris and seborrhea.) In general, antiandrogens suppress terminal hair growth. Cyproteron (cyproterone acetate), not generally available in the United States, has demonstrated some success. Temporary side effects of this drug in some patients have included weight gain, swelling of the legs, dry skin, itching, depression, and loss of libido; long-term effects remain unknown.

For some women with hirsutism believed to be related to excess production of ovarian androgens, the use of an oral contraceptive, particularly Demulen, to suppress ovarian secretion, may be beneficial. For those with adrenal oversecretion, the short-term use of oral prednisone or *dexamethasone* to suppress the adrenal gland has met with some success. However, because of their potential side effects, the long-term use of steroids is not generally recommended for treating hirsutism.

Aldactone (spironolactone), another oral antiandrogen, seems thus far to be the most promising drug treatment for hirsutism. Although it is not FDA-approved for this use, Aldactone has been available for many years in the United States as a diuretic. Recent trials of this drug for hirsutism and acne have been encouraging, and side effects have been few. However, the long-term safety and efficacy of Aldactone for use in hirsutism awaits more extensive and rigorous testing. For now, its major disadvantage is that it takes at least a year before any benefit is seen.

Finally, it should be clear that the perfect antiandrogen is not yet available; no current drug can completely suppress terminal hair growth or completely reverse the condition. Thus, the various cosmetic measures described above remain the mainstays of treatment.

GOING TO EXTREMITIES: HEALTHY NAILS AND FEET

A super skin deserves to have super complements. Well-groomed nails make hands appear more graceful and give a finishing touch to your overall appearance. When beautiful, they reflect not only a healthy concern for yourself but a sense of self-confidence. Although it can be argued that feet don't get the same kind of exposure, nevertheless they make a statement about you and how you've kept them; a smooth, well-manicured foot completes the picture of total skin health.

But of course, neither nails nor feet are really ornamental. Nails protect your fingertips, particularly the sensitive nail beds below the nail. They enhance your sense of light touch. They are also useful for picking up things such as coins and sheets of paper. Just as important, they act as windows to your general health; doctors often use them as clues to the presence of underlying illnesses.

Leonardo da Vinci called the foot a masterpiece of engineering. In the course of an average day, the feet of an active person sustain the impact of about 5 million pounds. As any podiatrist will tell you, a complex relationship exists between the general condition of the bones, ligaments, tendons, and so forth, *within* your feet, the condition of the overlying skin, and your overall health.

In order to remain healthy, your nails and feet need proper care. This chapter discusses the keys to such care, the uses and abuses of nail cosmetics, and ways to prevent and treat a variety of common, distressing problems that affect nails and feet.

ANATOMY OF A NAIL

Nails are much more complex than they appear (see Figure 13.1). Like the uppermost layer of your skin, nails are composed of tightly bound layers of nonliving materials. The *nail plate,* or simply, the nail, is largely composed of keratin, the same protein composing your skin and hair.

Nail strength is believed to be a function of both composition and shape. The epidermis of your skin is primarily composed of soft keratin. By contrast, your nails, like your hair, are composed of hard keratin, and nail hardness is largely attributed to the high sulfur content of hard keratin. Furthermore, the characteristic shape of the nail—that is, the front-to-back and side curvatures of your nails—imparts greater strength than a flat surface.

In addition to keratin, small amounts of calcium, phosphorus, and trace metals such as chromium, selenium, and zinc are found in the nail plate. Nails are relatively porous, and some investigators believe that the calcium in nails is not a natural constituent but is absorbed from the outside (from soaps, etc.). Others, however, maintain that calcium is a normal constituent of the nail.

Regardless of the controversy, almost everyone agrees that calcium contributes little, if anything, to nail hardness. The importance of the other trace substances in nails is still unknown. Finally, *phospholipids,* found in the uppermost and lower layers of the nail plate, are believed to be responsible for nail flexibility.

The *nail matrix* is the living and growing area of your nail. Special cells within the matrix ceaselessly grow and divide and produce new nail. Unlike hair, which grows in cycles, your nails grow continuously throughout your life. Any damage to the matrix can result in distorted nail growth and deformed nails; permanent damage to the matrix results in permanent deformity of the nail.

Most of the nail matrix is hidden from view below the skin of the *posterior nail fold,* which is located at the base of the nail plate. Pressure on the nail by the posterior nail fold is believed to be one reason that your nails grow forward, rather than straight up. Another reason may be that nail matrix cells are

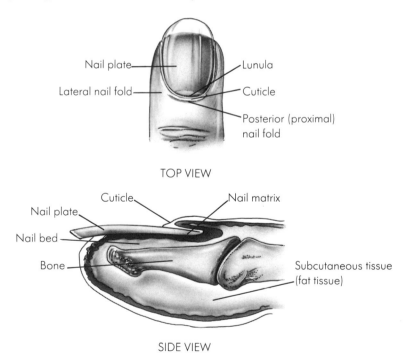

TOP VIEW

SIDE VIEW

Figure 13.1   Normal nail unit

oriented in a forward direction. The *lunula,* the white, crescent-shaped area at the base of your nail, is the only area of the matrix visible to the naked eye.

The *cuticle,* the opaque skin fold at the base of your nail, is basically an extension onto the nail plate of the epidermis of the finger or toe. By no means an imposing structure, the cuticle still serves a very important function: It protects the base of the nail from irritation and infection.

The *nail bed,* which lies directly below the nail plate, is soft, thick, and grooved, and serves to cushion the nail plate. The nail bed plays no part in the formation of the nail plate; however, it contains many small blood vessels that oxygenate and nourish the nail matrix and specialized structures called *glomus bodies,* which are responsible for the regulation of the blood supply to the digits in cold weather. The nail bed also acts as something of a safety net; if you should lose a nail for any reason, the nail bed can compensate by hardening to form a tough protective barrier.

FACTS ABOUT YOUR NAILS

Nails grow about ¼ inch each month. The actual growth rate varies among people but is constant with any one person. However, nails on the same hand or foot grow at slightly different rates. The average time for fingernails to grow from the base to the free edge is about six months. Toenails grow at about one-third to one-half the rate of fingernails and take from twelve to eighteen months to grow from base to edge. Nails grow faster during childhood, pregnancy, in summer, and in hot weather. Playing the piano, typing, and nail biting also speed up nail growth. Curiously, in most cases, the longer the finger, the faster the nail growth. Thus, the middle fingernail grows the fastest, followed by the ring and index fingernails. Nails on your right hand generally grow faster than those on your left.

Normal growth patterns may be adversely affected by such things as winter, cold weather, general illness, and malnutrition.

As a rule, nail growth also slows as a person ages. Between the ages of twenty-five and ninety-five, the rate of nail growth gradually falls to nearly 50 percent of what it was during youth. In general, nails, especially toenails, tend to become thicker, more irregular, and misshapen with age.

PROPER NAIL CARE

To ensure strong, beautiful nails, you must always be mindful of what I believe is the first and most important rule of proper nail care: *Be kind to your nails.* This means making a special effort to protect them from injury. It means avoiding using your fingernails as tools. It means using a pencil to dial the telephone, not rummaging around the bottom of your handbag, and remembering to pick things up with your fingerpads instead of your fingernails. It also means wearing protective gloves, such as rubber gloves, at work (depending on the nature of your work), when performing household chores, while gardening, or while pursuing your favorite hobbies. It especially means using protective gloves when washing dishes or changing diapers. Exposure to household soaps, detergents, and solvents can overly degrease, dry, and damage your nails, making them rougher, more brittle, and more likely to split. And being kind to your nails also means refraining from overdoing home *or* professional manicures, which if performed clumsily may damage sensitive structures such as the cuticle and pave the way for infection and other nail conditions.

Finally, proper nail care means knowing about the safety and correct use of the nail cosmetics currently on the market. Used correctly, nail-care products can enhance the beauty of your nails and keep them strong and healthy. Used incorrectly, they can be the source of many problems.

CLIPPING, FILING, AND TRIMMING YOUR NAILS

Nails need to be clipped and trimmed regularly. To prevent unnecessary problems, clipping and filing must be performed gently and properly. In addition, trimming overgrown cuticles must be executed with special care. Some simple guidelines, therefore, are in order.

Ingrown nails, particularly ingrown toenails, are among the most common problems resulting from an improper clipping technique. They occur when a sharp corner of a nail embeds itself like a knife into the nearby nail fold. Swelling, tenderness, pain, and infection are frequent complications. To prevent ingrown nails, clip or cut your nails *straight across,* rounding them only slightly at the edges. When filing your nails, use only the fine side of the emery board or a diamond file. Always file your nails toward the center instead of toward the sides. Finally, to bevel the edges of your nails, hold the emery board at about a 45-degree angle and pass the fine side of the board around the edges of your nails.

Your cuticles are especially important structures and must be manipulated carefully. Before working on them, soak them in warm water for a few minutes; it helps to soften them so that they can be more easily manipulated and trimmed. To prevent unnecessary pressure and damage to the underlying nail matrix, push back wide or unsightly cuticles *gently* with your fingertips or a towel. Don't use orange sticks, metal nail files, or "cuticle pushers"; used incorrectly, these cause unnecessary trauma, which can result in the subsequent development of unsightly horizontal ridges and furrows in your nails. Special cuticle creams and oils intended to soften cuticles and keep them soft are no more effective than regular skin moisturizers. An ordinary all-purpose moisturizer or even plain olive oil used after soaking will do the job nicely and should be applied to the nail folds as well.

STRENGTHENING YOUR NAILS

Good health, good nails? Unfortunately, not always. Even with proper nail care, brittleness and splitting may occur. These are not uncommon problems among women between the ages of thirty-five and fifty, and nail dryness is a contributory factor in many instances. While there is no cure for constitutionally fragile nails, practicing the following simple nightly regimen can be helpful. Soak your fingertips, nails completely submerged, in lukewarm water for ten to fifteen minutes. Gently pat them dry and immediately apply a potent moisturizing lotion directly over your nails. For best results, your nails should still be moist and soft from soaking. I generally prescribe Lac-Hydrin Lotion (available by physician prescription only) for this purpose. Complex-15 (a moisturizer containing phospholipids) may also be helpful. In general, special nail creams with a granulated consistency for smoothing nails are seldom necessary.

DON'T WASTE YOUR TIME AND YOUR MONEY

If you suffer with nail problems, you've probably heard of or tried many supposed remedies from friends or relatives. Gelatin has been, and still is, frequently recommended for strengthening weakened, splitting nails. Sold in powder or capsule forms, gelatin, a protein, is supposed to nourish and harden nails when taken daily. Unfortunately, gelatin remains of unproven value and is probably useless. For one thing, the protein in nails is keratin, which differs from the protein found in gelatin. For another, any protein in the gelatin is broken down by your stomach and intestines into its components and is no more taken into the growing area of your nails than any of the other nutrients you eat.

Calcium supplementation has also been touted to promote nail growth and hardness. This idea gained some support recently, following the observation that some women taking calcium supplements for a bone-thinning disease called *osteoporosis* claimed to have noticed faster-growing and stronger nails. As I mentioned earlier, nails naturally contain very little calcium and some, if not most of it, comes from the environment. It is, therefore, extremely unlikely that taking calcium supplements can be of any real value, except perhaps psychological. On the other hand, taking large amounts of calcium without a physician's supervision is not without its potential risks. Overconsumption of calcium supplements in a vain attempt to help strengthen nails can be dangerous to your general health and should be avoided *unless* prescribed by your physician.

Finally, several other remedies deserve brief mention. These include the use of B-complex vitamins, high doses of vitamin A, and seaweed. Iron may be a hard metal, but unless you have been found to have iron-deficiency anemia, iron supplements will not help to strengthen your nails. The test of time has proven all of these remedies valueless.

NAIL COSMETICS

Generally speaking, great care and expertise go into the manufacture of nail cosmetics. It is remarkable that manufacturers have been able to formulate products that are basically uniform in color and consistency, easy to apply, quick drying, water resistant, and relatively resistant to chipping. Nail cosmetics didn't really exist before the 1920s, except for ordinary paints and shellacs. Today there is an almost staggering array of nail-care cosmetics, including nail polishes, base coats, top coats, nail polish removers, nail hardeners, nail conditioners, nail menders, and artificial nails.

Nail-care cosmetics are estimated to account for less than 10 percent of reactions to all cosmetics. Considering the overwhelming numbers of people who use these products every day, it is truly remarkable that so few untoward reactions occur. Nevertheless, they can and do occasionally occur.

NAIL POLISHES

Americans spend about $200 million annually for nail polishes alone. Polishes, or nail enamels as they are also called, are intended to add color to your nails and protect them. The active ingredients in nail polish include *nitrocellulose, pigments, resins,* and *plasticizers.* As a rule, to permit better adherence of polish to your nails, nail enamels do *not* contain oil or wax moisturizing bases.

Derived from plant cellulose, nitrocellulose is the main film-forming, waterproof, varnishlike ingredient in nail polish. It imparts toughness and durability. Some nail polishes also contain nylon fibers for thickening and strengthening nails. Pigments (colors) and sometimes pearlizers (shimmer producers) are added to give the polish its final color and shade. Resins improve its adhesion and gloss. Finally, plasticizers add gloss and make polish less brittle when dry.

When putting on nail polish, take care to apply it evenly to the nail plate and avoid inadvertently spreading it onto your cuticles or the surrounding nail folds.

The continued use of some very darkly colored nail enamels, particularly dark reds or browns, can occasionally lead to deep discolorations of your natural nails. Some of the pigments in these enamels tend to leak out of the nail varnish and penetrate into your nail. Interestingly, the color of the stain often differs from the color of the polish, e.g., a deep red polish may stain the nail yellow. Although this is disconcerting, it represents no permanent nail damage; discolorations generally grow out with the nail.

Nail polishes are occasionally responsible for allergic reactions. Naturally, if you already know that you are allergic to all polishes, you should avoid using them altogether. Instead, you can use a buffing paste and chamois buffer to give your nails a high gloss. However, buff gently to avoid irritation. If you find that you are allergic to a specific nail polish color, switch brands. If after switching brands you are still allergic, switch colors. If you continue to have problems but still wish to use nail polishes, see your dermatologist, who can perform special patch tests to determine which ingredients you are allergic to.

NAIL POLISH REMOVERS

Acetone or acetone derivatives are the active ingredients in nail polish removers, and they are quite effective. However, too frequent use can damage the nail by removing some of the cementing substances that hold the nail plate together. Moreover, acetone is equally capable of degreasing normal skin and can be quite drying and irritating. For that reason, always rinse off your hands thoroughly after using nail polish removers. Finally, when choosing a nail polish remover, look for ones that contain oil or lubricant additives; these ingredients can help to lessen some of acetone's drying action.

BASE COATS AND TOP COATS

Base coats are essentially clear nail polishes intended to coat the nail before regular nail polish is applied. By providing this type of undercoat, base coats help nail polishes to adhere better. They also help to prevent nail and nail polish chipping.

Top coats, which differ little from base coats, are intended to be applied directly on top of regular nail polish for the purpose of increasing glossiness and preserving the finish. Unfortunately, in certain sensitive people, both base coats and top coats can be irritating or allergenic. In most cases, I have found that a sufficient rest period from all nail cosmetics usually enables these people to use nail polishes safely again—minus base coats or top coats—without a recurrence of their problem.

NAIL HARDENERS AND BUILDERS

Nail hardeners, which are liquids containing formaldehyde or formaldehyde-releasing ingredients in 5 to 10 percent concentrations, are intended to prevent nail chipping, fraying, and peeling. When applied regularly to your nails, they work.

Unfortunately, formaldehyde and its derivatives are common irritants and allergic sensitizers. These chemicals can cause a variety of nail problems, including excessive dryness and brittleness, discoloration, discomfort, separation of the nail from the nail bed, nail loss, and even bleeding under the nail plate. Irritation of the surrounding skin and cuticle may also occur. Unhappily, these reactions may last for weeks or even months before resolving.

Given the number of adverse reactions, it is hardly surprising that the FDA has restricted the sales of nail hardeners. Those available in the United States today are really modified nail polishes in which the amount and quality of the resin have been altered slightly. Even in Europe, where true nail hardeners are still sold, those containing formaldehyde must so state clearly on the product label.

If you choose to use nail hardeners, do so only occasionally. *Limit their application to the tips of your nails.* There is little sense in subjecting the entire nail plate to the hardener when the tips of your nails are ordinarily the sites most likely to split or fracture. Finally, avoid spreading hardeners onto your cuticles or the surrounding skin where they can be particularly irritating.

Nail builders are protein-containing liquids often advertised as being capable of "nourishing" or "feeding" your nails. As I mentioned earlier, since nails are composed of nonliving protein, there is no way that they can be "nourished" or "fed" from the outside. Nevertheless, the protein in nail builders can serve to fill in any shallow pits or other fine surface irregularities present on your nails. Like a base coat, this allows nail polish to go on more smoothly and adhere better.

ARTIFICIAL NAILS

Three basic types of artificial nail products are currently available, and each is composed of water-impermeable plastics.

Glue-on preformed artificial nail kits frequently contain acrylate adhesives. Allergic reactions to these products are quite common, and acrylates may provoke irritation in the nearby cuticle and surrounding skin. The overuse of glue-on nails can result in brittleness, splitting, fraying, and discoloration of the natural nails.

A second type of artificial nail is a preformed nail with an adhesive backing, which you can simply press on. Because no glues are necessary for binding them to your natural nails, this type of nail generally causes the fewest problems.

Sculptured nails, the third type of artificial nail, are created by a salon technique. A metallized paperboard template is placed around your fingertips, and sculptured nails are formed upon the surface of your natural nails by the application of layers of acrylic polymers. These polymers are then molded (sculpted) to the desired length and thickness. The bonding between the prosthetic and natural nails is permanent. A number of people have experienced severe allergic reactions, infections, and pain with sculptured nails. And, if for any reason the artificial nail must be removed, surgery is usually needed because of the tight bonding between the prosthetic and natural nails.

The prolonged use of any type of artificial nail can cause injury, even permanent damage, to your natural nails. Because they cover your natural nail and do not permit the evaporation of any moisture that accumulates under them, softening and lifting off of the underlying nail may occur, particularly if the artificial nails have been left in place for several days. Artificial nails, most especially sculptured nails, account for a very substantial percentage of adverse reactions to all types of nail cosmetics.

Overall, I advise against the use of all types of artificial nails. However, if you really want to use them, I suggest the press-on nails. But whatever you use, *remove all types of artificial nails as soon as possible.* They should not be left in place for more than a few days at a time.

COMMON NAIL PROBLEMS

NAIL INJURY

Trauma to your nail or nail matrix or repeated exposure to certain chemicals can result in temporary or even permanent damage to your nails. Accidents, such as striking your fingernail with a hammer or getting it caught in a door, often cause bleeding and bruising of the soft tissue under the nail. The often frightening-looking black-and-blue mark that usually forms under the nail following these types of injuries may take several weeks or months to disappear (i.e., to grow out normally).

Occasionally, bleeding under your nail may continue, and the mounting pressure of the accumulated blood may cause severe pain. In this case, your doctor may need to pierce your nail painlessly with a red-hot, flame-heated paper clip to release the trapped blood, a measure that usually produces immediate relief.

Injury to your nails can have both immediate and long-term effects on their appearance. If the nail matrix is only mildly injured, ridging, the development of white spots, separation of the nail from the nail bed, and even temporary nail loss may subsequently occur. Once they have developed, these problems persist for months until a new, healthy nail grows out. If the matrix is severely damaged or destroyed by trauma, however, a permanently distorted *(dystrophic)* nail develops. In general, the extent of nail deformity following injury depends upon the extent of the nail matrix damage.

Less serious forms of trauma limited to the nail, such as nail biting or the tic of using the index fingernail to scratch the thumbnail, result in unsightly nails, but no permanent damage to the nail unit. Although often easier said than done, merely breaking the habit in these cases permits nails to regrow normally.

DISCOLORATIONS

Nail discoloration can result from numerous causes. The presence of underlying illnesses, such as certain liver, kidney, or glandular diseases; the ingestion of certain drugs; injury to the nail or its matrix; and certain inflammations and infectious diseases such as fungus infections and psoriasis are among the more common conditions that occasionally give rise to nail discolorations. Cirrhosis of the liver and kidney disease are associated with whitening of the nails. Some of the other conditions are discussed in the following sections. Fortunately, many of these conditions are treatable and should be brought to the attention of a dermatologist.

Thin brown streaks that run from the base of the nail to the tip are quite common in black people and are perfectly normal and no cause for concern. In most instances, these streaks represent ordinary moles (beauty marks, birthmarks) located under the nails. Similar brown streaks in whites, in whom they are much more uncommon, however, should be brought to the immediate attention of a dermatologist. While, in most cases, they may simply represent ordinary moles or traumatically induced black-and-blue marks under the nails, the possibility of malignant melanoma (chapter 10) must be excluded.

A few of the more common chemicals and drugs that *occasionally* cause nail discolorations are listed below:

RESORCIN (topical antiacne drug): can cause yellow-brown nails

TETRACYCLINE (common antiacne antibiotic): can cause yellow-brown nails

MINOCYCLINE (antiacne antibiotic): can cause bluish-gray discoloration

BETA-CAROTENE (vitamin A derivative): can cause yellowish discoloration

CHLOROQUIN (antimalarial drug): can cause bluish-brown discoloration

NICOTINE (from cigarettes): can cause brown nails

NAIL POLISHES, base coats, nail hardeners: can cause yellow-brown nails

INK: can cause discoloration depending upon the ink color

Finally, *pseudomonas,* a particular bacterial infection of the nails, is responsible for the development of a deep green discoloration of the nails. This infection is not uncommon among people whose hands are continually in water, such as professional dishwashers, bartenders, waiters, and nurses. Soaking the nails daily in a solution of equal parts of white vinegar and water for several weeks usually cures this infection.

BRITTLE AND SPLITTING NAILS

Nail brittleness and splitting tend to become more of a problem as people age. In some people, conditions such as poor circulation and arthritis may contribute to these problems. In younger people, however, contact with harsh detergents or other cleansers, and the overuse of nail polish removers, nail hardeners, or artificial nails are common causes of brittleness and splitting. While there is no cure, the use of protective gloves when appropriate, the routine use of nail polish for nail protection and splinting, the infrequent use of nail polish removers, and the avoidance of nail hardeners and artificial nails are advisable. Soaking your nails nightly in lukewarm water followed by the liberal application of an all-purpose moisturizer can also be helpful.

HANGNAILS

Hangnails are actually splits in the skin along the sides of nails that usually form on excessively dry and cracking skin. They may also result from paper cuts, overaggressive manicuring, or the nervous habits of picking and nail biting. At times, hangnails may be responsible for causing a good deal of discomfort or even pain. They also tend to catch on clothes or other objects. The proper nail care (outlined above) and the use of protective gloves when washing dishes or clothes help to prevent dryness and hangnail formation.

Treating hangnails is simple. *Carefully* snip them off with a clean, fine pair of scissors or a cuticle clipper. Avoid the temptation to pull the tip off a hangnail. This usually results only in ripping more deeply into the tender flesh at its base. Following clipping, the base of the hangnail usually heals like any other simple cut.

BACTERIAL, FUNGAL, AND YEAST INFECTIONS

When damaged in any way by trauma, irritation, or allergy, the nail folds, the skin surrounding your nails, become subject to a variety of bacterial, fungal, and yeast infections. If left untreated, these infections usually affect nail appearance, growth, and color. If the infecting organisms attack the nail matrix, permanent nail deformities may occur.

BACTERIAL AND YEAST INFECTIONS

Cuts and breaks in the skin around your nails commonly occur as a result of accidental injury, splinters, nail biting, improper manicuring, and excessive dryness. They are especially common in persons whose hands are constantly wet, such as dishwashers, bartenders, and waiters. In general, normal skin is quite resistant to infection; however, a break in the skin paves the way for the entrance of bacterial and yeast infections. Candida, the same organism responsible for causing common yeast vaginitis, is the most frequent fungus to attack the skin *surrounding* the fingernails. *Staphylococcus aureus* (or just plain staph) is the most common bacterial germ to do so.

Paronychia is the medical name for the infection that results when either bacteria or yeasts attack the skin around your fingernails, particularly the posterior nail fold (see Figure 13.1). An acutely infected nail fold is typically red, irritated, swollen, pus-filled, and painful. Temporary infection can cause nail ridging. More prolonged paronychia can result in the formation of severe nail distortion and discoloration or even complete destruction of the matrix.

Of course, prevention, as outlined earlier, is the best form of therapy for bacterial or yeast paronychia. When paronychia is severe, your doctor may have to drain any accumulated pus, examine the material under the microscope, culture it, and begin oral and topical antibiotic or antiyeast therapies. If treatment is initiated early, the nails gradually regrow normally. Untreated infections, however, or those for which treatment was delayed, may result in permanent damage to the nail matrix; this, in turn, may result in permanently misshapen nails.

Besides yeasts, other kinds of fungi, most commonly *Trichophyton rubrum* (the ringworm fungus), are capable of directly attacking the nail plate. These fungal infections produce thickened, lusterless, deformed, ridged, and yellowish nails. In addition, they can cause whitish flaking and pitting of the nail surface, and the formation of thick, crumbling, powdery debris below it. Although they usually require many months of combined oral and topical antifungal therapy, fungal infections of the nails are curable in many instances. Consultation with a dermatologist is important.

PSORIASIS

Psoriasis is an inflammatory condition that can affect the skin, scalp, and nails (chapter 8). When it involves the nail unit, psoriasis can be damaging in a number of ways. In many respects, such damage resembles that caused by fungal infections (see above).

The more common nail changes seen in psoriasis include pitting, horizontal furrows, crumbling, whitish or yellowish discolorations, and loosening and lifting of nails. In more severe cases, fingernail psoriasis is associated with a potentially destructive rheumatoid-arthritis-like inflammation of the joints of the fingers (psoriatic arthritis). Although no cure is yet available for psoriasis, a variety of therapies have been found helpful. Psoriatic nail dystrophy may be treated by the application of high-potency topical corticosteroids such as Temovate cream, or by therapeutic injections of corticosteroids such as Kenalog suspension. The application of the anti-skin-cancer cream Efudex (chapter 10) has also been found helpful in some cases. Prompt evaluation, treatment, and follow-up by a dermatologist are essential.

COMMON FOOT PROBLEMS

Selecting healthy footwear is an extremely important part of proper foot care. Unfortunately, it may not guarantee you complete freedom from developing some common foot problems. Some of these are hereditary and can even occur when shoes are not worn, although they can be aggravated by wearing improperly fitted shoes.

Bunions, high and *low arches* (flat feet), and *gout* are examples of hereditary foot problems. Such conditions represent congenital defects in foot structure, function, or metabolism. A bunion is an enlargement of the joint behind the great toe or small digit.

As the affected joint becomes increasingly deformed, the involved toe and other toes are pushed out of alignment. Arch problems may cause tiredness, discomfort, and pain in the feet. Finally, gout, a metabolic disease in which uric acid crystals are deposited in the joints, often affects the great toe. Swelling, tenderness, and pain are common. More detailed discussion of these conditions is outside the intent and scope of this book. However, if you suffer from any of these problems, particularly gout, medical consultation is strongly advised.

In keeping with the sole's primary function to protect and cushion your foot, the skin there is ten times thicker than elsewhere on your body. Nevertheless, despite this degree of protection, skin problems occur there, as well as on the more delicate skin on the top and sides of the feet. The following sections are devoted to the prevention and treatment of several of the most frequently encountered problems affecting the skin of your feet. Two very common foot conditions, athlete's foot and plantar warts, are discussed in chapter 9, and the management of excessive perspiration, another fairly common foot condition, is covered in chapter 14.

ROUGH SKIN

Dry, scaly skin, particularly on the heels of your feet, is a rather common problem and one that some people seem more prone to develop than others. In addition, habitually walking barefoot or wearing loose sandals can often contribute to this problem. If rough skin is a problem for you, you may find relief by simply applying an all-purpose moisturizer to your feet regularly. As explained in chapter 3, for best results, moisturizers should be applied immediately after your bath or shower, when your skin is still moist or wet. If roughness and scaliness persist, see your dermatologist, who can prescribe, if necessary, a more potent prescription moisturizer, such as Lac-Hydrin Lotion, or a keratolytic agent (a peeling medication) to help remove scales and smooth the roughened skin.

BLISTERS

Blisters on your feet may develop for a variety of reasons. Highly inflammatory fungus infections of the feet (tinea pedis), particularly those caused by the organism *Trichophyton mentagrophytes,* often cause blistering, weeping, and oozing. Contact allergies (contact dermatitis) to the chemicals in footwear, particularly leather-tanning agents, rubber and rubber cements, and shoe and sock dyes, may be responsible in certain sensitive people for the development of itching, redness, swelling, and small blisters, primarily involving the thinner skin on the more sensitive tops and sides of the feet.

Acute contact allergy of the feet is treated in the same way as contact dermatitis arising elsewhere on the skin (chapter 9). Whenever a contact allergy is suspected, an attempt should be made to identify and eliminate the offending allergen(s) in order to prevent possible recurrences; patch testing is often helpful in this regard. Once the culprit allergen(s) has been determined, your dermatologist may refer you to a shoe shop that specializes in producing custom-made shoes free of allergenic materials. Keeping your feet dry is an important self-help measure to prevent leaching out of potential allergens by sweat.

Fungal infections of your feet are diagnosed and treated in the same manner as those located elsewhere on your skin (chapter 9). Once tinea pedis is cured, however, you should wear a freshly laundered pair of socks each day, keep your feet clean and dry, and regularly use antifungal powders such as ZeaSorb-AF or Desenex, to minimize the chance of recurrence. Since warm, moist places are ideal sites for fungal overgrowth, antifungal powders should be dusted liberally into your socks and shoes and onto your feet, especially between your toes.

Larger blisters are most commonly caused by mechanical factors, such as rubbing and irritation from ill-fitting socks, shoes, or boots. These *friction blisters,* as they are appropriately called, are typically quite painful. If broken, blisters may become secondarily infected by bacteria, for which blister fluid makes a nourishing culture medium. To minimize this risk you must be extremely careful not to tear away the thin blister roof.

Treating friction blisters is usually easy. Eliminate the cause and the problem disappears. Opening the blister and draining it alleviates pain; however, to prevent infection, the blister roof should be retained. To release the fluid and alleviate the pressure, you must first thoroughly cleanse the area with alcohol. Using an alcohol-cleaned needle, puncture one or two sides of the blister *at its base.* Next, gently express its watery contents by pressing firmly on the blister roof. Finally, reclean the treated area with alcohol, then cover with a topical antibiotic such as Polysporin ointment, and a Band-Aid. Blisters treated in this way generally dry up completely in a few days and heal without a scar.

FISSURES

Fissures are simply breaks in the skin. They generally occur between the toes or around the heels. However, fissures can be extremely painful and can even cause considerable disability. Gait problems or shoe irritation are frequently responsible for the development of heel fissures, while fissures between your toes usually result from inadequate drying after bathing or showering. On the other hand, overzealous drying with a rough towel has been known to cause them and should be avoided.

Depending upon the specific cause(s) of your fissures, your dermatologist or podiatrist may simply advise the use of powders or corn starch to keep the area dry. In addition, your doctor may prescribe the use of compound *tincture of benzoin,* a sticky liquid that acts as a sealant, thereby protecting the fissures from further trauma and irritation and permitting faster healing. Once the fissures have healed, you should make sure to gently but thoroughly dry the web spaces between your toes after your bath or shower and routinely dust on some talcum powder.

CORNS AND CALLUSES

Corns and calluses on your feet result from persistent and prolonged friction and pressure on the skin. Abnormal foot function is the most common predisposing cause of these conditions; feet that possess any abnormalities of gait or even subtle abnormalities in the internal alignments of the bones, ligaments, and tendons are more prone to developing corns and calluses. This is because malalignments in the internal anatomy of the feet, referred to as *biomechanical abnormalities,* often lead to abnormal rubbing and irritation within your shoes. For example, people with a *hammertoe* deformity, an abnormality in which the toe is bent upward in a flexed position, are especially prone to corn formation over the affected area. Finally, corns and calluses frequently result from wearing poorly fitted shoes, especially those that pinch your two outside toes.

Corns and calluses are composed of the same cellular elements. They are largely *hyperkeratoses,* that is, markedly thickened areas of skin (Figure 13.2). To the naked eye, however, corns appear round or cone-shaped, and possess tips (sometimes mistakenly called *roots*) that point into the skin instead of outward. These points act like needles or nails driven into your skin. Appropriately, the medical term for them is *clavi* (Latin for "claws"). Because of this, corns are frequently extremely painful.

While most corns are found on the outside of your toes, *soft corns* are found between the toes (Figure 13.2). These tend to be whitish, moist, soggy, and soft; hence their name. *Seed corns,* groups of tiny pinhead-size corns, most often develop on the soles.

Calluses, or *callosities,* are thickenings of skin that form over bony prominences. Calluses are the skin's means of protecting its deeper structures from repetitive outside irritation. Calluses are not usually painful, but like corns, they occasionally can cause considerable pain and disability. The heels and the center of the balls of the feet, especially in women who frequently wear high heels, are common locations for callus formation.

Temporary relief from corn and callus discomfort may be obtained by covering them with either protective (nonmedicated) corn pads, small circular spot Band-Aids, or moleskin. Soft corns may be temporarily helped by drying the web spaces between your toes thoroughly and separating the toes with lambswool. To shrink corns and calluses, soften them first by soaking them

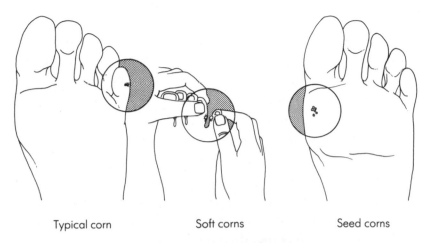

| Typical corn | Soft corns | Seed corns |

Figure 13.2 Types of corns

for ten or fifteen minutes in lukewarm water. They are easily manipulated when moist. Pat dry and while the skin is still relatively moist, you may thin the corns and calluses by gently abrading them with a pumice stone (a piece of volcanic glass pressed into a rough-textured stone, purchased in any drug store) or a metal file. Unless advised by your doctor, you should avoid using scissors, razors, callus parers, and medicated pads.

Naturally, for long-term relief, evaluation and treatment by a dermatologist or podiatrist is advised. Custom-made insoles, *orthotic devices,* or ready-made insoles, such as Spenco Insoles, may be recommended by your doctor to stabilize your feet, redistribute body weight, or simply cushion your feet. Depending upon the individual circumstances, surgery is sometimes necessary to rectify the underlying biomechanical abnormality.

INGROWN TOENAILS

An ingrown toenail forms when a sharp edge of your toenail acts like a knife and penetrates deeply into the fleshy skin next to it, the lateral nail fold. This usually results from cutting your nails too short or too far back at their corners. Obesity and constitutional problems, such as possessing abnormally curved toenails or unusually large big toes, are other causes of ingrown toenails. The big toe is most frequently affected.

At first, you may notice only slight redness and tenderness. If the condition is allowed to continue, however, swelling, pain, and a pus-filled discharge will follow. Without proper medical attention, severe infection can result, and can even spread more deeply to involve the underlying bone.

In most cases, ingrown toenails are preventable. Wear shoes wide enough and long enough to minimize pressure on your toenails. (Tight, pointed-toe, Italian-cut styles are more likely to cause problems.) Being careful to cut your toenails straight across (preferably with nail clippers) and flush with the underlying pads of the toes is another important self-help measure. Leave your nail edges *slightly* rounded, rather than with sharp points.

Mild cases of ingrown toenail can usually be treated at home. Soaking the affected toe daily in warm water by itself is usually quite soothing and can speed healing. Packing a sterile wisp of cotton under the affected nail edge in some cases can lift the nail edge far enough away from the surrounding flesh to allow healing and subsequent normal nail growth.

If secondary infection should occur, or if the condition otherwise worsens, see your doctor. Occasionally, the entire nail or a portion of it will need to be surgically removed (*total* or *partial nail evulsion*), in order to allow it to grow back normally. If you continue to suffer from recurring ingrown toenails despite these medical therapies, your doctor may suggest the use of caustic chemicals or surgery to permanently destroy the portion of the nail matrix that continues to give rise to the ingrown portion your nail. Fortunately, in most cases this procedure, known as *matricectomy,* is rarely necessary.

SPECIAL CARE FOR SPECIAL PLACES

*B*y this point you have probably realized that your skin is not one uniform organ from the top of your head to the tips of your toes. Individual areas of your skin differ in a number of important ways. Therefore, to maintain healthy skin, each area of your skin has to be cared for with regard to its own unique requirements. Several regions of your skin, specifically the genital and anal areas and the underarms, require special consideration. This chapter addresses the common problems affecting these sites, how to prevent them, and what to do about them if they occur.

GENITAL AREA

GENITAL DEODORANTS

Genital deodorants, or "feminine hygiene sprays" as they are frequently called, are largely unnecessary. Genital deodorants, which generally contain antiseptics and fragrances, are commercially available as aerosol sprays, aerosol powder sprays, and premoistened towelettes.

To varying degrees, most healthy women have natural vaginal odors. The vulva—that is, the vagina and its surrounding lips—contains many special sweat glands known as apocrine glands (chapter 1). Apocrine gland secretion is normally odorless. However, as part of their metabolism, skin bacteria, which ordinarily colonize the vulva harmlessly, act to break down these secretions, and it is these breakdown products that cause vaginal odor.

Tight-fitting jeans, underwear, and panty hose contribute to odor production by reducing sweat evaporation and providing a warm, moist environment in which the odor-causing bacteria flourish. Besides odor, tight-fitting garments can cause vulval inflammation, itching, and even infection. Doctors have appropriately nicknamed the condition "panty hose dermatitis."

Foul-smelling vaginal odors, particularly when accompanied by a discharge, are abnormal. Such odors may be due to various infections or vaginitis. Common infectious causes of foul-smelling vaginal secretions include *nonspecific vaginitis,* a bacterial infection caused by the organisms *hemophilus* or *gardnerella; Candida* (yeast) infections; and *Trichomonas* and *Chlamydia* infections (chapter 15). In addition, forgotten tampons or diaphragms and occasionally menstrual fluid may be responsible for such odors. In these cases, removal of the foreign object, followed by soap and water cleansing, quickly eliminates the problem. Medical attention should be sought for any condition that does not clear up promptly with simple measures.

Attention to genital hygiene prevents many of these problems. Routine gentle soap and water cleansing and keeping the area dry are more effective measures—and certainly safer ones—for controlling vaginal odors (and preventing infection) than the use of deodorant sprays. In addition, vaginal deodorants may sting, irritate, or burn this sensitive area. In a few instances, these products have been associated with urinary tract infections. They have also been responsible for swelling and true allergic contact dermatitis. Finally, but quite important, by masking a problem, vaginal deodorants may delay seeking proper medical intervention. In sum, avoid feminine deodorant sprays and seek dermatologic or gynecologic attention if you have any specific questions or problems.

VAGINAL DOUCHING

In general, advertising notwithstanding, vaginal douching is unnecessary for *routine* genital hygiene. Occasionally, however, gynecologists or dermatologists may prescribe douches to treat certain bacterial or fungal infections of the vagina. Sometimes they also recommend them for preventive use in people who tend to suffer recurrent episodes of vaginitis.

The ingredients contained in commercial douches sometimes cause irritation with routine daily use. In some cases, they can injure the cells lining the vagina or the nearby urethra and even predispose one to vaginal infections or urinary tract infections. They may upset the delicate acid-base balance within the vagina. They can wash away natural lubricants. Finally, they can reduce or eliminate the bacteria that normally colonize the vagina and whose presence is necessary to maintain the optimum acid-base balance there.

Commercially available douches typically contain five major types of ingredients: detergents and alkalis for cleansing, antiseptics for suppressing bacteria, emollients for lubrication, acids for approximating the normal vaginal acid environment, and fragrances. In general, you should avoid using a douche more than once or twice a week, unless, of course, your doctor recommends it.

ANAL ITCHING

Anal itching, or *pruritus ani,* as doctors call it, can be a very annoying and embarrassing problem. It is also responsible for many sleepless nights. It is especially common in males. Since anal itching is accompanied by an intense urge to scratch, and since such scratching is not feasible in public, anal itch is an extremely troubling problem for the sufferer. In severe cases, itching and the desire to scratch may become an obsession.

The diagnosis of pruritus ani is usually reserved for those cases where no clear-cut disorder can be found to account for anal itching. Conditions causing anal and *perianal* (the skin region around the anus) itching and inflammation include atopic dermatitis, contact dermatitis, psoriasis, and seborrheic dermatitis (chapter 8). Bacterial, fungal, and yeast infections (chapter 9) and pinworm infestation are other common causes of this condition. Finally, swellings and growths, such as hemorrhoids, anal polyps, and anal skin tags can also cause intense itching. If you suffer from anal itching, you should see your dermatologist. Satisfactory treatments are available for each of these conditions; most important, treating the underlying condition generally ends the itching.

Irritation from the presence of fecal material on the anal skin is believed to be the most common cause of pruritus ani, and one not associated with the presence of other skin diseases. The anus is composed of a series of circular folds of delicate flesh. These folds often serve as traps for fecal material and shield it from being wiped away with toilet tissue. Feces contain certain bacteria whose metabolic products have been found capable of provoking itching. Perspiration and trapped feces then combine to cause anal irritation. In some cases, especially in older people, weakening of the anal sphincter may contribute greatly to the problem. The observation of underwear streaked with feces is generally an excellent clue to the cause of the irritation.

In many cases of pruritus ani, simply paying greater attention to proper anal cleansing is usually all that is necessary to put an end to irritation and itching. For people with more persistent problems, however, I usually recommend the use of soft, white, unscented facial tissues instead of ordinary toilet tissue. Facial tissue tends to be gentler than even the gentlest toilet tissues. After each bowel movement, place a small amount of a mild moisturizing lotion, such as Moisturel or Balneol, on a clean facial tissue and gently massage the anal region to remove any entrapped fecal material. Residual moisturizer need not be wiped away and can serve as both lubrication and protection. If necessary, for additional protection or comfort, apply the moisturizer again at bedtime. For those with particularly sensitive anal skin and those with poor anal sphincter tone, the hygiene regimen just described must be followed for life. If not, recurrence of the problem is likely.

UNDERARM PROBLEMS

Sweating and odor represent the two most common underarm problems. Like the genital and anal areas, your underarms possess special apocrine sweat glands (chapter 1), which become active only after puberty. However, an offensive odor is produced when sweat is acted upon by the bacteria that normally colonize your armpits. These bacteria are particularly active in the warm, moist areas of your underarms and groin, where evaporation does not occur readily. *Deodorant soaps, deodorants,* and *antiperspirants* have been formulated to deal with perspiration and odor.

DEODORANT SOAPS

Few experts will disagree that regular soap and water cleansing is the single most effective way of reducing underarm odor; when perspiration and bacteria are washed away, there can be no odor produced. The major drawback of plain soap and water cleansing for body odor is that bacteria and perspiration soon return. Deodorant soaps, which contain antibacterials such as *triclocarban* (Safeguard and Dial) or *triclosan* (Lifebuoy), can be helpful in suppressing bacteria and prolonging the antiodor effects of soap and water cleansing.

Unfortunately, some people, particularly those with naturally dry or sensitive skin, may find these soaps too irritating and drying to use on a regular basis. Those with normal skin may use these soaps more liberally if necessary. However, since there are no odor-producing glands on the face and neck, I generally suggest that you use more gentle soaps for cleansing these areas (chapter 3) and reserve deodorant soaps for body use.

DEODORANTS

Simply defined, deodorants are cosmetics that are intended to reduce body odor. Deodorants may contain fragrances for masking odor, and/or antiseptics for reducing the numbers of odor-producing bacteria. The less bacteria on your skin, the less sweat they can break down into odor. Triclosan is a common antiseptic found in many deodorants. Not surprisingly, underarm deodorants today are seldom exclusively antibacterial formulations; most of them contain antiperspirant ingredients, as well.

ANTIPERSPIRANTS

As the name clearly suggests, antiperspirants are products that contain ingredients capable of reducing perspiration wetness. While various brands of antiperspirants differ in their abilities to control sweating, to be considered a true antiperspirant, a product must reduce the amount of sweating by at least 20 percent. Despite what the ads say, no antiperspirant currently available completely eliminates sweating. In fact, in the armpit, less than half of all sweat ducts are susceptible to the action of these antiperspirants.

By reducing sweat production, antiperspirants ensure that the odor-producing surface bacteria have less ammunition to use. Most antiperspirants contain aluminum salts *(aluminum chlorohydrate* or *aluminum chloride),* which are believed to reduce perspiration production by physically blocking the sweat ducts by plugging them with aluminum-containing casts. In general, lotion, cream, stick, and roll-on antiperspirants work more effectively than aerosols and pose no inhalation risks.

Surprisingly, adding more active ingredient to a particular antiperspirant does not necessarily make the product more effective. Put another way, antiperspirants that are advertised as "extra-dry" or "extra-extra-dry" may not necessarily be better than their less "dry" counterparts. Because they need time to plug the sweat gland ducts, aluminum antiperspirants generally require several hours before they reach their maximal effectiveness and also tend to be more effective after several applications. Therefore, to maximize your antiperspirant's effectiveness, you would do better to apply it first at night and then once again the following morning, rather than only in the morning.

EXCESSIVE SWEATING

Most healthy people sweat heavily on hot, humid days. However, some people sweat profusely all of the time and in some cases, the sweat literally can be seen pouring off them. *Hyperhidrosis* is the medical name for this condition. In most cases, the causes of excessive sweating are unknown. For people who suffer from it, the problems of persistent wetness, odor, and clothing stains can cause extreme and continued embarrassment and psychological distress. Frequently, people with an underarm sweating problem also suffer from profuse sweating of their feet and hands, making the simple, social act of shaking hands a nightmare.

Fortunately, hyperhidrosis can be treated. For milder cases, dermatologists may prescribe antiperspirants that are stronger than those commercially available. Some people are helped by the higher concentrations of aluminum chloride found in Xerac-AC lotion or Drysol. These products are more effective when applied at bedtime and again in the morning for the reasons discussed in the preceding section. Unfortunately, many people find these antiperspirants too irritating, especially when applied to the sensitive armpit region. For more severe cases of sweating, or for those that have not responded well to other topical therapies, your doctor may prescribe topical anticholinergics such as *scopolamine hydrobromide* or certain oral anticholinergic agents such as Robinal PH to reduce sweat gland stimulation. For palm and sole hyperhidrosis, your doctor may recommend that you soak your hands and feet in 10 percent *Formalin* or 10 percent *glutaraldehyde solutions* to cause a sweat duct blockage within the horny layer of your skin.

Finally, *tap water iontophoresis,* which consists of exposing the excessively sweaty areas of your body to a small electric current, is sometimes successful. The exact mechanism by which iontophoresis works still remains unclear. One theory maintains that it may have something to do with inducing a temporary clogging of the sweat glands within the horny layer of the skin. A second theory maintains that iontophoresis blocks sweating by disturbing the electrical gradient believed necessary for normal sweat flow within the sweat ducts.

Until recently, iontophoresis could be performed only in the dermatologist's office, a clinic, or a hospital and required the use of expensive equipment; further, multiple patient visits were required. Now, however, relatively inexpensive home units are available. A few years ago, Drionics, a home iontophoresis device, was introduced in the United States. It consists of a battery-powered generator that acts as a source of electric current. The current is delivered to the affected area through water-saturated wool pads suspended in small plastic boxes. Early reports concerning the success of this product for reducing excessive sweating have been encouraging. Unfortunately, iontophoresis is only a *treatment* for hyperhidrosis, not a cure. Even when successful, these treatments must be repeated every four to six weeks.

SEX AND
YOUR SKIN

*I*ncreased sexual freedom in our society has brought with it increases in certain kinds of skin problems; hence, achieving super skin is no longer solely a matter of proper skin care, but one of safe sex, too. Your sexual habits *can* be a source of many skin problems. This chapter covers the signs, symptoms, prevention, and treatments of many common sex-related conditions.

At one time, *venereal disease (VD)* referred to three common diseases: *syphilis, gonorrhea,* and *chancroid.* More recently, it became apparent that a wide variety of bacterial, viral, and other parasitic diseases traditionally not included in this category could likewise be transmitted through intimate body contact. To signal this change, doctors began referring to all these conditions as *sexually transmitted diseases (STDs).* While syphilis and gonorrhea are still very much a part of the list of common sexually transmitted diseases, *herpes, AIDS, genital warts, molluscum contagiosum, lice,* and *scabies* now top that list. Interestingly, the original venereal diseases are now the least common.

Most sexually transmitted diseases start either within the skin or have prominent skin manifestations at some point in the course of the illness. For that reason, all sexually active people should familiarize themselves with the signs and symptoms of the more common STDs so that they may reduce their risk of acquiring or spreading these infections and prevent unnecessary complications. This is the first and one of the most important steps in safe sex.

Fortunately, most sexually transmitted diseases are preventable, and cures are currently available for many of them. If you think you might have a problem, you should consult your family physician, internist, dermatologist, gynecologist, hospital STD clinic, or local department of health. Confirming a diagnosis of sexually transmitted diseases usually requires that your doctor perform a combination of special microscopic examinations, blood tests, and bacterial or viral culture studies.

GENERAL METHODS OF PREVENTION

Despite the fact that we are fortunate to have cures for a number of the sexually transmitted diseases, the old adage "an ounce of prevention is worth a pound of cure" is still worth heeding. Research continues actively in the pursuit of preventive vaccines for some of the more common STDs, such as herpes. Unfortunately, such vaccines are still investigational and are not commercially available. In the meantime, other measures must be followed to minimize the risk of illness.

Complete abstinence from sex is the only *guaranteed* means for preventing sex-related illnesses. For most people, however, this is hardly practical or desirable. Barring complete abstinence, only two types of measures are believed to be useful for preventing the spread of STDs: careful selection of sexual partners, and the use of barrier methods of contraception.

Limiting sexual relations to only one partner (provided that the partner is not already infected) appears to carry no risk for acquiring an STD. Unfortunately, some of the STDs may not produce any immediate symptoms, so infected people may be impossible to identify. Nonetheless, simply reducing the number of sexual partners and avoiding people who are themselves definitely known to have many other sexual partners are likely to reduce the chances of your exposure to an infected person.

Barrier methods of contraception, which are intended to prevent unwanted pregnancy, may also prevent the spread of STDs. These include condoms, diaphragms, and vaginal spermicides. Condoms, when used properly and consistently, may prevent the deposition of contaminated semen and likewise physically protect penile skin from contamination by vaginal secretions. A diaphragm provides a physical barrier for deposition of contaminated secretions upon the cervix, an important site for STD infection. Spermicides, designed to inactivate sperm cells, have also been shown to inactivate a wide range of STD germs. On the other hand, washing the genitals with soap and water, immediate urination after intercourse, and douching have *not* been shown to be effective methods for preventing the spread of STDs and should not be relied upon for that purpose.

SYPHILIS

Syphilis is a contagious condition caused by the bacterium *Treponema pallidum,* which belongs to a special class of bacteria known as *spirochetes.* The disease may be contracted through heterosexual or homosexual relations. Today syphilis can be treated easily, but it *can* be a dangerous condition if left untreated.

Syphilis is divided into four main stages—*primary, secondary, latent,* and *tertiary*—each with its own distinguishing features. In primary syphilis, the first sign of the disease is the development of a nontender sore, pimple, or cut, called a *chancre,* at the site where the germs entered the skin through microscopic cuts or abrasions in the mouth, vagina, or penile urethra. This may occur ten to forty days after sexual contact with an infected person.

Chancres frequently occur on the shaft of the penis, and on the lips or opening of the vagina. However, the initial sore(s) may go unnoticed, especially in women, where it may appear internally or be confused with some other form of irritation. Orogenital sexual relations with an infected partner can result in syphilitic sores in the mouth. Except for the sores, most people with this stage of syphilis feel otherwise healthy, although they usually do have swollen lymph glands in the groin area. The drainage from chancres is highly contagious, and pregnant women with syphilis can transmit the disease across the placenta to the unborn child. If left untreated, chancres disappear by themselves in one to five weeks.

The onset of secondary syphilis typically occurs six to twenty-four weeks later in an untreated case. A widespread, nonitchy body rash and a flulike illness consisting of headache, fever, sore throat, and joint pains appear. Occasionally, smooth-surfaced, wartlike growths (condylomata lata) also appear in the genital or anal regions. The rash of secondary syphilis teems with germs and is highly contagious.

If left untreated, the infecting bacteria of syphilis are capable of remaining inactive within the body for many years (latent syphilis) or years later may cause serious consequences (tertiary syphilis). These include heart and blood vessel disease (cardiovascular syphilis) and neurological diseases (neurosyphilis) such as paralysis, insanity, and blindness.

The diagnosis of syphilis in its early stages is based upon an evaluation of the history and clinical features of the condition and several laboratory tests. Smears of lesions of primary or secondary syphilis are examined with the aid of a special microscope (dark field microscopy). A screening blood test known as the VDRL may also be ordered. Results of a positive screening test can be confirmed by the use of a second blood test known as the FTA. In cases of suspected tertiary syphilis, examination of the cerebrospinal fluid may be required.

None of these consequences need happen, however. If you notice any ulcerated sore or rash on yourself or on others with whom you have intimate contact, seek medical attention right away. Syphilis can be cured by the use of antibiotics, most frequently intramuscular penicillin. Persons allergic to penicillin may be treated with oral tetracycline or erythromycin. Primary, secondary, and latent syphilis of less than one year's duration are usually treated in a single session. Patients who have had syphilis for more than one year are generally treated once a week for three successive weeks.

CHANCROID

Chancroid is another venereal disease that starts as sores. Like syphilis, it is caused by a bacterial germ, *Hemophilus ducreyi,* and may be contracted through heterosexual or homosexual contact.

Unlike syphilis, chancroid is much more common in men than in women, and is responsible for severe pain both at the site of the sores and in the groin lymph glands. Chancroid sores are generally surrounded by a reddish halo, are foul-smelling, and also much more pus-covered, ragged, and irregular than those observed in syphilis. Irritation and swelling of the penis can be quite pronounced. Sores may first appear as early as one to three days after sexual exposure. These typically heal spontaneously, within a few days even without treatment.

The diagnosis of chancroid depends upon the history and clinical picture. Examination of smears made from the ulcer base and special bacterial cultures is often necessary to clinch the diagnosis.

Like syphilis, chancroid is curable by antibiotics. A ten-day course of oral *erythromycin* or *trimomethoprim/sulfa* is usually sufficient. About 15 percent of the time, a mixed infection of syphilis and chancroid may be contracted and people with this are said to have *mixed chancres.* In those cases, both conditions require treatment with antibiotics.

HERPES

Herpes, or more correctly, herpes simplex infection, is a widespread STD. About 20 million people have genital herpes and about 500,000 new cases are diagnosed each year. The Centers for Disease Control (CDC) noted a 90 percent increase in patient visits to private practitioners in the United States for genital herpes in a recent five-year period. Countless more people have herpes infections of the mouth and lips (so-called cold sores or fever blisters). Today, herpes infections are largely spread by direct physical contact, primarily through kissing or sexual intercourse.

Herpes simplex infections of the oral or genital areas are caused by two closely related viruses, *herpes simplex type I* and *herpes simplex type II,* which are cousins of the virus responsible for chicken pox. Not that many years ago, herpex simplex I virus was responsible for the overwhelming majority of all cases of lip sores, cold sores, or fever blisters, and herpes simplex II for nearly all cases of genital herpes. However, since the sexual revolution in America in the 1960s and the overall change in attitudes toward orogenital sex, this pattern has changed somewhat. Herpes type II has become responsible for many cases of oral herpes and herpes type I for many cases of genital herpes.

INITIAL INFECTION

Herpes infections typically begin within a week to three weeks following physical exposure to an infected person. The virus invades the body through tiny breaks in the mucous membranes. Occasionally, a newly infected person may feel itching, burning, pain, or "pins-and-needles" sensations at the infection site within twenty-four hours before any outbreak becomes apparent. These symptoms, which appear before the actual breakout, are called *prodromal* symptoms. Subsequently, a group of small blisters on a red base appear, lymph glands may swell, and fever, headache, and muscular aches and pains may occur. In women, blisters may involve the labia, vagina, and cervix, while in men, the penis and scrotum may be involved. Urination may become painful. After one to two days, the blisters break and form painful, open sores. During the course of the next two to three weeks, the sores crust, dry up, and finally fade completely.

RECURRENCES

After the initial infection, the herpes viruses travel to the nerves near the spinal cord. Once there, they may remain inactive for days to years, but they do not disappear. Under certain stimulations, the herpes viruses may become active again, track back down the nerves toward the skin, and start the process of infection (Figure 15.1). When this happens, the resulting infection is called a *recurrence*.

A recurrent attack within three months of the first outbreak occurs 50 to 75 percent of the time. These infections may be triggered by periods of heightened nervous tension, physical illness, heat, sun exposure, mechanical irritation, sexual activity, and menstrual periods. However, the triggering stimulus for many recurrences is still not known. Fortunately, in many cases, as time passes, recurrences become fewer and further between and less severe.

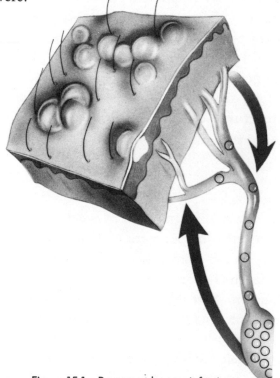

Figure 15.1 Recurrent herpes infection:
reactivated virus tracks down the nerves to the skin.

Recurrent infections, which are often preceded by prodromal symptoms, tend to be less severe than the initial attack, and usually last three to five days. The frequency of recurrences varies greatly. A person may have none, just one, or many episodes. In general, infrequent recurrent infections of herpes amount to nothing more than a nuisance and inconvenience. However, when recurrences are frequent, herpes can interfere with a person's sex life and can be a source of much emotional pain and embarrassment.

POSSIBLE SERIOUS COMPLICATIONS

Herpes has been associated with some serious medical consequences. If the infection becomes transferred to the eye after touching an oozing sore, a severe infection known as *keratitis* may result; this can lead to permanent destruction of the cornea; if left untreated, severe impairment of vision or even blindness can result. In addition, passage of a baby through a herpes-contaminated birth canal can lead to severe herpes infection in the newborn. Pregnant women with a history of recurrent herpes attacks are generally cultured for herpes each week beginning with the thirty-sixth week of pregnancy. If a mother is found to have active genital or cervical herpes at the time of delivery, obstetricians generally elect to deliver the newborn by Cesarean section.

PREVENTION

The best advice on prevention is to avoid physical contact with anyone with active herpes sores. If you and your partner both have herpes, refrain from contact when the condition is active; having herpes in one area doesn't prevent you from getting it in another location. You should consider the condition most contagious from the time you experience the first symptoms of tingling, etc., until the crusts have completely dried up and fallen off. Unfortunately, some people are known to shed virus in between attacks, and women in particular may suffer asymptomatic episodes of recurrences, making possible the unintentional spread of herpes. Therefore, whenever possible, you should use barrier methods such as condoms, diaphragms, and spermicides for additional protection. Naturally, if you have active herpes sores, you should wash your hands thoroughly before touching any other areas of your body (or someone else's) to prevent starting new areas of infection.

DIAGNOSIS AND TREATMENT

The diagnosis of the typical case of herpes is usually made on clinical appearance only. In less straightforward cases, your doctor may take a scraping from the base of an active blister and examine it under the microscope for the presence of the multi-nucleated, giant-size cells characteristic of herpes infections (*Tzanck smear*). Viral cultures and blood tests for herpes may also be needed in some cases.

No cure is yet available, though every year someone comes up with a new remedy that is supposed to work. Among the many "cures" that have so far proven ineffective are the consumption of large amounts of vitamins (particularly C, E, and B-12), Lactobacilli (acidophilus), zinc, lysine, and other dietary modifications, and the use of DMSO. If you have herpes, don't waste your time and money and don't harm yourself with treatments that don't work. See your doctor.

The antiviral drug *acyclovir* (Zovirax) represents a major breakthrough in herpes treatment. Although it neither cures herpes nor prevents initial infection, Zovirax has been found to be effective, in ointment form, for shortening the duration and severity of initial infections. For best effect, it must be applied five times a day for five days from the very onset of symptoms.

In capsule form, Zovirax is used not only to shorten the duration and severity of initial infections, but to entirely prevent, or sharply suppress, the outbreak of recurrent infections. To treat an initial outbreak, one must take one capsule five times a day for ten days; for control of recurrent infections the dose is usually one capsule five times daily for five days. To prevent recurrent infections altogether or to reduce their frequency and severity, the usual dosage is one pill three times daily. To date, no significant untoward reactions have been observed during one-year courses of continuous therapy. For those who suffer from frequent, or occasionally seemingly nonstop, physically and psychologically disabling recurrent episodes of herpes, Zovirax can provide significant relief.

Active research to develop a vaccine that will prevent initial herpes outbreaks continues. Experimental trials are currently under way, but it will be years before a vaccine will be available for general use. Unfortunately, vaccines will not cure those who already have herpes.

GENITAL WARTS

You learned about warts in chapter 9. The genital or venereal wart *(condyloma acuminatum)* deserves special note. Like other types of warts, genital warts are caused by certain strains of the human papillomavirus (HPV) and are now one of the most common sexually transmitted diseases. They may be spread by direct or indirect contact and by *autoinoculation* (self-spread from one area of your body to another). Genital warts frequently occur along with other STDs. All sexual partners of people with venereal warts should be examined by a dermatologist.

Typically, venereal warts are slowly enlarging viral growths that can infect any region of the anal and genital areas. If left untreated, they may become extremely large. They typically appear as flesh-colored, soft, velvety, cauliflowerlike, heaped-up vegetations on the skin or mucous membranes.

COMPLICATIONS

Once believed to be only a nuisance, anogenital warts have become of greater concern to the medical community. At least three viral strains causing venereal warts have been linked to the formation of precancerous changes and cancer of the cervix and genital area in women. Nearly 90 percent of all cervical cancers are now believed to be linked to the wart virus. Controversy exists about whether venereal warts are also associated with certain growths on the penis; some recent evidence points in this direction. In addition, passage of a newborn through a wart-contaminated birth canal may result in the development of certain tumorous growths called *laryngeal papillomas* in the throat of the newborn.

PREVENTION

Sexual contact should be avoided while one or both partners are affected. The use of a condom can also be helpful. If you are the sexual partner of a male with a history of genital warts, you should have a checkup with a gynecologist. Internal examination and Pap smears are extremely important in these cases.

DIAGNOSIS AND TREATMENT

The diagnosis of wart infections is generally straightforward. A biopsy may be performed when any doubt exists on clinical grounds. Dermatologists use a variety of methods to cure venereal warts. They may be removed by electrosurgery, cryotherapy, excision, or chemical application. A caustic chemical, *podophyllin,* is used in varying concentrations to treat genital warts. Several applications spaced at weekly intervals are often quite effective. Sometimes new warts appear as old ones are destroyed. In addition, warts may be quite tenacious and are known to recur in a fair number of cases. To limit the spread of warts, it is best to treat them when they are still small.

MOLLUSCUM CONTAGIOSUM

Molluscum contagiosum, a viral condition that had previously been found primarily in children, on the face and upper part of the body, is now more commonly found in the genital region of sexually active young people. Molluscum contagiosum has been associated with other STDs in as many as 67 percent of cases. The virus is in no way related to the viruses responsible for warts, as some people mistakenly believe. As its name implies, it is a contagious condition, usually beginning fourteen to sixty days after exposure. Autoinoculation occurs frequently.

The molluscum virus typically causes the formation of relatively small, pearly, flesh-toned or whitish bumps on the skin, the center of which is frequently depressed. Lesions of molluscum may occur alone or in groups and may be numerous. Molluscum contagiosum seldom causes any symptoms, although if individual lesions grow large, they may become inflamed and irritating.

Diagnosis is usually made by examination alone. No special tests are ordinarily needed, although occasionally a biopsy may be needed for confirmation. Home or office treatments are the same as for treating common warts. As in the case of warts, new, invisible colonies of molluscum can start while other areas are under treatment. It is important, therefore, to return to your dermatologist for follow-up to be sure that all new growths are treated.

SCABIES

Scabies is a highly contagious skin disease caused by a nearly invisible parasitic bug, *Sarcoptes scabiei,* the "itch mite." Scabies is not an infection, but an *infestation.* The scabies mite burrows into the skin, thereby causing irritation and allergy. Scabies is acquired largely through close physical contact, but may also be spread through contaminated clothing, linens, and towels. There is a four- to six-week incubation period between the time of exposure and the outbreak of the rash.

The rash typically affects the web spaces between the fingers and toes, back of the hands, wrists, elbows, armpits, breasts, beltline, genital area, and buttocks; the face is spared. Typically, the rash is extremely itchy, particularly at night, and may appear as grayish white, threadlike streaks, tiny blisters, and scratched, pimplelike bumps. The itching is believed to be an allergic reaction to the mites' feces. The threadlike streaks represent the burrows where the mites hide and lay their eggs.

DIAGNOSIS, PREVENTION, AND TREATMENT

In many cases, the diagnosis can be made on clinical grounds. In less clear-cut cases, a scraping of an involved area of skin is needed. Since tetracycline-containing solutions fluoresce under ultraviolet light, painting a scabietic burrow with tetracycline followed by Wood's light examination is another helpful confirmatory test.

Scabies is a curable condition. Kwell and Scabene lotions, which contain the potent pesticide *lindane,* are most often prescribed for it. Eurax lotion and sulfur ointments are alternative forms of treatment. The lotion is applied to all the affected areas at bedtime and rinsed off in the morning. Sexual partners of infected persons are frequently treated simultaneously to prevent the condition from "Ping-Ponging" back and forth between partners. All intimate apparel should be either hot-water laundered or dry-cleaned.

Unfortunately, infestation with scabies does not confer any permanent immunity against future attacks. In fact, if you have had scabies before, subsequent attacks generally occur after shorter incubation periods and are more severe. Daily shampooing, good personal grooming habits, and not sharing clothing, bedding, or towels with friends are good methods for preventing scabies infestations. Above all, intimate contact with anyone complaining of a rash that is especially itchy at night should be avoided until a dermatologist has been consulted.

LICE

Lice infestation, or *pediculosis,* is another form of parasitic infestation. It is sometimes confused with scabies. Once believed to be a disease exclusively of lower socioeconomic groups and overcrowding, lice infestation affects people of all ages, races, and socioeconomic groups. Three types of lice infest humans: head lice, body lice, and pubic or "crab" lice. All three types feed by biting the skin and sucking blood. Lice infestation is highly contagious, and all forms cause severe itching. Head and body lice are transmitted from one person to the next by direct contact with infested hairs or contact with intimate apparel, combs, hats, etc. Pubic lice are spread largely by sexual contact.

In general, lice reproduce very rapidly and their eggs, called *nits,* hatch every seven to ten days. Mature lice survive for about one month. Body lice deposit their eggs within the seams of clothing and bedding folds. Head and pubic lice lay their eggs directly upon the hair strands within infested areas.

If you look closely at the involved areas of a person infested with head or pubic lice, you may occasionally see adult lice. More often, however, you will find very small, whitish, dandruff-like eggs firmly attached to the hair shafts—the hallmark of these types of lice infestation. Nits are most likely to be found on the back of the head and around the ears. Body louse infestation, however, is usually signalled by long scratch marks. Pubic lice may also infest the eyelashes, armpit, and beard areas.

COMPLICATIONS

Breaks in the skin due to scratching can result in complicating bacterial infections and abscesses. Body lice can also be carriers of other, more serious epidemic diseases, including *typhus* and *relapsing fever.* Pubic and head lice have not been found to be carriers of other diseases. Fortunately, improved sanitation and hygiene have made body lice uncommon in the United States. By contrast, pubic lice infestation remains a common, sexually transmittable condition.

DIAGNOSIS, PREVENTION, AND TREATMENT

Finding adult lice and nits confirms the diagnosis; special tests are seldom needed. Naturally, attention to personal cleanliness and avoidance of direct contact with infected persons are the best ways to prevent lice infestation. Not sharing intimate apparel, bedclothes, linens, towels, combs, brushes, hats, and other personal items is another effective method.

Two types of medications have proven effective in curing lice infestation. One contains lindane (Kwell, Scabene), the same medication recommended for scabies. The second medication is another pesticide, *pyrethrin* (Rid). Despite treatment with these agents, which kill both lice and nits, nits often remain firmly attached to the hair shafts. Understandably, this is often of great concern to many people, but it need not be. To dislodge nits, you can rinse your hair with a solution containing one part water and one part plain white vinegar and then comb thoroughly with a fine-tooth comb. As with scabies, all intimate apparel and items that have been in contact with the infested areas should be hot-water laundered or dry-cleaned.

DISEASES CAUSING ABNORMAL SECRETIONS AND DISCHARGES

Although this chapter is devoted to those sexually transmitted diseases that involve the skin, brief mention of the common venereal diseases typically causing abnormal vaginal or urethral secretions or discharges is warranted.

The four most common conditions associated with abnormal penile, vaginal, or anal discharges include *Candida vaginitis, Trichomonas vaginalis, nonspecific urethritis (NSU),* and *gonorrhea.* If you or anyone you know is suffering from an abnormal discharge, medical attention should be sought as soon as possible to prevent complications. Happily, diagnosis is usually not difficult and cures are available for each of these conditions.

Candida, a common yeast infection (also discussed in chapter 9), is a frequent cause of vaginal and penile irritations (particularly in uncircumcised males). Redness and swelling of the affected areas are common, and intense itching and a cheesy white discharge are characteristic of this condition. Examination of scrapings under the microscope and a fungal culture are confirmatory. The use of topical broad-spectrum antifungal agents, such as Spectazole or Nizoral creams, is curative in most cases. Specific antiyeast preparations such as Mycolog ointment may also be prescribed. In some cases, sexual partners may serve to continually reinfect each other. When this is suspected, both partners should be examined and treated simultaneously.

Trichomonas infection is caused by a parasitic organism called a *protozoan* (an *amoeba* is another example of a protozoan). While trichomonas affects both men and women, many men infected with it experience no symptoms. As a result, such *asymptomatic carriers* may spread the condition to others unwittingly. In women, trichomonas infection typically causes a cream-colored, thick, and frothy vaginal discharge. Itching and pain upon urination also occur frequently. Once again, sexual partners may pass the infection back and forth to each other, so doctors generally treat both partners simultaneously.

Nonspecific urethritis (NSU), or as it is also known, *nongonococcal urethritis (NGU),* is a very common sexually transmitted infection of the *urethra,* the canal for urination. NSU is caused by a variety of bacterialike organisms, including Chlamydia, an organism believed to cause more than one-half of all cases. *Ureaplasma* is another common organism responsible for NSU. The symptoms include pain or burning upon urination and the production of a scant, watery, or milky urethral discharge. If the condition is permitted to persist, the discharge will usually become thicker. Once again, it is advisable to treat steady sexual partners simultaneously to prevent repeated reinfections. The possible consequences of untreated NSU include infection, damage, and scarring of the reproductive system, which may lead to sterility *(pelvic inflammatory disease, PID).* In fact, Chlamydia is the major cause of PID in the United States. Gonorrhea is the next most common cause.

Gonorrhea is a bacterial infection that can affect the genital and anal areas. In many women, the disease may produce no symptoms or only a mild discharge. On the other hand, for most men, painful urination and a thick, mucus- and pus-filled discharge is common. Anal infections of gonorrhea in males usually result from anal intercourse, and in females may result either from anal intercourse or contamination from nearby vaginal secretions. Contrary to a popular myth, you cannot contract gonorrhea from toilet seats. If left untreated, gonorrhea may result in serious consequences. Permanent damage to the sex glands and organs that can make it impossible for a woman to become pregnant can occur.

AIDS

A complete discussion of the *Acquired Immunodeficiency Syndrome (AIDS)* and its multitude of signs and symptoms is beyond the scope of this book. However, since AIDS does give rise to several skin manifestations, and since it is having such an enormous impact upon our society, a brief discussion is warranted.

Without doubt, AIDS, a fatal disease caused by a virus known as the *human immunodeficiency virus,* or *HIV,* is probably the most serious and widespread epidemic of our time. (Until recently, the AIDS virus was commonly known as the HTLV-III/LAV virus.) As the word *immunodeficiency* implies, the infecting virus seriously impairs the body's immune mechanisms, that is, its ability to fight infections. In 1981, AIDS was first diagnosed largely within the gay communities of New York and Los Angeles. At one time thought to be a disease confined to homosexuals, at present three groups appear to be at greatest risk of contracting this illness: homosexual males, hemophiliacs, and intravenous drug abusers. Other groups, including promiscuous heterosexuals and those having intercourse with prostitutes, may also be at increased risk of AIDS infection.

Fortunately, for most people outside of these high-risk categories, the AIDS virus is not very contagious. Not only does the virus *not* survive long outside the body, soap and water, chlorine, and other household bleaches quickly destroy it. AIDS is not believed to be spread by casual contact; intimate contact with the secretions of infected people is believed to be essential for contracting the infection. As evidence of its low degree of contagion, only a handful of health-care workers caring for AIDS patients have fallen victim to this disease.

Nevertheless, it has become increasingly important to know about one's intimate partners. This means knowing more about your partner than his or her profession or the type of clothing he or she prefers. It means knowing about your partner's life-style and medical conditions. It is particularly important to learn whether your partner is bisexual or an intravenous drug abuser. It is clear that the greater the number of sexual encounters with

AIDS-infected partners, the greater the likelihood for contracting the infection. Spermicides, vaginal jellies, and diaphragms appear to be of little benefit in preventing the spread of this condition. According to the U.S. Surgeon General, "barring abstinence, condoms are believed to offer the best means for protection yet available."

The skin plays host to a variety of manifestations of AIDS. A once rare type of malignant blood vessel tumor called *Kaposi's sarcoma* has been seen in as many as 40 percent of AIDS sufferers. The lesions of Kaposi's sarcoma appear as reddish, pink, purple, or brownish bumps in the skin. In addition to Kaposi's sarcoma, certain familiar rashes and growths appear even more commonly in AIDS victims, are more widespread, and often more stubborn and resistant to treatment in these patients than in healthy people. Skin conditions that frequently plague AIDS patients include warts, molluscum contagiosum, yeast infections, canker sores, herpes simplex, shingles, and especially seborrheic dermatitis (chapter 8). In addition, a characteristic abnormality of the tongue, known as *hairy oral leukoplakia,* in which the sides of the tongue develop whitish, thickened plaques, has been observed with increased frequency among AIDS patients.

Although no cure for AIDS is currently available, millions of research dollars are being committed to this end. Hope remains for the development of a vaccine to prevent its further spread and for more effective methods for treating people already infected, arresting its progress and reversing the process.

For more information about AIDS, consult your doctor, or write to the U.S. Department of Health in Washington, D.C., or your local board of health. Finally, the VD national hotline, 1-800-227-8922, may also be contacted for more information about AIDS, as well as other sexually transmitted diseases.

SIXTEEN

PREGNANCY AND YOUR SKIN

*M*ost of you have probably heard about the wonderful glow or radiance of pregnancy. It has been claimed that pregnant skin is skin at its best, and this is certainly the case for many women. Pregnancy, or *gestation,* as doctors sometimes refer to it, probably can be best considered a variation of normal health in which unique hormonal, physiological, and emotional alterations affect profound changes in your skin, as well as many other organs.

Among the many skin changes that may be brought about by pregnancy are stretch marks, blood vessel overgrowths, the formation of "broken" blood vessels, the appearance of new moles, the darkening of old ones, generalized skin darkening, and skin yellowing. In addition to widespread itching, there are several different kinds of severe, itchy, hivelike rashes that are unique to pregnancy. Finally, other more common skin conditions, such as acne, atopic dermatitis, and psoriasis can be affected by pregnancy. These problems and others and their treatments are the subject of this chapter. Not to worry. With proper care and supervision, pregnant skin *can* be radiant.

PREGNANCY PRODUCTS

Certain cosmetic manufacturers have recently attempted to create a market for skin-care products specially formulated for the mother-to-be. Directing their advertising to the pregnant woman's concerns about doing the right things for herself and her developing baby, the manufacturers of these cosmetics would have you believe that their products can perform such wonders as preventing or reducing stretch marks, "firming" and "toning" your skin, improving circulation, and soothing tired muscles. Unfortunately, none of these claims can be substantiated scientifically. In the main, these products are simply moisturizers. Probably the greatest benefit you can derive from any of these pregnancy products is the psychological lift you get from pampering yourself. However, you can achieve the same results for a lot less money if you treat yourself to a nice warm bath and follow it by gently massaging in an all-purpose moisturizing cream or lotion.

"NORMAL" SKIN CHANGES IN PREGNANCY

A number of skin changes may occur during pregnancy. Some of these are referred to as *physiological* changes; that is, they occur so commonly that they are considered an expected (normal) part of pregnancy. In most cases, physiological changes are believed to be linked to the hormonal changes that take place during pregnancy, and while they usually do not affect the health of either the mother or fetus, they may be quite distressing cosmetically.

Other conditions represent true diseases specifically related to pregnancy. Such illnesses may not only cause symptoms in the mother, but in some cases may even threaten the health or life of the developing fetus. These diseases are discussed later in this chapter.

SKIN COLOR CHANGES

Hyperpigmentation, or overpigmentation of the skin, occurs commonly during pregnancy; about 90 percent of pregnant women develop this to some degree. Hyperpigmentation is usually mild and ordinarily appears as further darkening of areas of the body that are already darkly pigmented. These areas characteristically include the *areolae* of the breasts (the pink rim of tissue around the nipples), the armpits, vulva, anus, and inner thighs. The *linea nigra,* a dark line that extends along the midline of the abdomen from the pubic bone to the *umbilicus* (belly button) and sometimes as high as the chest, is another commonly involved site. Actually, this line is always present on your abdomen and just becomes darker with pregnancy. Before pregnancy, the line is appropriately called the *linea alba,* or white line.

Ordinary freckles *(ephelides),* some types of scars, and many moles (birthmarks, beauty marks) may also darken during pregnancy. Such changes are generally harmless and nothing to worry about. However, since such malignant moles (malignant melanomas) and their precursor lesions (dysplastic nevi) are likewise hormone-sensitive and may be stimulated by pregnancy, you should bring any suspicious changes in a mole to the attention of a dermatologist. Most often, your doctor will need only to reassure you that there is nothing to worry about. Where any problem is suspected, however, a biopsy is performed for confirmation (see chapter 10).

This preferential darkening of certain skin areas is believed to take place because those areas ordinarily contain greater concentrations of pigment cells. It may also be due to a heightened sensitivity to hormonal stimulation in these areas. Hyperpigmentation, which is generally more pronounced in dark-haired, dark-complexioned women, usually begins within the first trimester. Continued darkening generally occurs throughout the remainder of the pregnancy, and frequently diminishes after delivery. As a rule, however, affected sites do not entirely return to their prepregnancy color. For example, although pink prior to first pregnancy, nipples typically turn brown during pregnancy and remain so thereafter. Since hyperpigmentation conditions are harmless, reassurance is all the therapy that is ordinarily needed.

MELASMA

Melasma (the "mask of pregnancy") is a special kind of hyperpigmentation that involves the face. It may appear to some extent in 50 to 75 percent of all pregnancies and is also more common in darker-skinned and dark-haired women. It also occurs in up to one-third of women who take birth control pills. Melasma most commonly affects the central area of the face—forehead, cheeks, nose, upper lip, and chin. At times, it may affect the cheeks and the nose only or, less commonly, the area over the angles of the jawbones. Melasma is believed to be caused by a combination of overexposure to the sun and hormonal and genetic factors. In the majority of cases, melasma disappears within twelve months following delivery.

Except for the appropriate use of high-SPF sunscreens and protective clothing, few preventive measures for hyperpigmentation are available. Perfumed cosmetics, which occasionally cause hyperpigmentation problems following sun exposure, should be avoided. For persistent hyperpigmentation, masking cosmetics may be used to cover the blotchiness (chapter 5). Bleaching creams or lotions containing *hydroquinone,* such as Melanex, are occasionally used with some success. More recently, in preliminary studies, a combination of hydroquinone and Retin-A has been found successful, bringing satisfactory depigmentation in eight to twelve weeks.

BLOOD VESSEL CHANGES

Several different kinds of blood vessel problems are common in pregnancy, although they do not differ from those seen in nonpregnant women. However, during pregnancy blood vessel abnormalities generally increase in size, as well as number.

Spider nevi (sometimes called *spider hemangiomas* or *spider telangiectasias*) are actually dilations of small arteries known as *arterioles.* The adjective *spider* is descriptive; small blood vessels characteristically radiate away from the faintly pulsatile center of the arteriole and look like the rungs of a spider's web. While spider nevi are ordinarily seen in slightly more than 10 percent of nonpregnant women, they appear in more than two-thirds of all pregnant women. Their development is believed to be related to the high levels of circulating estrogens. Spider nevi typically involve the neck, face (particularly around the eyes), and arms, in that order, and appear during the second through the fifth months of pregnancy.

Most spider nevi that develop during pregnancy fade after delivery; three-quarters of them fade by the end of the second month after delivery. However, they seldom disappear completely. Moreover, recurrences and enlargement during subsequent pregnancies may occur. Treatments aimed at completely removing spider nevi are generally postponed until after delivery to allow for maximum spontaneous resolution. Low-voltage electrodessication applied to the central, "feeder" arteriole usually eradicates the spider completely. During pregnancy, masking cosmetics may be used as needed.

The development of telangiectasias, or "broken" blood vessels, is also common. In fact, telangiectasias are not "broken" blood vessels, but may be considered *varicosities* (dilations) of tiny, superficial blood vessels (capillaries) in the skin. They are most noticeable on the face, neck, shoulders, and back. Like spider nevi, telangiectasias often fade within a couple of months after delivery. If they persist, they are managed in the same way as spider nevi, i.e., by the use of masking cosmetics or electrodessication.

"Cherry" hemangiomas are small developmental abnormalities of blood vessels. They are flat or pimplelike and vary in color from purple to brilliant red; hence "cherry." Cherry hemangiomas spontaneously occur in as many as 5 percent of all pregnant women, usually beginning within the first trimester and continuing to enlarge slowly toward delivery. The upper chest, abdomen, and back are the usual locations for their development. Most cherry hemangiomas persist after delivery but may be removed by simple electrosurgery or a combination of shave excision and electrosurgery (chapter 10).

Palmar erythema, or more simply red palms, also occurs frequently during pregnancy, particularly during the first trimester. Approximately two-thirds of white women develop them. In some women redness affects the base of the thumb as well as the fleshy area directly opposite it near the wrist. In others, there may be a mottled purple and pallid discoloration of the entire palm. Red palms and spider nevi often occur together, and high estrogen levels are postulated as the cause of both. Other presumed causes include a genetic predisposition and the effects of the high blood flow characteristic of pregnancy.

In general, this harmless condition fades on its own about one week after delivery.

Purpura and *cutis marmorata* are two other blood vessel problems common during pregnancy. *Purpura,* or black-and-blue marks, often appear during the last half of pregnancy and are believed to be the result of increased capillary fragility and leakage due to backup pressure. (Delicate flaplike structures—venous valves—attached to the inner walls of your veins at 2-inch intervals help return blood flow by limiting backflow due to gravity. When these venous valves malfunction, backflow and pooling occur.) Purpura is an innocuous condition and no therapy is necessary; the problem disappears after delivery.

Cutis marmorata, a bluish mottling of the skin of the legs, can also occur. In this condition the blood vessels demonstrate an exaggerated sensitivity to stimuli that causes them to constrict and dilate. Circulating estrogens are believed to be responsible for this sensitivity, which doctors refer to as *vasomotor instability.* Cutis marmorata disappears after delivery; here again, reassurance is the only treatment necessary.

VARICOSE VEINS   The development of varicose veins can pose a big problem during pregnancy. They appear in more than 40 percent of pregnant women, most commonly in the legs. Varicose veins are responsible not only for swollen, discolored legs, but chronic leg fatigue and ankle swelling. *Hemorrhoids,* which are actually varicose veins in the anal region, are also common during pregnancy and can cause bleeding and pain.

Varicose veins in pregnancy are believed to result from a number of factors working in concert. For one thing, blood flow from the uterus (womb) increases markedly during pregnancy. Since blood returning to the heart from the legs drains into the same larger veins as blood returning from the womb, blood vessel congestion and backup into the legs occurs. Moreover, because the hormones of pregnancy have a tendency to overly relax blood vessel walls, the veins in the legs are more prone to overstretching and dilating as a response to increasing backup pressure. Finally, the continuously increasing size and weight of the uterus during the later months of pregnancy places an additional downward force on the already overstressed blood vessels of the legs, causing pooling in the lower limbs. Prolonged sitting and standing and the use of elastic garters and panty girdles may also contribute to increased backflow pressure (Figure 16.1).

A hereditary predisposition for the development of varicose veins is believed to exist. If your mother had them during her pregnancy, you stand a good chance of having them during yours. You may inherit a trait for having weak vein walls or too few valves, exacerbating backflow problems.

While varicose veins may shrink somewhat after delivery, they

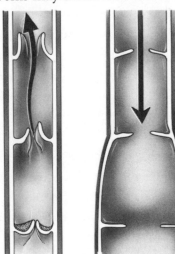

Normal vein and valves

Varicose vein resulting from weakened vein walls, malfunctioning valves, and increased backflow

Figure 16.1 The development of varicose veins

seldom do so completely. During pregnancy, the aim of therapy is to keep the veins collapsed without compromising circulation. Helpful measures include avoiding excessive weight gain, exercising regularly, and avoiding constricting round garters, tight girdles, and panty-leg girdles. In addition, you should make a conscious effort to keep your legs elevated above the midline as much as possible when resting. Many people think that merely elevating their legs on a hassock, for example, is sufficient. It isn't. You must keep your legs *above heart level* to promote blood return to your heart. Further, sleeping on your side, rather than on your back, minimizes uterine pressure on underlying blood vessels and facilitates adequate blood return.

Finally, your doctor may recommend a variety of elastic support hose. Jobst stockings, which may be obtained with a doctor's prescription, are custom-made support stockings composed of an elastic core surrounded by a combination of Dacron and cotton. For precise fit, measurements are taken along the entire length of each leg at 1½-inch intervals. Such measurements ensure that the right degree of counterpressure is applied to each area of your legs. To be most effective, support hosiery must be worn throughout the day. For optimum benefit, you should put them on *before* you get out of bed in the morning (before the legs have a chance to swell from standing). The continued use of support hose is often required after delivery.

Definitive treatments for varicose veins include the injection of sclerosing agents to scar closed the dilated vessels, and a surgical procedure, *venous stripping and ligation,* for removing the abnormal veins. Naturally, the choice of treatment depends on your individual circumstance.

EDEMA   Varicose veins may cause swollen ankles, but fluid retention, resulting in swelling (*edema*) of the ankles, as well as of the eyelids, face, hands, and feet, frequently occurs during gestation. About 70 percent of pregnant women develop ankle edema and about 50 percent develop eyelid edema, both of which are believed to be due to hormone-induced salt and water retention and leaky capillaries.

Doctors generally treat this form of edema in much the same way as they do the swelling from varicose veins. In addition, they may recommend a restricted salt intake. In severe cases, diuretics (water pills) may be prescribed. This condition almost invariably disappears spontaneously after delivery.

ORAL CONDITIONS

PREGNANCY "TUMORS"   The so-called pregnancy tumor has nothing at all to do with malignancy, as some people fear. It is a special type of abnormal, rapid blood-vessel overgrowth involving the gums. Pregnancy tumors usually begin somewhere between the second and the fifth months and most often arise within the ridges of gum tissue that normally project between your teeth, known as the *interdental papillae*. They may also develop on the inner cheeks or tongue.

Pregnancy tumors are generally soft, smooth, shiny, reddish purple or pinkish red fragile masses; they may hang from stalks or sit on broad bases and project over the surrounding teeth. Because they are so fragile, these growths frequently break down into open wounds *(ulcers)* and bleed. Dermatologists commonly refer to pregnancy tumors as *pyogenic granulomas.* These growths are believed to result from a combination of estrogen stimulation and irritation from cavities, tartar buildup, or extensive dental work. Nor surprisingly, their typically rapid appearance and growth is alarming to most women and prompts them to seek medical attention.

Since they ordinarily shrink considerably within several months following delivery, surgery is often postponed until that time. To help reduce tumor size, good oral hygiene must be maintained and any factors causing local irritation should be eliminated. Surgery is the treatment of choice when a pregnancy tumor causes bleeding, ulceration, infection, or interference with eating. Rapid regrowth of the tumor following surgical removal occurs frequently in these cases.

PREGNANCY GINGIVITIS   A condition related to pregnancy tumors is called *pregnancy gingivitis* and is believed to develop to varying degrees in nearly all pregnant women. It is an inflammation of the gums that usually begins in the first trimester and increases in severity until delivery. Lesions of pregnancy gingivitis are pink to red, smooth, glossy, and swollen. Ulceration, bleeding, and discomfort are common. Since pregnancy tumors develop in approximately 2 percent of women with pregnancy gingivitis, the condition may be considered a forerunner to pregnancy tumors. The causes, prevention, and treatment of this condition are the same as for pregnancy tumors.

STRETCH MARKS

Stretch marks, or *striae gravidarum,* develop in the majority of pregnant white women, usually toward the end of the second trimester or the beginning of the third trimester; black and Asian women seldom develop them. Stretch marks, which quite commonly occur on the breasts and abdomen, may also occur on your upper arms, lower back, buttocks, thighs, and groin area. As the involved areas grow tremendously larger during pregnancy, overstretching of the skin, which results in the tearing of collagen and elastin fibers, is believed to be the primary cause of this problem; rapid gains or losses of weight during pregnancy further aggravate the tendency.

Stretch marks first appear as pinkish or reddish streaks; after delivery they develop fine wrinkles along the surface and turn an ivory white or whitish lilac color. Stretch marks are permanent, although they fade and become less noticeable with time. Massaging them daily with a moisturizer when you first notice them may promote fading; however, the use of specific anti-stretch-mark creams is of no proven benefit.

SKIN TAGS

Skin tags usually begin to appear during the second half of pregnancy, varying in size from pinpoint to more than ¼ inch in diameter. In general, they are soft, fleshy, and flesh-colored or slightly pigmented, and hang from a slender stalk. Like regular skin tags, they develop on the face, neck, chest, armpits, under the breasts, and on the inner thighs. They occasionally disappear after pregnancy; however, the vast majority become larger with time. Removal, which is usually deferred until after delivery, is the same as for ordinary skin tags (see chapter 10).

HAIR AND NAIL CHANGES

Several kinds of hair and nail changes may occur during pregnancy. These include hair loss, excess hair growth, distorted nail growth, and the development of abnormal nails.

HAIR LOSS

Anagen effluvium, or hair loss that occurs during the active growing phase of the hair cycle, occasionally occurs during the latter part of pregnancy. In addition, some women experience a male-pattern-like baldness late in pregnancy. This usually consists of a mild frontal and temple hair loss. While in both cases of hair loss the precise causes remain unknown, most authorities agree that complete recovery can be expected after delivery. No therapy is necessary other than reassurance.

Postpartum telogen effluvium, or hair loss after delivery, is described in chapter 12. The causes for this condition may include the stresses of delivery and changes in hormonal balance. Telogen effluvium usually begins between one and five months after delivery and may continue for several months. Most often, although unfortunately not always, hair spontaneously regrows completely between six and fifteen months after the onset of the condition.

HIRSUTISM

Excess hair growth, or hirsutism (chapter 12), can be triggered by pregnancy. Most pregnant women experience this problem to some degree, but it is generally more noticeable in dark-skinned, dark-haired women who exhibited a tendency for excess hair growth *before* pregnancy. The excess hair growth is usually more pronounced on the upper lip, cheeks, and chin; however, it may also affect the arms, legs, breasts, and back. Both fine lanugo hairs and coarse terminal hairs may be produced.

Most lanugo hairs fall out within six months after delivery. On the other hand, the terminal hairs usually remain. Several methods for treating hirsutism are described in chapter 12. Recurrence of the problem with subsequent pregnancies is common.

NAIL CHANGES

A number of nail changes may occur during pregnancy, including the development of overly brittle or overly soft nails; the formation of horizontal grooves along the nail plate; separation of the nail plate from the underlying nail bed; and the accumulation of thick debris under the nail. The cause of these changes is unknown. However, if you develop these nail changes, you should follow the recommendations for proper nail care discussed in chapter 13 to prevent aggravating the problem.

ACNE

Sebaceous gland activity also increases during pregnancy, particularly during the last trimester. As a result, many women complain of oily skin during this time. However, the effects of pregnancy on acne are unpredictable; some cases improve, possibly as a result of increased estrogen levels, and others worsen.

OTHER PREGNANCY CHANGES

Several other physiological changes occur during pregnancy. For example, for unknown reasons, eccrine sweat gland production increases, which means you can expect to sweat a lot more during pregnancy. Increased sweating may be related to an overactive thyroid or to the weight gain of pregnancy.

Early in the first trimester, sebaceous glands located within the areolae of your breasts begin to enlarge into small brownish bumps known as *Montgomery's tubercles*. In fact, the presence of these bumps is considered an early sign of pregnancy.

Blood vessel congestion and dilation are responsible for changes in the genital area. Early on such changes impart a bluish purplish hue to the vagina and cervix. Later in pregnancy, the vulva becomes fuller and broader. In the past, before the advent of today's laboratory tests to confirm pregnancy, these clinical signs were used by obstetricians to establish pregnancy.

Finally, in many cases, pregnancy seems to favorably affect two common skin conditions: psoriasis and atopic dermatitis (chapter 8). While psoriasis tends to improve during pregnancy, alas it returns after delivery, although the severity of the condition following delivery is usually no worse than before pregnancy. Atopic dermatitis also tends to improve during pregnancy, but, like psoriasis, returns to the prepregnancy state afterward.

JAUNDICE AND PRURITIS

Two conditions common to pregnancy span the divide between what can be considered normal changes expected during pregnancy and the abnormal conditions discussed in the following sections. These are jaundice, or yellowing of the skin and whites of the eyes, and pruritus, or itching. During the last trimester of pregnancy, a number of hormonally induced chemical alterations within the liver normally occur. As a result, the liver generally becomes somewhat more sluggish in its ability to clear certain waste products. Usually these changes in liver function are subtle and of little consequence, and the condition is referred to as *physiological jaundice.* However, occasionally liver function becomes so compromised that recurrent episodes of jaundice result. In more severe cases, the liver becomes swollen and tender, and nausea, vomiting, and intense itching occur.

No effective therapies for physiological jaundice are currently available. Fortunately, following delivery, all signs and symptoms of this condition usually resolve promptly. Recurrences are common with successive pregnancies, although the severity of these episodes may vary.

Approximately 20 percent of women complain of itching at some point during pregnancy. In many cases, it is a relatively minor problem involving only a small, localized area, often the abdomen. However, in others, pruritus can be a widespread, incapacitating condition affecting most of the body. Sometimes itching may begin as a localized problem as early as the third month, only to progress to generalized itching in the last trimester. Some experts believe that common pregnancy-related itching is due to minor abnormalities in certain of the liver's metabolic activities, leading to the accumulation of *bile salts* within the skin. Although capable of eliciting itching, these changes in liver function are generally too subtle to cause other signs and symptoms of illness such as jaundice.

In the following sections, a variety of abnormal rashes and skin conditions unique to pregnancy are briefly discussed. In each of these conditions, itching plays a major role. However, when no cause can be found for itching, the condition is technically known as *idiopathic* (unknown cause) *pruritus* or *pruritus gravidarum* (itching of pregnancy). Since simple pregnancy itching is considered a diagnosis of exclusion, doctors attempt to rule out all other causes before making this diagnosis.

Pruritus gravidarum usually disappears on its own after delivery. In some milder cases, simple reassurance that this will happen is all the treatment that is necessary. The use of moisturizing lotions and oatmeal baths may be soothing, particularly if your skin tends to be dry. Since tight-fitting clothing and warm, humid weather aggravate the condition, these should be avoided. For more severe or widespread cases of itching, topical corticosteroid creams and oral antihistamines may be prescribed. Occasionally, ultraviolet light B (UVB) treatments may be recommended. Administered over a three- to five-day period, ultraviolet treatments have been reported successful in diminishing the itchiness for a substantial number of patients.

ITCHY RASHES OF PREGNANCY   A number of rashes unique to pregnancy may occasionally complicate this period. These conditions are referred to by dermatologists as the *pruritic dermatoses of pregnancy*. Some of these conditions are quite rare, so the facts about them are still in the process of being sorted out. One recent classification listed seven disorders, but universal agreement among experts about the classification of these conditions does not yet exist. A detailed discussion of these conditions is beyond the scope and intent of this chapter. However, because they affect the skin during pregnancy, and especially because in certain cases they threaten the health and life of the developing fetus, four of them are briefly described.

The *toxemic rash of pregnancy* usually begins in the last week of pregnancy. Reddish or pinkish pimplelike bumps, hives, and large reddish elevations affect the abdomen and the extremities. While itching is intense, no other symptoms or signs appear and the fetus remains unharmed. Treatment is directed toward alleviating the symptoms.

Another, similar condition is *pruritic urticarial papules and plaques of pregnancy,* or *PUPPP* for short. PUPPP is being diagnosed with increasing frequency these days, probably due to increased physician awareness. This condition usually begins in the third trimester and also appears as reddish or pinkish pimplelike bumps, hives, and elevations affecting the *upper* arms and legs and abdomen. Interestingly, the eruption may begin within stretch marks. While itching can be severe and debilitating, both mother and fetus are otherwise unaffected. Symptomatic therapy and reassurance are all that are needed, and PUPPP disappears rapidly after delivery. Fortunately, the condition does not seem to recur with subsequent pregnancies.

A third rash of pregnancy is known as *herpes gestationes.* Despite the name, this condition has nothing whatever to do with herpes infections. In fact, it is believed by some to be a variant of a nonpregnancy blistering disease known as *bullous pemphigoid.* Herpes gestationes may begin any time from the second week of pregnancy to the period shortly after delivery. The rash, which consists of reddish or pinkish pimplelike bumps, elevations, and small and large blisters, can affect the entire skin surface. Itching can be severe and fetal mortality may occur in as many as 30 percent of cases. In addition to the usual forms of anti-itch therapy, high doses of systemic corticosteroids may be prescribed to control the rash. Herpes gestationes may recur with subsequent pregnancies.

Impetigo herpetiform is another misleadingly named condition. This rash has nothing to do with either impetigo or herpes. Impetigo herpetiform may begin anytime from the first to third trimesters. Pustules on a reddish base are the typical lesions in this condition. At first, skin fold areas such as the groin may be involved; later, however, the entire torso of the body may be affected. Itching in this case is minimal or absent, but the patient feels extremely ill. Fetal mortality is significant. Here again, systemic corticosteroids may be needed. This condition may recur with subsequent pregnancies.

USING MEDICATIONS DURING PREGNANCY

One of the most important admonitions that can be given to a pregnant mother is to *avoid, if possible, using any drugs at all throughout pregnancy.* (For that matter, elective surgical treatments of any minor conditions should also be postponed until after delivery.) You should especially try to avoid taking any medications during the critical first trimester of pregnancy when fetal organ development takes place. While there are times, such as in treating some of the more serious conditions described above, when drugs must be taken, *never take any drug or OTC preparation unless your obstetrician approves it.* If a medication is prescribed, it is especially important to follow all dosage directions carefully.

Fortunately, over the years a number of medications have proven safe for use during pregnancy. For pain and fever relief *acetominophen* (Tylenol) is considered safe. It has not been associated with the development of any congenital malformations. Aspirin and other salicylates, on the other hand, should be avoided. Taken in the third trimester, salicylates can prolong gestation and labor and increase the likelihood of bleeding complications.

Many antihistamines have proven safe for use in pregnancy, particularly *chlorpheniramine* (Chlortrimeton). Some reports exist linking *diphenhydramine* (Benadryl) to the development of oral clefts. However, diphenhydramine and another very effective antihistamine, *hydroxycine* (Durrax, Atarax), may be safely used during the second and third trimesters. (On the other hand, since they are known to pass into the milk, you should avoid all antihistamines when nursing, unless advised by your physician.)

Systemic penicillins, cephalosporins, and most *erythromycins* are generally believed to be safe for use during pregnancy. However, *tetracyclines, trimethoprim/sulfa* combinations, and *erythromycin estolate* should not be taken.

The administration of oral corticosteroids has been linked with the development of cleft palate and congenital cataracts, particularly when taken during the first trimester. However, systemic corticosteroids have been used safely in many cases when they have been needed to treat certain serious disorders that have flared up during pregnancy. Nevertheless, they are used only when their potential benefits outweigh the risks.

Topical corticosteroids may be used during pregnancy, particularly during the second and third trimesters. However, to minimize absorption and reduce the risk of any potential problems, the lowest-potency steroid to do the job is usually selected and applied to the smallest area to control or arrest the problem.

Finally, while oral antifungal agents are not recommended for use during pregnancy, potent, broad-spectrum topical antifungal agents such as *clotrimazole* (Mycelex, Lotrimin) and topical anti-yeast medications such as *nystatin* (Mycostatin) have proven safe.

GOOD SKIN IS POSSIBLE AT ANY AGE

*H*owever much we all may resent it, growing older is a fact of life. Fortunately, growing older these days doesn't necessarily mean having to look or feel bad; with a little extra attention, good skin is possible at any age.

While most of us have some general notion of what body aging is all about, in fact it is a complex process that results in both increased vulnerability and reduced adaptability to environmental stresses. Every organ in your body ages in its own way and at its own rate. Skin aging results from the combined effects of the natural aging process *and* the accumulated impact of lifelong environmental assaults.

It has been estimated that approximately 65 percent of all people over the age of sixty-five have at least one skin condition that could benefit from dermatological care. This chapter focuses on those conditions that are especially common in or unique to older people or follow a different course in older people than in young people. The cosmetic treatments for wrinkling, sagging, and unattractive fat distribution; basic skin care and mainte nance; proper selection and application of makeups; regular attention to preventing and treating common skin conditions; the sun; and skin growths have all been addressed in earlier chapters.

Mature skin differs from young skin in a number of ways (chapter 1). Basically, skin aging is divided into chronological aging (i.e., your natural, inherited family trait for aging) and photoaging (i.e., sun-induced, or more precisely, ultraviolet light–induced aging resulting from years of accumulated exposure). The structural, functional, and metabolic changes in your skin that characterize chronological aging parallel the aging and degenerative changes in other body organs. Because of this, investigators are studying skin aging for clues to organ aging in general. Since senior citizens represent the fastest-growing segment of the American population—more than 30 million and climbing—the study of aging and its consequences is of no small importance.

In brief review, some of the major changes in skin structure and functions associated with chronological aging include thinning of the uppermost layer of the skin (the epidermis); diminished production of collagen; degeneration of elastin fibers; the development of abnormalities within the many small, delicate blood vessels supplying the skin; diminished sweat gland activity; decrease in the number of pigment cells (melanocytes) in skin and hair; steady decline in oil (sebacous) gland secretion; and deterioration of the skin's immune system. Photoaging is a separate process and largely involves damage to collagen and elastin fibers within the midlayer of the skin (the dermis).

Skin aging doesn't begin at age sixty-five. Different segments of your skin age at different rates. For example, deterioration of elastin fibers begins as early as age thirty, becomes more pronounced by age fifty, and eventually involves the majority of fibers by age seventy. Similarly, the abnormalities involving the small blood vessels become pronounced after age seventy. Pigment cells remain fairly constant in number and function until middle age, after which they begin a steady decline. Finally, oil and sweat gland secretions follow a steady decline after young adulthood.

These changes and others have profound effects on skin health and appearance and on general health and longevity. For example, thinning and flattening of the epidermis leads to impairment of the skin's extremely important barrier functions, causing problems by allowing certain drugs and irritants to be more easily absorbed. It may also increase skin susceptibility to shearing stress, thereby promoting blister formation; this may explain why removing taped bandages and Band-Aids so often rips skin in the elderly. Degeneration and decreased production of the supporting and elastin fibers also slows wound healing. Moreover, deterioration of the small blood vessels may reduce the rate at which allergens or irritants are cleared from the skin. Decreased sweat production impairs body temperature regulation. Diminished oil gland secretion may contribute to skin scaling and flakiness. Decreases in pigment cell numbers and functioning may permit greater ultraviolet light damage and thereby enhance photoaging. And this decrease is also responsible for the graying and whitening of your hair, long held to be hallmarks of aging. Finally, diminished skin immunity may pave the way for recurrences of certain infections, such as shingles (chapter 9) or the development of skin cancers (chapter 10).

The effects of photoaging are profound (chapters 2 and 5). They include wrinkling and sagging, the development of leathery skin, mottled discolorations (e.g., liver spots) and "broken" blood vessels, and the formation of precancers of the skin and skin cancers.

While it is obvious that the impacts of chronological aging and photoaging over time combine to effect sweeping changes in skin appearance, it has become increasingly apparent that concern for one's appearance changes little with age. However, swayed by the belief that it is almost inappropriate to demonstrate concern for one's appearance during later life, many physicians push aside cosmetic issues when dealing with older patients. In my private practice, I have treated quite a number of men and women in their eighties for such problems as the removal of wrinkles and liver spots. Actually, concern for one's appearance at any age is a sign of emotional health—a sign that the individual is still interested and involved in life. Moreover, deterioration in appearance can trigger or aggravate depression, which is a big problem in later life.

Given the emphasis on good looks and youthful appearance today, choosing the most flattering shades and colors of cosmetics and knowing the best ways to apply them become even more important for older people. Consulting with a trained cosmetologist to learn the most effective makeup techniques for *you* can be one of the most worthwhile steps toward achieving glowing skin. In fact, some studies have shown that learning how to give yourself a professional-looking makeover (facial cosmetics and hairstyling) provides significant beneficial short- and long-term effects upon self-image, the ability to socialize with others, and the establishment or restoration of a more positive attitude toward life in general. For these reasons, I believe that one of the most important steps you can take is to treat yourself to a professional makeover. Try it. You'll like it.

COMMON SKIN PROBLEMS

Certain skin conditions affect many people as they get older. (Rashes, infections, and growths that affect everyone are covered elsewhere in this book.) These conditions include dry skin; noninfectious rashes such as acne rosacea (adult acne); infections such as shingles; and growths such as seborrheic keratoses (heaped-up age spots), acrochordons (skin tags), sebaceous gland hyperplasia (overgrown oil glands), precancers, skin cancers, and cherry hemangiomas. They also include hair problems, such as androgenetic alopecia (male/female pattern hair loss) or hirsutism (excess facial and body hair), and nail problems such as the development of duller, thicker, more brittle and ridged nails.

PRURITUS (ITCHING)

Itching is the most common symptom in dermatology and alerts us that something is wrong. It can range in severity from being a simple passing annoyance to severe and relentless enough to precipitate mental depression and thoughts of suicide. The sensations of itching and pain are so closely related that itch is often considered a subthreshold pain. It is a very common complaint of the elderly and often severe enough to prompt consultation with a dermatologist.

In most cases the cause of itching is unknown, and the condition is referred to as *senile pruritus*. About one-third of the time, however, severe, widespread itching is linked to the presence of a significant, underlying medical problem. These include kidney and liver disease, an overactive thyroid, diabetes, adverse drug reactions, and blood cell malignancies such as leukemia. Dermatologists generally make an effort to exclude these causes in any individual over sixty-five who complains of itching in the absence of an apparent skin rash.

Dry, rough, scaly skin is believed to play a contributing role in itching in a fair proportion of cases. By age seventy most people are affected to some degree by dry skin *(xerosis, asteatosis)*. Wintertime can make matters even worse; low humidity and cold and chapping conditions outdoors and dry heat indoors contribute to what dermatologists often call "winter itch." In extreme cases of dryness, the skin, especially on the lower limbs, cracks and fissures. This itchy, disfiguring condition is fittingly known as *eczema craquele* (French for "marred with cracks").

Repetitive scratching and rubbing of itching places can result in two other related conditions: *lichen simplex chronicus (neurodermatitis)* and *prurigo nodularis*. Thickened, scaly plaques involving the nape of the neck, lower legs, forearms, and anal and genital regions typify lichen simplex chronicus, while firm, scratched, reddish brown pimple-size or pea-size bumps involving the arms and legs characterize prurigo nodularis. Stress is believed to play a role in the development and continuance of both these conditions. Both can be quite disfiguring.

Severe itching requires medical intervention. If it is found to be related to an underlying condition, treating that condition will often relieve the itching. You can minimize dryness by using gentle cleansers (chapter 3) and moisturizers (chapter 4). In the majority of cases where no cause can be found, the use of topical steroids and antihistamines may be helpful. For localized areas, intralesional steroid injections can be extremely valuable. In addition, since *menthol*, phenol, and *camphor* have long been known to cool and soothe skin, moisturizers containing these ingredients, such as Sarna lotion, may be particularly useful for controlling generalized itching. Or you might try other anti-itch topicals, such as Pramgel *(pramoxine)* and Eurax lotion *(crotamiton)*. Finally, for additional comfort, wear loose-fitting, soft cotton clothing rather than tight-fitting clothes and scratchy woolen garments.

CONTACT DERMATITIS

Contact dermatitis, or allergy to certain substances that come into contact with your skin, is discussed more fully in chapter 8, but it is important to stress here that older people are at risk of developing contact dermatitis for several reasons. First, as skin ages its barrier function diminishes, and it is less efficient in protecting against environmental assaults. Second, there is a diminished ability to clear irritants and allergens from the dermis, leading to an accumulation of these substances. Finally, dry skin, which commonly plagues older people, tends to be more easily irritated.

In general, the treatment of contact dermatitis is the same for people of all ages: Avoid the offending allergen.

STASIS DERMATITIS

Stasis dermatitis is a type of eczema that deserves special mention. It represents one of several complications of what doctors refer to as *venous insufficiency disease* and arises over areas with underlying poor venous circulation and varicose veins. Stasis ulcers are another common complication of venous insufficiency (see below). As with other forms of eczema, itching is the most troublesome symptom of stasis dermatitis. The affected skin typically appears reddish, swollen, and flaky.

The precise nature of the link between venous blood vessel problems and the development of stasis dermatitis remains unclear. However, eczema of the legs against a backdrop of varicose veins and other evidence of venous insufficiency is highly supportive of the diagnosis.

The use of topical corticosteroid creams and ointments is generally effective for controlling the problem. Avoid anti-itch preparations containing diphenhydramine or *caine* derivatives (e.g., *benzocaine*) since you may, with stasis dermatitis, be at an increased risk for developing contact dermatitis to these ingredients.

ANGULAR CHEILITIS

Angular cheilitis *(angular stomatitis)* is an inflammation at the corners of the mouth, where the upper and lower lips join, characterized by redness and moist cracking. Angular cheilitis may also spread to involve the mucous surfaces of the lips.

A number of factors are believed to contribute to the development of angular cheilitis. For example, age-related loss of teeth and bone may predispose one to loss of the vertical dimensions of the mouth and result in overclosure of the jaws and moisture retention in the folds at the corners of the mouth. Decreased facial muscle tone may likewise contribute to the development of sagging skin folds and overclosure of the mouth. Drooling during sleep and excess saliva production, common in older people, also leads to moisture accumulation at the corners of the mouth. Finally, yeast infections and deficiencies of iron or B-complex vitamins can be responsible for angular cheilitis, particularly in individuals already predisposed to the condition.

Treating angular cheilitis consists of rectifying its causes. Denture and teeth problems should be treated to improve normal bite and restore the normal vertical dimensions of the mouth. The use of the injectable collagen implant Zyplast (chapter 11) to reduce the depth of the moisture-accumulating folds at the corners of the mouth may be extremely helpful in some cases. When confirmed, yeast infections should be treated and nutritional deficiencies corrected. Mycolog ointment for eliminating yeast infection and Westcort ointment for reducing inflammation are effective treatments. And the routine application of zinc oxide as a nighttime barrier ointment can be especially helpful if you have a drooling problem.

CHONDRODERMATITIS

Chondrodermatitis nodularis helicis is an extremely painful nodule or bump on the top of the ear. Chondrodermatitis usually affects only one ear, and in most cases affects men over the age of forty. The nodules generally range in size from ¼ inch to ½ inch in diameter and tend to be very firm and flesh-colored, often surrounded by a faintly reddish border and covered with a thin scale or crust. Pressure on the affected ear or cold temperatures often cause considerable pain or discomfort.

Chondrodermatitis is believed to result from constant trauma to the ear, such as from sleeping continually on one side or using a telephone receiver or headset on one side only. Sun damage to the delicate tissues of the ear may also play a contributing role by further weakening the tissue there. In addition, the ear's naturally poor blood supply and absence of a cushioning, protective fat layer may be other predisposing factors.

Diagnosing chondrodermatitis usually presents little difficulty. Occasionally, in less clear-cut cases, a biopsy may be needed for confirmation. The injection of intralesional steroids can prove beneficial in some cases. However, cryosurgery or simple office surgical removal of the bump, under local anesthesia, are considered the treatments of choice.

VENOUS LAKES

Venous lakes are simply accumulations of blood within dilated veins; they typically occur on the exposed areas of the face, lips, ears, and neck as blue to bluish black, compressible bumps. Many people are satisfied to be reassured that the condition is harmless and has no potential for becoming malignant. For those bothered by the appearance of venous lakes, simple electrosurgery, performed under local anesthesia, removes them in a matter of minutes with excellent results and little chance of recurrence.

SENILE PURPURA

Senile purpura are black-and-blue marks or bruises that develop spontaneously over the backs of the hands, forearms, and occasionally on the legs. It is a rather common condition. Age- and sun-damage—related degeneration of the supporting connective tissue of the blood vessels in the skin and loss of fat are believed to account for the markedly increased blood vessel fragility characteristic of this condition. The blood vessels in people with senile purpura are so fragile that the slightest incidental traumas to the skin, such as brushing against a tabletop or resting the elbows on a table, lead to blood vessel breakage. The black-and-blue marks sometimes become so large that they cover most of the forearm. It is usually either the frightening size of the bruises or the frequency with which they occur that prompts people to seek medical attention.

The diagnosis is quite straightforward and is usually based upon the clinical appearance alone, but a detailed history to exclude the use of medications associated with bruising, such as aspirin, oral steroids, or nonsteroidal anti-inflammatory agents, is usually taken. Sometimes the physician may order some additional blood tests to be certain that no internal causes of abnormal clotting exist.

Simple reassurance remains the best therapy for senile purpura. The use of masking cosmetics can be helpful for people who are troubled esthetically by the problem. Finally, vitamin C supplements are occasionally recommended to help clotting, but the value of this treatment remains unproven.

LEG ULCERS

Enlarged veins are quite common in older people and represent an impairment in the ability of the large veins of the legs to maintain blood flow toward the heart. Such impairment results from either a weakness in the walls of the leg veins or in the failure of their one-way valves to maintain forward flow. In general, women develop varicose veins about four times more often than men; the hormonal and circulatory stresses of pregnancy are believed to play a major role in their later development. In addition, a hereditary predisposition for developing them is also believed to be a factor in many cases.

SYMPTOMS   The effects of venous insufficiency can range from mild to severe. Mild cases exhibit the presence of unsightly bluish, bulging, tortuous blood vessels, and generally do not require medical attention. More troublesome cases promote the development of stasis dermatitis (see above), as well as the typical skin changes of prolonged venous insufficiency: reddish brown mottling of the skin and dark brown patches. In severe cases, *venous (stasis) ulcers* may develop.

Stasis ulcers can be disabling for many. In the United States alone, more than 600,000 people are estimated to suffer with this problem, and this number is likely to rise dramatically because of the ever-increasing population of older people. Interestingly, in Sweden, where accurate figures are kept and are readily retrievable, stasis ulcers have been found to affect as much as 0.4 percent of the entire population.

When venous circulation of the lower extremities is compromised, any injury to the skin leading to a break, regardless of how small, may fail to heal properly and result in the development of an ulcer (an open sore in the skin). Characteristically, stasis ulcers have jagged edges and pinkish, moist, weeping bases *(exudative ulcers)*. They are typically painless, but they often enlarge with time and may persist for many months and occasionally for years. Quite commonly, even after complete healing, the area may reulcerate (break down) and the problem start all over again.

TREATMENT   The diagnosis of venous ulcers requires the exclusion of other relatively common causes of leg ulcers. A careful history and physical examination must be performed. Special tests to assess blood flow may also be needed. If pus is present and infection suspected, a bacterial culture of the ulcer base or drainage fluid may be obtained.

The choice of conservative medical therapy versus more aggressive surgical therapy for venous leg ulcers depends upon the individual circumstances. The mainstays of conservative leg ulcer treatment include daily cleansing, *debridement* (removing dead tissue), the treatment of infection when present, and the use of special dressings. Ulcers may be cleansed with hydrogen peroxide, *aluminum chloride* solution (e.g., Domeboro), *acetic acid* solution (vinegar and water), or *silver nitrate* solution. Ointments containing protein-dissolving enzymes, such as Travase and Elase, or special water-absorbing *dextran polymer beads* (Debrisan) may be prescribed to chemically debride the ulcers. More recently, newer semipermeable wound dressings composed of water and plastic polymers (similar to soft contact lenses) have been found to speed healing and reduce pain. These include Vigilon, Duoderm, and Opsite dressings. Oral and topical antibiotics are prescribed when infection complicates ulcer healing.

Special elastic support stockings (discussed in chapter 16) may be prescribed. In order to push the blood upward against gravity, these stockings are fitted to provide the most pressure on the lower portion of the legs. Elastic pressure-gradient stockings usually have to be replaced every four to five months owing to stretching and loss of effectiveness for controlling fluid accumulation. In addition, exercises such as walking, jogging, or bicycling, which involve the contraction of the calf muscles, also aid circulation by squeezing blood back toward the heart.

When chemical therapies for removing dead tissue fail or are inadequate, the surgical excision of nonliving, decaying (nonviable) tissue may be necessary. It is essential to remove this tissue since healing is delayed and the risk of infection increased by its presence.

When healing is slow or does not progress despite all attempts at conservative therapy, your doctor may suggest skin grafting. This consists of removing an ulcer-sized segment of healthy skin from another area of the body. The healthy skin is then placed over the ulcer and the graft is stitched in place. By contrast, *pinch-grafting* consists of the transplantation of tiny plugs of healthy skin tissue to the ulcer site. (Donor pinch grafts are usually taken from the thighs, under local anesthesia.) Often successful, the pinch-grafting procedure allows healthy skin to migrate outward from the small grafts, ultimately covering over the entire ulcer site with new epidermis.

Finally, other forms of surgery may be directed at the underlying venous problems. These include sclerotherapy, or the injection of a scarring agent to chemically close off varicose veins, and venous stripping and ligation surgery for removing varicose veins. These procedures are best performed by a vascular surgeon.

NONVENOUS LEG ULCERS   Other common causes of leg ulcers include clogged arteries *(arteriosclerosis),* diabetes, and *hypertension* (high blood pressure). Leg ulcers caused by clogged arteries tend to be located below the ankles, on the toes or the tops of the feet. They are usually round, dry (nonexudative), and of a pale, grayish color. Arteriosclerotic ulcers are generally extremely painful. The rest of the foot may be pale in color, and the pulses may be weak or absent. *Intermittent claudication* (a condition in which cramping pain in the feet, hips, or legs forces you to stop walking) is a common symptom resulting from clogged arteries within the legs.

Leg ulcers resulting from high blood pressure usually involve the outer ankle regions. They tend to develop in people who have had uncontrolled or poorly controlled high blood pressure for a long time. Although these occasionally affect men, women in their forties and fifties are most commonly affected. Like arteriosclerotic ulcers, hypertensive leg ulcers are generally dry and extremely painful.

Finally, diabetic foot ulcers usually form beneath thick calluses and pressure points, such as the soles of the feet. These ulcers tend to be deeply infected, foul-smelling, and have moist borders. They are usually painless, however, owing to diabetic impairment of nerve function.

With some variations or modifications, the basic methods for managing nonvenous leg ulcer conditions are the same as those described above for stasis ulcerations: cleansing, debridement, and the use of dressings. For arterial ulcerations, however, the legs should *not* be elevated; the aim is to aid arterial circulation away from the heart toward the feet and toes. For the same reason, elastic pressure stockings are not prescribed for this condition; by applying pressure near the feet, they can further compromise arterial circulation. In the cases of both hypertensive and diabetic ulcerations, the key to effective management is control of the underlying condition; in other words, high blood pressure must be brought under control and sugar metabolism strictly regulated. Finally, while skin grafting procedures are useful in some cases of stasis ulcers and occasionally diabetic ulcers, skin grafts generally do not take well and have proven of little value in the care of either arterial or hypertensive leg ulcers.

After all is said and done, skin aging *is* inevitable. But with our current technology it need no longer be so painful to bear. Glowing skin for the golden years is no longer just a possibility, but a reality.

WHAT'S ON THE HORIZON

*A*dvances in the diagnosis and treatment of skin conditions are taking place so rapidly that no chapter on what's new and exciting could possibly cover all of them. Therefore, I have chosen to highlight a few that I find fascinating and are likely to have profound effects upon skin care and general health in the not-too-distant future. These are the *ultrasound scan, computer imaging in the evaluation of skin disease, lasers, tissue expansion techniques, transdermal patches, an antitumor vaccine,* and *artificial skin.* However, it is important to remember that each of these techniques is still in its developmental or experimental stages and, with the exception of computer imaging, it may be some time before they may be available for general use.

ULTRASOUND

Ultrasound, or the use of echo sound waves, has been available for years. Instruments known as *transducers,* which contain high-frequency electronic components, convert sound waves into recognizable patterns on video monitors. Originally perfected to detect submarines during World War II, ultrasound techniques were later adapted for medical uses. For several years now, ultrasound has been used by obstetricians to view the developing fetus safely through the use of reverberated sound waves without having to expose it to harmful, birth defect–causing X-rays. Ultrasound has also been employed successfully in fields such as gastroenterology (stomach and intestinal disorders) and cardiology (heart diseases), to diagnose gall bladder problems, diseases of other abdominal organs, and heart valve problems without need for X-rays or invasive or risky surgical procedures.

Most recently, ultrasound has made its way into the study of skin disorders. A particular type of ultrasound device, known as the *A-scan ultrasound,* is being evaluated as a noninvasive, nonsurgical alternative to biopsy (chapter 10). Imagine: no cutting into the skin, no pain, no stitches, no healing time! In addition, the results of A-scan testing are available within a minute; there is no waiting several days for the biopsy report from the pathology laboratory.

Using an A-scan, researchers have been able to distinguish among fatty, fibrous, and cellular material, as well as tissue edema (swelling). They have also been able to determine exactly which layers of the skin are affected by a certain disease and to take measurements of the abnormal tissue. Finally, A-scans have been helpful for confirming the diagnosis of such conditions as moles, warts, and keloids.

Currently, researchers are continuing to compare the microscopic appearance of various lesions with their appearance on the A-scan, in the hope that they will be able to improve their diagnostic acumen with ultrasound. The aim is eventually to replace biopsies wherever possible.

COMPUTER IMAGING

Not surprisingly, computers have made a place for themselves in the field of dermatology. Computerized networks of databases under the aegis of the American Academy of Dermatology allow dermatologists access to vital information about drugs, information from the burgeoning scientific literature, and other valuable information for diagnosis and treatment of skin disorders. However, most recently, computers are also being used directly in diagnosis and patient evaluation.

It has been known for some time that the overall prognosis for a patient with malignant melanoma (chapter 10) is related to the depth of invasion of the cancer at the time it is diagnosed. As a rule, the greater the depth of tumor invasion, the worse the outcome. Not long ago, some researchers demonstrated that the volume of the tumor is a far better indicator of prognosis than depth. Using the biopsy material from patients with malignant melanoma, these researchers used a computer to reconstruct a three-dimensional picture of the cancer in each patient. The computer then used the three-dimensional model to calculate the volume of the tumor in each case. Although still experimental, these measurements have permitted more accurate prognoses than any measurements previously available. Thus, this computer-imaging technique makes it possible for patients to decide more intelligently upon treatment alternatives. For example, those who know that their prognosis is grave may elect to pursue more radical or experimental forms of therapy. This computer technique should be available for more general use in the early 1990s.

Digital image analysis, another new computer technique to enter the skin arena, was developed by NASA for topographical analysis of the moon's surface. In skin research, digital image analysis is not only the newest, but probably the most reliable experimental method yet available for evaluating dry skin in the laboratory.

In this process video images of the skin are converted to mathematical terms (digitized) and transmitted to a computer for graphic display. The computer is capable of "reading" a video camera view of either a photograph of the skin or a slide of skin scales; it translates varying levels of brightness within the skin into three-dimensional graphic representations. Using this method, the degree of skin scaliness can be very accurately evaluated and visualized. Digital image analysis can be especially useful for judging the effect of moisturizers on your skin. Considering the numbers of people who suffer with dry-skin problems and the constant quest for the ideal moisturizer, digital image analysis promises to be a very useful investigative tool in skin-care research.

LASERS

Lasers, another high-tech advance in dermatology, are simply intense, focused beams of selected wavelengths of light. A variety of different lasers are available, each with its own wavelength and its own particular therapeutic strengths. For some time now, the argon laser has been used successfully to treat disfiguring port-wine stains, and the carbon dioxide laser has been used to perform a variety of dermatologic surgical procedures.

However, an exciting new form of laser therapy, *photodynamic laser therapy,* is currently being evaluated in the treatment of a variety of cancers, including basal cell cancer, squamous cell cancer, melanoma, Kaposi's sarcoma, and metastatic breast cancer. The procedure consists of the prior administration of a photosensitizing substance known as *hematoporphyrin derivative (HPD)* followed by laser irradiation. It has been found that seventy-two hours after the systemic administration of HPD to a patient with these cancers, most of it is preferentially taken up by the malignant tumor cells. The reason for this selective uptake is not known. By itself, HPD does the tumor tissue no harm; however, when subjected to laser irradiation from either the argon-pumped dye or gold-head vapor lasers, HPD is converted into substances that are toxic to the tumor cells, killing them. Topical formulations of HPD are currently in development. The results of photodynamic laser therapy are preliminarily encouraging; however, much additional research is needed to determine whether lasers can live up to their initial promise in this area.

But that's not all. Lasers have been found to have some other potentially useful functions. Recent evidence suggests that low-energy lasers, such as the helium-neon laser, might be useful for stimulating speedy wound healing. Experiments in animals and humans suggests that collagen production is stimulated by low-energy laser irradiation and that this may account for enhanced wound healing following laser treatment. This may be especially important for managing traumatic or surgical wound healing in elderly or chronically ill patients who characteristically exhibit poor wound healing.

Along the same lines, neodymium:YAG and argon lasers have been used to weld together surgical wounds, a method that would replace stitches. In some studies, laser-welded surgical wounds healed not only with as much strength as conventionally stitched wounds, but with esthetically more acceptable results. Since stitches in the skin act as a potential focus for inflammation and infection and are annoying to most people, eliminating them from surgery is an obvious advantage. In this field, too, more research is needed to confirm these encouraging initial findings.

TISSUE EXPANDERS

To exploit the elastic capacity of your skin, reconstructive surgeons have developed the technique of tissue expansion. The procedure is intended to safely stretch skin in areas where it is quite tight or inelastic. Simply, a tissue expander implant is a high-grade, reinforced silicone bag (which is available in standard sizes or can be custom made) attached to a long, thin tube. The implant device is usually positioned between the skin and the underlying muscles. Saline solution (salt water) is injected through the tube into the silicone expander to enlarge the implant and stretch the overlying skin. After the desired expansion is achieved—the time may vary from weeks to months—the implant is removed. One obvious advantage is that the expanded skin matches the color and texture of normal skin.

Tissue expansion techniques have been used successfully for breast augmentation surgery, after mastectomy for breast cancer, and for stretching the surrounding skin after any large growth or abnormality has been surgically removed. Most recently, tissue expanders have been used after scalp reduction surgery for hair-loss problems to stretch the remaining hair-bearing areas and make them cover larger areas more efficiently (chapter 12).

TRANSDERMAL PATCHES

Using your skin as a route for administering drugs is a particularly exciting development. Transdermal patches, or skin patches, use your skin as a route for the controlled release of drugs into your system, offering an additional means for delivering potent medications to your circulation. Previously this could be accomplished only by the oral, intramuscular, and intravenous injection routes. Transdermal drug delivery has the additional advantages of being painless and nonirritating to the gastrointestinal system.

Transdermal patches are multilayered disks about the size of a small coin. They contain a reservoir for holding a drug and an adhesive-coated polymer membrane through which the drug passes to the skin at a controlled rate. Low but effective drug levels can be maintained in this fashion for up to several days, depending upon the drug being used.

Transderm-Scop, a *scopolamine* patch, is one such delivery system. Worn on the relatively permeable skin behind the ear, scopolamine patches have been used successfully to control motion sickness, radiation sickness, and the untoward side effects of certain anticancer treatments. Astronauts in the U.S. space shuttle program have worn them for motion sickness control.

Transdermal patches also have been used to deliver nitroglycerin and other nitrates employed in the treatment of heart disease. *Angina* (exertional heart pain), *congestive heart failure,* and *myocardial infarction* (heart attack) have all been treated successfuly in this manner in selected patients.

Currently, transdermal patches are being developed to deliver *estradiol* to postmenopausal women requiring estrogen replacement therapy and to deliver the antihypertensive medications *timolol* and *clonidine hydrochloride* to people with high blood pressure. In a recent modification of the transdermal skin patch designed to *limit* systemic absorption and confine drug release to the skin, salicylic acid, incorporated into a special skin patch delivery system, has been successfully used to treat warts.

The long-term success of transdermal patches and their place in our overall drug arsenal remains to be clarified. Concerns about the overall safety and efficacy of the transdermal delivery system still exist, including whether skin patches deliver suboptimal drug levels; whether drug tolerance will ultimately develop by using the skin route; and whether the skin with its inherent variability can actually control the input of certain drugs satisfactorily. Another concern is the frequency of development of contact dermatitis to a drug delivered in this way, which has been observed with transdermal nitroglycerin and clonidine. Nevertheless, the prospects for modifying the transdermal skin-patch delivery systems to be more effective and less problematic are promising.

ANTICANCER VACCINES AND THERAPY

The dream of discovering a vaccine against cancer is hardly new, but recently we have come one step closer to realizing that dream. Based upon our ever-increasing understanding of how the immune system works, a tumor vaccine against malignant melanoma (chapter 10) was recently developed and tested. For more than five years, researchers at the Thomas Jefferson University School of Medicine in Philadelphia have been conducting basic and clinical research toward realizing the goal of vaccinating a patient against his/her own tumors.

Their theory holds that each of us retains the capacity to mount an immune response to kill off tumors that start in our body. However, for reasons that are as yet unclear to these researchers, certain cells, known as *suppressor T-cells,* squelch the body's protective immune response and permit malignancies to grow and eventually kill. Using an anticancer drug, *cyclophospha-mide,* in low doses, these researchers have been able to dampen the suppressor lymphocyte reaction and thereby enhance the body's immunological reaction to the tumor.

They have further attempted to enhance natural immunity by vaccinating patients in their skin with extracts of their own malignancy. The vaccine is readministered every four weeks for six months. In the original study, two of the twenty patients with malignant melanoma who had not responded to any previous form of conventional therapy demonstrated striking improvement in their condition. The results are preliminary, but encouraging, and experimental studies continue.

Finally, another triumph of technology, genetic engineering, offers promise in the field of anticancer therapy. Clinical trials are to begin shortly with a genetically engineered drug, *melanoxin.* In laboratory tests, melanoxin has been found to kill human melanoma cells. In preliminary animal testing, melanoxin was found to spare healthy cells, while targeting melanoma cells for destruction. The drug works by zeroing in on the receptor sites of malignant melanoma cells. Once attached to the melanoma cell, the drug delivers its deadly payload, *diphtheria toxin,* ten times more deadly than cyanide. The outcome of these clinical trials has exciting implications for the whole field of anticancer therapy, not just melanoma treatment.

ARTIFICIAL SKIN

Technological advances are not limited to better ways to diagnose and treat skin diseases. Research actively continues in the field of creating artificial or synthetic skin. Artificial skin has been used primarily to treat burn victims who have had large areas of their skin destroyed. The ideal skin substitute must be capable of preventing infection and reducing fluid losses and must not be rejected by the body's immune system.

Recently at the Massachusetts Institute of Technology, investigators produced a biodegradable skin substitute, called stage I skin. This skin, which appears to stimulate new skin growth, is composed of calf collagen, *chondroitan-6-sulfate* (a complex sugar derived from shark cartilage), and silicone rubber. After physicians suture stage I skin in place, they find that fibrous tissue–producing cells, called *fibroblasts,* migrate to the synthetic skin and lay down a new "dermis." The investigators aptly refer to the new dermis as *neodermis.* After about three weeks, when the calf collagen within the stage I skin has been largely degraded, the stage I skin is removed and small pieces of epidermis from other areas of the patient's body are then transplanted over the neodermis; within several days a completely new epidermis forms. While the new skin appears to function like natural skin, it lacks hair follicles and sweat glands.

Even more recently, these same MIT researchers have improved upon stage I skin and have developed what they call stage II skin. Stage II skin uses the same complex membrane of stage I synthetic skin except that the membrane is seeded with the patient's own skin cells. In this procedure, a biopsy is first taken of the patient's normal skin and a suspension of pure basal cells created. Within two hours of the biopsy, these cells are seeded by a special process into the collagen-sugar-silicone complex of stage I skin. The advantage of this technique, according to its developers, is that while neodermis is being made, neoepidermis is also being made, making it unnecessary to perform additional surgical procedures at a later date to transplant the epidermis (as is currently required when stage I skin is used).

Today, the development of artificial skin is still in its infancy, and much, much more needs to be learned. Trading new skin for old may seem like a dream come true to those who are troubled by certain skin problems, such as acne, wrinkling, and skin cancers. However, the day in which you may "unzip" your skin and put on a new one is conceivably somewhere over the horizon. At the very least it is a tantalizing thought—and it certainly would be a short cut to achieving super skin. However, until such time as science can provide that miracle, and others, you've got to continue to work at preserving and protecting the one and only skin that nature gave you.

INDEX

A

abdominoplasty, 185–186
abscesses, 139–140
acetone, 39, 99, 214–215
acid mantle, 6, 33
acne, 10, 76, 87, 93–109
 antibiotics for, 100–102
 controlling, 96–108
 cosmetics and, 66, 67, 69, 70, 71, 72, 98
 cysts, 95, 96, 100, 103, 104, 108, 176
 dermatologist's care for, 100–108
 development of blemishes in, 95–96
 foods and, 97
 hormones and, 94, 199
 medications for, 33, 38, 40, 46, 49, 97, 98–100
 moisturizers and, 47, 48, 49, 54, 56
 myths about, 97
 perioral dermatitis, 93, 109
 in pregnancy, 266
 rosacea, 86–87, 93, 108–109, 152, 180, 275
 scars, 94, 95, 96, 100, 104–105, 106, 174
 soaps and, 38, 97, 98
 stress and, 82, 94–95, 109
 sun and, 16, 24, 97
 surgery, 103–104
 vulgaris, 93, 94–108, 204
Acquired Immunodeficiency Syndrome (AIDS), 253–254

acrochorda, *see* skin tags
actinic keratoses, 160–161
age spots ("liver" spots), 17, 153–154, 156, 274, 275
 concealing, 68–69
 removing, 173
aging, skin, 3–4, 11–13, 272–284
 angular cheilitis in, 278–279
 chondrodermatitis in, 279
 chronological (natural), 11–12, 14, 17–18, 273, 274
 contact dermatitis in, 277
 cosmetics and, 66
 dryness and, 44, 45
 leg ulcers and, 280–284
 liposomes and, 52
 moisturizers and, 43
 pruritus (itching) in, 275–277
 senile purpura in, 280
 solar-induced (photoaging), 6, 11–12, 14, 17–19, 51, 124, 273, 274
 stasis dermatitis in, 277–278
 venous lakes in, 279–280
AIDS, 253–254
alcohol, in cosmetics, 39–40, 68, 73–74
alcohol use, 86–87, 109, 180
allergies:
 to antibiotics, 141
 to cosmetics, 47, 50, 54, 55, 60, 65, 71, 214, 215
 to deodorant soaps, 37
 dermatitis and, 111, 115–118, 224, 230–231, 277
 to drugs, 87

allergies *(continued)*
  to foods, 113, 126
  to footwear, 224
  to fragrances, 55, 73
  to genital deodorants, 230–231
  hypoallergenic products and, 74
  to injectable collagen, 108
  to lanolin, 47, 54–55
  to nail products, 214, 215, 216
  seborrhea and, 119
  stress and, 95
  sun and, 16, 24
  tests for, 118
alopecia, 194–197
aluminum chloride, 234, 235, 282
aluminum salts, 39, 234
American Academy of Dermatology, 156–157, 287
American Cancer Society, 14, 85, 142, 156–157
amino acids, 49–50
androgens, 94, 196, 197, 199, 204
anemia, 76, 196
angular cheilitis, 278–279
anthralin, 122, 123, 195
antibiotics:
  for acne, 100–102
  for bacterial skin infections, 140–141
  for sexually transmitted diseases, 240–241
  sun and, 16, 17, 24
  for venous ulcers, 282
  for yeast infections, 132
anticancer vaccines and therapy, 291–292
anticoagulants, 16, 195
antifungal agents, 129–130, 131, 132, 224, 251
  pregnancy and, 271
  sun and, 16
antihistamines, 113, 114, 115, 122, 137, 268, 271, 277
antioxidants, 63, 64
antiperspirants, 234–235
anus:
  gonorrhea infection of, 252
  itching of, 231–233
apocrine sweat glands, 8, 9, 13, 36, 230, 233

arthritis, psoriatic, 122
astringents, 39–40, 98, 99
athlete's foot, 128, 130
autoimmune diseases, 194–195

B

bacterial skin infections (pyodermas), 137–141
  diagnosing and treating, 140–141
  medicated soaps and, 38
  of nails, 219, 220–222
  from whirlpool baths, 90, 137–139, 140
balding, *see* hair loss
basal cell cancers, 142, 148, 149, 157–158, 288
basal layer (stratum germinativum), 5–6, 7
bathing, 40–41, 52–53
beauty, 167–169
benign skin growths, 151–156
  cysts, 151–152
  lipomas, 155–156
  sebaceous gland hyperplasia, 152–153
  seborrheic keratoses, 154
  skin tags, 154–155
  solar lentigines, 153–154
benzocaine, 24, 278
benzoyl peroxide, 38, 40, 98, 99, 100
beta-carotene, 28, 76, 219
bicycling, 80
biopsies, 143–147, 160, 286
  excisional, 144, 146, 147
  incisional, 146, 160
  punch, 144, 146, 160, 194
  scissor, 144, 145–146
  shave, 143, 144, 145
birth control pills, 109
  hair and, 193, 204
  sun and, 16, 17
  yeast infections from, 132
bismuth oxychloride, 66, 72
black-and-blue marks (purpura), 260, 280
blackheads (open comedones), 95, 96, 99, 108
  removing, 103–104

blisters:
    friction, 224–225
    see also specific conditions
blood poisoning (septicemia), 140
blood pressure, high, 283, 284
blood vessels, 5, 7–8, 13
    aging and, 273, 274, 279–280
    alcohol and, 86–87
    "broken," *see* "broken" blood vessels
    junk foods and, 97
    Kaposi's sarcoma and, 254, 288
    nicotine and, 84
    in pregnancy, 258, 260, 267
    purpura and, 280
    stasis dermatitis and, 278
    syphilis and, 240
    varicose, 68–69; *see also* varicose
      veins
body odor, 9, 40–41, 229–231, 233,
    234
    deodorant soaps and, 36–37
body temperature, 4, 7, 9, 81, 274
boils, 139
breast surgery, 182–185
    augmentation, 182–184, 289
    complications of, 184
    reduction, 184–185
"broken" blood vessels (telangiectasias),
    17, 38, 68, 86, 108, 113, 148,
    149, 259
    aging and, 274
    alcohol and, 86
    concealing, 68–69
    in pregnancy, 259
    removing, 109, 148, 180–182
    spider veins, 180, 181–182, 258–259,
      260
bubble baths, 39
bullous pemphigoid, 269

C

calcium, 78
    in nails, 207–208, 212–213
calluses, 225–227, 284
camphor, 39, 277
cancer, 84, 291–292
    see also skin cancers

candida (yeast) infections, 132, 251, 254,
    278–279
    of nails, 221
    of vagina, 102, 221, 230, 251
canthaxanthin, 28
carbohydrates, 77, 78
carbuncles, 139–140
cataracts, 16, 271
cellulite, 89, 177–178
cellulitis, 140
cephalosporins, 271
chancres, 239–240
chancroid, 241
chemical peels, 105, 106, 143, 173–
    174
chemical stabilizers, 63, 64
cherry hemangiomas, 259–260, 275
chicken pox, 15, 135, 242
chlamydia infections, 230, 252
chondrodermatitis, 279
cigarettes, 84–85
clarifying lotions, 39, 40
clay, 66, 73
cleansers, cleansing, 31–41, 56
    abrasive (exfoliating), 38
    acne and, 97–98
    alcohol-based, 39–40
    bubble baths, 39
    categories of, 32–33
    creams and lotions, 32, 36
    ingredients in, 61
    itching and, 277
    moisturizers and, 46
    soaps, 33–34
clothing:
    atopic dermatitis and, 114
    as defense from sun, 20–21, 56, 258
    exercise and, 80
    itching and, 277
coal tar, 122–123
cocaine, 87, 88
cocoa butter, 48
cold sores, 15, 242
collagen:
    in cosmetics, 7, 49–50, 56, 106–
      107
    in skin, 7, 13, 17, 49, 78, 106, 264,
      273, 289

collagen injections, 180, 278
  for scars, 50, 105, 106–108
  for wrinkles, 50, 174–175
comedones:
  closed (whiteheads), 95, 96, 97, 108
  extraction of, 103–104
  open (blackheads), 95, 96, 99, 108
computer imaging, 286–288
condoms, 239, 245, 247, 254
congenital nevi, 160, 163–164
contact lenses, 68, 72
contraceptives:
  oral, see birth control pills
  sexually transmitted diseases and, 238,
    239, 245, 254
corns, 225–227
corticosteroid(s):
  creams and ointments, 109, 113–114,
    120–121, 122, 138, 222, 268, 278
  injections, 152, 176, 177, 195
  oral, 270, 271
cortisone, 115, 122, 126
cosmetics, 57–74, 275
  acne and, 66, 67, 69, 70, 71, 72, 98
  alcohol-based, 73–74
  blushers, 67, 72
  bronzers, 27
  choosing, 59–63
  concealers, 66–67, 71
  cream-based, 66–70
  exercise and, 80–81
  eye, 67–68, 70, 71–73
  foundations, 66
  fragrances in, 109
  hypoallergenic, 74
  ingredients in, 6–7, 59–65
  lip, 70–72
  masking, 68–69, 258, 259
  pencil, 70, 71–72
  powder-based, 63, 64, 72–73
  removing, 36, 68
  skin type and, 10–11
  stage, 69–70
  topical medications vs., 43, 57
cosmetic surgery, 143, 167–186
  abdominoplasty, 185–186
  for acne scars, 104–105
  breast, see breast surgery

  for "broken" blood vessels, 109, 148,
    180–182
  choosing doctor for, 171–173
  for keloids and "proud flesh" scars,
    176–177
  liposuction, 177–179
  microlipoinjection, 179–180
  motives for having, 170–171
  smoking and, 84–85
  for wrinkles, 18, 173–175
"crab" lice, 249–251
cracked skin, 111, 116, 122, 128, 276
cradle cap, 118–119
cryosurgery, 155, 158, 160, 161, 164
cryotherapy, 135, 148, 149–150, 153,
  154, 177, 247
curettage, 144, 145, 148, 154, 158, 160,
  161
cuticles, 209, 211
cutis marmorata, 260
cysts:
  acne, 95, 96, 100, 103, 104, 108, 176
  sebaceous, 151–152

D

dandruff (seborrhea), 118–121, 122, 204
deodorant(s), 234
  genital, 229–231
  soaps, 36–37, 233–234
depilatories, 200, 202–203
depressants, 87
dermabrasion, 105–106, 164
dermatitis (eczema), 111–121
  atopic, 112–115, 267
  bubble baths and, 39
  chondro-, 279
  chronic, 111–112, 117
  contact, 115–118, 224, 230–231,
    277
  dry skin and, 46, 47
  facial, 10–11
  hand, 116, 118
  irritant, 117–118
  medicated soaps and, 38
  neuro-, 276
  nummular, 111, 115
  perioral, 93, 109

poison ivy (poison oak; poison sumac), 116–117
  psoriasis vs., 121
  ringworm vs., 129
  seborrheic, 10–11, 111, 118–121, 122, 254
  stages of, 111
  stasis, 277–278, 281
  stress and, 82, 276
  subacute, 111, 117
dermis, 4–5, 7–8
  aging and, 12, 13, 273
detergents, 31, 32, 33, 34–35, 39
diabetes, 276, 283–284
  skin tags and, 155
  yeast infections and, 132
diaphragms, 239, 245, 254
dicloxacillin, 140
diet, 75–79, 77–79, 109
digital image analysis, 287–288
discoloration, *see* pigmentation
diuretics (water pills), 16, 17, 46
DNA, 49–50
DNCB, 195
douching, 231, 239
drinking, 86–87, 109, 180
drug abuse, 83, 87–88, 253
dry skin, 10, 11, 44–46
  aging and, 13, 275, 276
  astringents and, 40
  cleansing, 35, 36, 39, 41, 233
  computer imaging and, 287–288
  on feet, 223
  foundation makeup and, 66
  moisturizers and, 46, 49, 54, 55
  nummular dermatitis and, 115
  seborrheic dermatitis vs., 119
  wrinkles and, 45
dust, 114
dysplastic nevi, 160, 161–163, 257

E

ears, nodules on, 279
eccrine glands, 4, 8, 9, 13, 266
eczema, *see* dermatitis
edema, 262–263
eggs, in moisturizers, 49, 52, 65

elastin:
  in cosmetics, 7, 49–50, 65
  in skin, 7, 13, 17, 49, 78, 264, 273
electrocautery, 135
electrocoagulation, 148
electrodessication, 148, 152, 158, 259
electrolysis, 148, 180–181, 203–204
electrosurgery, 109, 148, 153–154, 155, 160, 247, 260, 279–280
emollients, 43, 62
emulsifiers (surfactants), 31–32, 62, 64
emulsion stabilizers and viscosity builders, 63, 64
epidermis, 4–7, 209
  aging and, 12, 273, 274
  layers of, 5–7
epinephrine, 126
erysipelas (St. Anthony's fire), 140
erythromycin, 101, 102, 140
  pregnancy and, 271
  for sexually transmitted diseases, 241
estrogen, 17, 51, 259, 260, 263
excision surgery, 105, 144, 146, 147, 153, 247
exercise, 79–81, 83
exfoliating cleansers, 38
exudative ulcers, 281
eyelids, 108, 262
eye makeup, 67–68, 70, 71–73
eyes, 16, 87, 108, 109, 244

F

facelifts, 84–85, 174
facial telangiectasias, 180–181, 182
fat, body, 8, 12, 89, 177–180
fats, in diet, 77, 78
fat suction surgery, 177–179
fat transfer surgery, 179–180
FDA, *see* Food and Drug Administration
feet, 206–228
  arch problems with, 222, 223
  blisters on, 224–225
  bunions on, 222–223
  corns and calluses on, 225–227, 284
  fissures on, 225
  gout and, 222
  ingrown toenails on, 227–228

feet *(continued)*
  ringworm of, 128
  rough skin on, 223
  sweating of, 235
feminine hygiene sprays, 229–231
fever blisters, 242
fissuring (cracking) of skin, 122, 225
flaky skin, 6, 55, 122, 274
  see also dry skin
folliculitis, 22, 37, 137–138
  from whirlpool baths, 90, 140
Food and Drug Administration (FDA),
    22, 29, 45, 51, 59, 107, 124, 180,
    204, 215
foods, 78
  acne and, 97
  allergies to, 112–113, 126
fragrances, 55, 73–74, 109, 258
freckles, 17, 156, 257
friction blisters, 224–225
fruits, as cosmetic ingredients, 8, 37–38
fuller's earth (kaolin), 21, 66, 72
fungal infections and rashes, 120,
    128–132
  on feet, 224
  hair loss from, 196
  medicated soaps and, 38
  of nails, 220–222
  ringworm, 128–130
  tinea versicolor, 130–131
  yeast, *see* yeast infections
furuncles, 139

G

gellants, 62, 64
genital:
  deodorants, 229–231
  herpes, 132–133, 241–246
  warts, 132–133, 246–247
glycerin, 35, 39, 40, 48
glycolic acid, 44
Goeckerman therapy, 123, 124
gonorrhea, 251, 252
griseofulvin, 17, 129, 130
growths, 142–164
  AIDS and, 254
  biopsy of, *see* biopsies

cysts, 151–152
eliminating, 148–151
lipomas, 155–156
sebaceous gland hyperplasia, 152–153
seborrheic keratoses, 154
skin tags, 154–155
solar lentigines, 153–154
see also skin cancers
gums, pregnancy and, 263–264

H

hair(s), 8, 187–205, 190
  aging and, 12–13
  anagen phase of, 189, 195–196, 265
  birth control pills and, 192, 204
  bleaching of, 191, 192
  breakage of, 191–192
  catagen phase of, 189
  conditioners for, 191
  dandruff (seborrhea) and, 118–121,
      122, 204
  dyes, 24, 191
  excess, *see* hirsutism
  growth of, 12–13, 189–190
  ingrown, 200
  lanugo, 266
  loss of, *see* hair loss
  normal, 188–190
  perming of, 192
  pregnancy and, 192, 265–266
  removing, *see* hair removal
  telogen phase of, 189, 192–194,
      265
  terminal, 189, 266
  thin or fragile, 13, 190–192
  vellus, 189
hair follicles, *see* pores
hair loss, 190, 191, 192–198
  aging and, 275
  alopecia areata, 194–195
  anagen effluvium, 195–196
  from drugs, 195, 196
  hereditary (androgenetic alopecia),
      196–198
  during pregnancy, 193, 265
  stress-induced (telogen effluvium),
      192–194

traction alopecia, 192
transplants for, 197–198
hair removal:
  bleaching, 201–202
  depilatories, 202–203
  electrolysis, 203–204
  pumicing, 200
  shaving, 201
  tweezing, 200
  waxing, 200–201
hairy oral leukoplakia, 254
hammertoe, 226
hands:
  dermatitis of, 116, 118
  pregnancy and, 260
  sweating of, 235
hangnails, 220
health, 75–90
heat radiation, 21
hemorrhoids, 260–261
herbs, as cosmetic ingredients, 37–38,
  49, 51–52
herpes, 15, 241–246, 254
  complications of, 244
  diagnosis and treatment of, 245–246
  genitalis, 132–133
  gestationes, 269
  initial infection with, 242–243
  prevention of, 244–245
  recurrences of, 243–244
  stress and, 82
  zoster (shingles), 132, 135–136, 254,
  274, 275
high blood pressure, 283, 284
hirsutism (excess hair), 198–199
  aging and, 275
  in pregnancy, 265–266
  treatments for, 204–205
histamine, 114, 125
hives (urticaria), 82, 87, 95, 125–126
honey, as cosmetic ingredient, 49, 52,
  65
hormones:
  acne and, 94
  androgens, 94, 196, 197, 199, 204
  estrogens, 17, 51, 259, 260, 263
  in moisturizers, 51
  stress and, 82

horny layer (stratum corneum), 5, 6, 12,
  44–45, 97, 122
  quick-tanning agents and, 27
  water content of, 43, 45
hot tubs, 90, 137–139
house-dust mites, 114
humectants, 47, 48–49, 50, 62
Hutchinson's melanotic freckles, 160,
  164
hyaluronic acid, 50
hydroquinone, 258
hyperhidrosis, 9, 235
hypertrophic ("proud flesh") scars, 174,
  176–177
hypoallergenic cosmetics, 74

I

"ice-pick" scars, 105, 106
immune system, 16, 82, 194, 273, 291–
  292
impetigo, 137
impetigo herpetiform, 270
infections, 127–141; see also specific types of
  infection
infrared radiation, 21, 24
injectable collagen, see collagen injections
insect bites, 126
intermittent claudication, 283–284
intradermal tests, 118
iodine, 76, 97
iontophoresis, 236
iron, 76, 78, 196, 278
itching:
  aging and, 275–277
  see also specific conditions

J

jaundice, 267–268
jewelry, 80–81, 117
jock itch, 128
jogging, 79–80

K

kaolin (fuller's earth), 21, 66, 72
Kaposi's sarcoma, 254, 288

keloids, 176–177, 286
keratin, 6,8,40,207, 212
keratosis pilaris (prickly hair follicles),
    124–125
kidneys, 137, 276

L

lactic acid, 44, 45, 48, 134
lanolin, 47, 54–55, 71
lasers, 288–289
leg ulcers, 280–284
lentigo maligna, 164
leukemia, 276
lice, 249–251
lichen simplex chronicus, 276
lipid film, 43
lip(s):
    makeup, 70–72
    sores on, 242
lipomas, 155–156
liposomes, 49, 52
liposuction, 156, 177–179
liquid nitrogen, 135, 149–150, 177
liver, 87, 267, 268, 276
"liver" spots (age spots), 17, 153–154,
        156, 274, 275
    concealing, 68–69
    removing, 173
lunula, 209
lupus erythematosus, 16, 69

M

magnesium silicates, 66, 72
makeup, see cosmetics
malignant melanomas, 142, 158–160,
    287
    congenital nevi and, 163–164
    detecting, 156–157
    dysplastic nevi and, 161–163, 257
    treating, 160, 288, 291, 292
marijuana, 87
masks, 70, 73
massage, 88–89
medications:
    cosmetics vs., 43, 57
    hair loss from, 195

sun and, 16, 17
    using, 138–139
melanin, 5–6, 29
    see also pigmentation
melanomas, malignant, see malignant
        melanomas
melasma, 258
menthol, 39, 277
mica, 67, 72
microcomedos, 95, 96
microlipoinjection, 179–180
milia, 151–152
milk, as cosmetic ingredient, 49, 52, 65
mineral oils, 47, 48, 54
minerals, 8, 77, 78–79
minoxidil, 195, 197
mites, house-dust, 114
Moh's chemosurgery, 148, 149, 158
moisturizers, 42–55
    acne and, 47, 48, 49, 54, 56, 98
    atopic dermatitis and, 115
    choosing, 53–55
    in cleansers, 34, 36
    exercise and, 80
    for feet, 223
    fragrances in, 55
    humectant, 48–49
    ingredients in, 7, 47–48, 61, 64–65
    itching (pruritis) and, 268, 277
    for nails, 211, 212
    occlusive, 47–48
    oil in, 54
    stretch marks and, 264
moles, 156, 162–164, 286
    under nails, 218–219
    pregnancy and, 257
    removal of, 145
molluscum contagiosum, 132–133,
        247–248, 254
monilia, 102
mouth, infections of, 132, 278–279

N

nail polish, 213–214
    allergic reactions to, 214, 215
    base and top coats, 215
    discoloration from, 219

hardeners and builders, 215–216, 220
removers, 214–215, 220
nails, 206–228
 aging and, 275
 anatomy of, 207–209
 artificial, 216–217
 brittle and splitting, 219–220
 calcium in, 207–208, 212–213
 care of, 210–213
 clipping, filing and trimming,
  210–211
 cuticle and, 209, 211
 deformities of, 218, 221
 discoloration of, 87, 218–219, 221
 growth of, 209–210
 hangnails and, 220
 infections of, 128, 129, 132, 219,
  220–222
 ingrown, 211, 227–228
 injuries to, 217–218
 pregnancy and, 266
 psoriasis of, 222
 strengthening, 211–213
 warts around, 133
National Cancer Institute, 14
natural moisturizing factors, (NMF), 43–
 44, 45
nerves, 7, 13, 135–136, 284
nervous tension, see stress
neurodermatitis, 276
niacin (vitamin B3), 76
nickel allergy, 81, 117
nitrocellulose, 213, 214
nits, 250, 251
NMF (natural moisturizing factors), 43–
 44, 45
nongonococcal urethritis (NGU), 252
nonspecific urethritis (NSU), 251, 252
nutrients, 7, 8, 76, 78
nystatin, 132, 271

O

obesity:
 ingrown toenails and, 227–228
 liposuction and, 177
 yeast infections and, 132
occlusive moisturizing ingredients, 47–48

oil glands, see sebaceous gland
oils, in moisturizers, 47–48, 54
oily skin, 10
 astringents and, 40
 cleansing, 34, 36, 38, 41
 cosmetics and, 11, 67, 72, 98
 hormones and, 94
 moisturizers and, 46, 54, 56
oral contraceptives, see birth control pills
orthotic devices, 227

P

PABA (para-aminobenzoic acid), 22, 23,
 24, 71
palmar erythema (red palms), 260
papillomas, see skin tags
papules (pimples), 93, 95, 96, 108, 204
parabens, 55
patch tests, 118, 224
pelvic inflammatory disease (PID), 252
penicillin, 141, 241, 271
penis, 239–240, 241, 242, 247, 251–
 252
perfumes, 73–74
petroleum jelly (petrolatum), 48, 54
pets, 128, 130
phenol, 173, 277
phospholipids, 44, 48
photosensitivity reactions, 16, 17, 28, 29
piezosurgery, 156
pigmentation, 5–6, 113
 aging and, 12–13, 273, 274
 chemical peels and, 174
 pregnancy and, 257–258
pigments, in cosmetics, 62, 67, 72, 213,
 214
Pill, the, see birth control pills
pills, swallowing, 138–139
pimples (papules), 93, 95, 96, 108, 204
pinch-grafting, 283
pinkeye, 87
pityriasis rosea, 136–137
placental extracts, as cosmetic ingredient,
 49, 51
plantar warts, 133
plastic surgery, see cosmetic surgery
pock-mark scars, 95, 176

poison ivy, 111, 116–117, 195
pores (hair follicles), 8, 9–10, 137
  alcohol-based products and, 39
  clogging of, 22, 47, 48, 66, 70, 96, 97, 99
  cysts and, 152
  prickly (keratosis pilaris), 124–125
  sun and, 16, 22, 97
post-herpetic neuralgia, 135–136
postpartum telogen effluvium, 265
precancers, 160–164, 274
  actinic keratoses, 160–161
  aging and, 275
  congenital nevi, 163–164
  dysplastic nevi, 161–163
  Hutchinson's melanotic freckles, 164
prednisone, 126, 136, 204
pregnancy, 255–271
  blood vessel changes in, 258–263, 281
  edema in, 262–263
  gonorrhea and, 252
  hair changes in, 193, 265–266
  herpes and, 244
  itching (pruritis) in, 267–268
  jaundice in, 267
  medications and, 103, 270–271
  nail changes in, 266
  "normal" skin changes in, 256–265
  oral conditions in, 263–264
  psoriasis and, 124, 267
  rashes in, 268–270
  skin color changes in, 257–258
  skin tags in, 155, 264–265
  stretch marks in, 264
  syphilis and, 240
  varicose veins in, 260–262, 281
preservatives, 63, 64
prickle cell layer (stratum spinosum), 5, 7
prickly hair follicles (keratosis pilaris), 124–125
prickly heat rash, 22
procaine, 24
propylene glycol, 48, 54
proteins, 49, 76, 77, 78
  in cosmetics, 49–50, 191
"proud flesh" (hypertrophic) scars, 174, 176–177
prurigo nodularis, 276

pruritic urticarial papules and plaques of pregnancy (PUPPP), 269
pruritis (itching):
  aging and, 275–277
  see also specific conditions
pseudomonas, 140, 219
psoriasis, 120, 121–124
  arthritis and, 122, 222
  coal tars and, 122–123
  concealing, 69
  dry skin and, 46
  eczema vs., 121
  of nails, 222
  nervous tension and, 82
  pregnancy and, 124, 267
  psoralens and, 29, 123–124
  ringworm vs., 129
  seborrheic dermatitis vs., 122
pubic lice, 249–251
pumice, 38, 200, 227
punch procedures, 106
purpura, 260, 280
pustules, 95, 96, 108, 109, 270
pyodermas, see bacterial skin infections

R

radiation therapy (radiotherapy), 148, 149, 158, 160
rashes, 110–126
  AIDS and, 254
  dermatitis (eczema), see dermatitis
  fungal, see fungal infections and rashes
  hives (urticaria), 82, 87, 95, 125–126
  in pregnancy, 268–270
  prickly hair follicles (keratosis pilaris), 124–125
  psoriasis, see psoriasis
  scabies, 248–249
  from syphilis, 240
red palms (palmar erythema), 260
refining lotions, 39
relaxation, 83, 84, 88–90
resorcinol, 38, 40, 98, 99
riboflavin (vitamin B2), 76
ringworm, 128–130, 221
royal bee jelly, as cosmetic ingredient, 49, 52, 65

S

St. Anthony's fire (erysipelas), 140
salicylic acid, 38, 40, 98, 99, 109, 120,
   134, 291
saunas, 89–90
scabies, 248–249
scalp:
   dandruff (seborrhea) and, 118–121,
      122, 204
   reduction surgery, 198, 290
   ringworm of, 128–129
   yeast, 119, 121
   see also hair
scars:
   acne, 94, 95, 96, 100, 104–105, 106,
      174
   concealing, 68–69
   cosmetic surgery for, 104–105, 106
   hypertrophic ("proud flesh"), 174,
      176–177
   "ice-pick," 105, 106
   injectable collagen for, 50, 105, 106–
      108
   keloids, 176–177
   pock-mark, 95, 176
   pregnancy and, 257
   self-inflicted, 82–83
scissor surgery, 144, 145–146, 155
sclerotherapy, 181–182, 283
scratch tests, 118
sebaceous gland(s), 8–9, 43–44, 96
   aging and, 13, 273, 274, 275
   cysts, 151–152
   dandruff and, 119
   overgrown (hyperplasia), 108, 152–
      153
   pregnancy and, 266
   seborrhea (dandruff), 118–121,122,
      204
   seborrheic dermatitis, 10–11, 111,
      118–121, 122, 254
   seborrheic keratoses, 154, 275
   sebum, 8–9
   selenium sulfide, 120, 131
   self-examination, 162–163
senile pruritus, 276
senile purpura, 280

sensitive skin:
   allergies and, 47
   astringents and, 40
   cleansing, 33, 34, 35, 36, 37, 39, 41,
      233
   moisturizers and, 46, 47, 48
sensitizing agents, 71
septicemia (blood poisoning), 140
serial puncture technique, 174–175
sexually transmitted diseases (STDs),
      237–254
   AIDS, 253–254
   antibiotics for, 240–241
   chancroid, 241
   genital warts, 132–133, 246–247
   herpes, *see* herpes
   lice, 249–251
   molluscum contagiosum, 132–133,
      247–248, 254
   preventing, 238–239
   scabies, 248–249
   syphilis, 196, 239–241
shampoos, 120, 122, 131
shave excision surgery, 143, 144, 145,
      260
shingles (herpes zoster), 132, 135–136,
      254, 274, 275
shoes, 225, 226, 228
showering, 40–41
silicone, 107
skiing, 24–25, 80
skin:
   aging of, *see* aging, skin
   artificial, 292–293
   as barrier, 4, 6–7, 274
   color, *see* pigmentation
   dry, *see* dry skin
   elasticity of, 7
   emotions and, 82–84
   grafting, 282–283, 284
   layers of, 4–8
   normal, 4–10, 35, 41
   nutrition, 7–8
   oily, *see* oily skin
   patches (transdermal patches), 290–
      291
   peels (chemical peels), 105, 106, 143,
      173–174

skin *(continued)*
  sensitive, *see* sensitive skin
  ten tips for healthier and younger-
    looking, 56
  types, 10–11, 19–20
Skin Cancer Foundation, 14, 142
skin cancers, 6, 16, 124, 156–160, 274,
  287, 288
  ABCD rule for detecting, 156–157
  aging and, 274, 275
  basal cell, 142, 148, 149, 157–158,
    288
  malignant melanomas, *see* malignant
    melanomas
  preventing, 156–157
  psoralens and, 29
  squamous cell, 148, 149, 158, 160,
    288
see also precancers
skin tags (acrochorda; papillomas), 146,
  154–155
  aging and, 275
  in pregnancy, 155, 264–265
smoking, 84–85
soaps, 31, 32, 33–34, 56
  acne and, 38, 97, 98
  additives in, 37–38
  atopic dermatitis and, 112, 115
  deodorant, 36–37
  liquid, 35–36
  medicated, 38
  moisturizers and, 46
  soapless (synthetic detergent soaps), 32,
    34–35, 56
  superfatted, 34
  toilet, 35
  transparent, 35
sodium thiosulfate lotions, 131
solar keratoses, 160–161
solar lentigines, 153–154
solvents, 62, 64
spermicides, 239, 245, 254
SPF (sun protection factor), 22–23, 25,
  26, 56
spider veins, 69, 180, 181–182, 258–
  259, 260
spironolactone, 197, 204–205
sports, 79

squamous cells, 5, 7
  cancers of, 148, 149, 158, 160, 288
staphylococci, 137, 140–141
staphylococcus aureus, 221
steam rooms, 89–90
steroid(s):
  injections, 104, 279
  oral, 126, 132, 136, 204
  topical, 115, 137, 138, 277
  see also corticosteroid
sties, 139
stimulants, 87
stratum corneum, *see* horny layer
stratum germinativum (basal layer),
  5–6, 7
stratum spinosum (prickle cell layer),
  5, 7
streptococci, 137, 140
stress, 81–84, 86
  acne and, 82, 94–95, 109
  atopic dermatitis and, 112
  hair loss from, 192–194
  hives and, 126
  seborrhea and, 119
stretch marks, 113, 264
subcutaneous tissue, 4
subcutis, 5, 8, 12
suction lipectomy, 177–179
sulfonamide antibiotics, 24
sulfur, 38, 98, 99, 109, 120, 249
sun blocks, *see* sunscreens
sunburst varicosities, 69, 180, 181–182,
  258–259, 260
sun exposure, 14–30, 71, 153, 279, 280
  acne and, 15, 16, 97, 109
  aging from, 6, 12, 14, 17–19, 51,
    273
  allergies and, 16
  "broken" blood vessels and, 180
  chemical peels and, 105, 174
  clothing and, 20–21, 56, 258
  conditions triggered by, 15–16
  dermabrasion and, 106
  moisturizers and, 46
  skin cancers and, 6, 16, 157, 158, 160
  skin types and, 19–20
  see also tanning
sunglasses, 21, 56

sunscreens and sun blocks, 18, 19, 21–
    25, 56
  acne and, 24
  allergies and, 24
  exercise and, 80
  hyperpigmentation and, 258
  ingredients in, 23, 61
  in lipsticks, 71
  Sun Protection Factor (SPF) of, 22–23,
    25, 26, 56
support hose, 262, 282
suppressor T-cells, 291–292
surfactants (emulsifiers), 31–32, 62, 64
surgery:
  hair loss from, 192
  see also specific procedures
surgical excision, 158
sweating, sweat glands, 8–9, 36–37, 41,
    80–81, 230, 233, 234–235
  aging and, 13, 273, 274
  allergens and, 224
  apocrine, 8, 9, 13, 36, 230, 233
  eccrine, 4, 8, 9, 13, 266
  excessive, 235–236
  nervous tension and, 82
  pregnancy and, 266
  sebaceous, see sebaceous gland
swimming, 26, 80
syphilis, 196, 239–241

T

talc, 21, 66, 72
tanning, 6, 14–30
  accelerator lotions for, 29–30
  artificial, 27–30
  blemishes and, 15, 16
  parlors, 30
  pills, 28–29
  tinea versicolor and, 131
tap water iontophoresis, 236
tars, 120, 122–123
telangiectasias, see "broken" blood vessels
tension, see stress
tetracycline, 17, 101–102, 109
  nail discolorations from, 219
  pregnancy and, 271
  for sexually transmitted diseases, 241

thickening, stiffening and suspending
    agents, 63, 64
tinea infections, 128–129, 130–131, 224
tissue expanders, 289–290
titanium dioxide, 21
tocopherol, 50
toothpaste, 109
topical medications, cosmetics vs., 43, 57
toxemic rash of pregnancy, 269
traction alopecia, 192
tranquilizers, 16, 17, 87
transdermal patches, 290–291
tretinoin (Retin-A; vitamin A acid), 51,
    100, 101, 150–151, 197, 258
trichomonas infections, 230, 251–252
triclocarban, 36, 233
triclosan, 36, 233, 234
tumors, see growths
tyrosine, 29–30

U

ultrasound, 285–286
ultraviolet light, 6, 16, 17, 21, 28, 30,
    49, 97, 124
  A (UVA), 21, 23–24, 26, 30, 123–
    124
  aging from, 51, 273
  B (UVB), 21, 23–24, 30, 123, 124,
    268
  therapy, 122, 123–124
  Wood's light, 129, 131, 194, 249
urea, 44, 48
ureaplasma, 252
urethral discharges, 251–252
uric acid, 52
urticaria (hives), 82, 87, 95, 125–126

V

vagina, 231, 239–240, 242, 251–252
  yeast infections of, 102, 132, 221,
    230, 251
varicella zoster, 135
varicose veins, 68–69, 180, 260–262,
    277–278, 281
vegetables, as cosmetic ingredients, 8,
    37–38

veins:
    aging and, 279–280
    see also blood vessels; venous
venereal disease, *see* sexually transmitted
    diseases
venous:
    insufficiency disease, 277
    lakes, 279–280
    stripping and ligation, 262
    ulcers, 280–283
veruccae, *see* warts
viprostil, 197
viral infections, 132–137
    pityriasis rosea, 136–137
    shingles, 132, 135–136, 254, 274,
      275
    warts, *see* warts
vitamin A acid (tretinoin; Retin-A), 51,
    100, 101, 150–151, 197, 258
vitamins, 7, 8, 15, 28, 49, 50, 51, 65,
    76, 77, 78–79, 102, 124, 245,
    278, 280
vitiligo, 69

W

warts, 15, 132, 133–135, 156, 247,
    248, 254, 286, 291
    genital, 246–247
    placebo effect and, 82
washing, *see* cleansers, cleansing
water pills (diuretics), 16, 17, 46
waxing, 200–201
weight, 76–77
whirlpool baths, 89–90
    folliculitis from, 90, 137–139, 140
whiteheads (closed comedones), 95, 96,
    97, 108
    removing, 103–104
witch hazel, 39, 99
wrinkles, 13, 18, 147, 274, 275
    collagen injections for, 50, 174, 175
    dry skin and, 45
    muscle tone and, 13
    removing, 173–175
    from smoking, 84

X

X-rays, 149

Y

yeast (candida) infections, 132, 251, 254,
    278–279
    of nails, 221
    of scalp, 119, 121
    of vagina, 102, 132, 221, 230, 251

Z

zinc, 78, 245
    oxide, 21, 22, 279
    pyrithione, 120